SPECULATIONS

SPECULATIONS

The Reality Club

John Brockman
Editor

PRENTICE
HALL
PRESS

New York   London   Toronto   Sydney   Tokyo   Singapore

"Reality and the Brain," "Psychotherapy Systems and Science," "The Two Faces of Creativity," "Speculation on Speculation," "Memes vs. Genes," and "What Narcissus Saw" previously appeared in *The Reality Club*, edited by John Brockman (New York: Lynx Books, 1988).
"The Two Faces of Creativity," by Morris Berman, originally appeared in *Coming to our Senses* (New York: Simon & Schuster, 1989).
"The Trilogy of *Homo Seriatim*," by William H. Calvin, originally appeared in *The Cerebral Symphony* (New York: Bantam Books, 1989).

PRENTICE HALL PRESS
15 Columbus Circle
New York, NY 10023

PRENTICE HALL PRESS and colophons are registered trademarks
of Simon & Schuster, Inc.

Library of Congress Cataloging-in-Publication Data

Speculations / John Brockman, editor.
    p.   cm. — (The Reality Club)
Collection of talks before the Reality Club.
ISBN 0-13-826215-2 : $10.95
I. Brockman, John, 1941–   .   II. Reality Club.   III. Series:
Reality Club (Series).
AC5.S67   1990
081—dc20   89-77353
                                                                                CIP

Designed by Irving Perkins Associates

Manufactured in the United States of America

10 9 8 7 6 5 4 3 2 1

First Edition

Contents

Introduction to
The Reality Club

JOHN BROCKMAN

The motto of The Reality Club is: To arrive at the edge of the world's knowledge, seek out the most complex and sophisticated minds, put them in a room together, and have them ask each other the questions they are asking themselves.

Since 1981 The Reality Club has held evening meetings once or twice a month, usually in New York. Each meeting consists of a one-hour talk or presentation by a speaker to Reality Club members. The floor is then open for lively, challenging, and often impolite discussion. We charge the speakers to represent an idea of reality by describing their creative work, their lives, and the questions they are asking themselves. We want them to share with us the boundaries of their knowledge and experience.

In selecting speakers we look for people whose exceptional creative work has expanded our notion of who and what we are. The following are among the more than 100 individuals who have previously accepted invitations to speak before The Reality Club, thereby becoming its members: space biospherian John Allen, biologist and author Isaac Asimov, Zen master Richard Baker-Roshi, anthropologist Mary Catherine Bateson, social critic Morris Berman, editor Stewart Brand, psychologist Jerome Bruner, actress Ellen Burstyn, neurophysiologist William H. Calvin, physicist Fritjof Capra, physicist Sidney Coleman, philosopher Daniel C. Dennett, essayist Annie Dillard, commentator Hugh Downs, nanotechnologist K. Eric Drexler, physicist Freeman Dyson, computer scientist Edward Feigenbaum, "chaos" physicist Mitchell Feigenbaum, theatrical director Richard Foreman, feminist Betty Friedan, zoologist Stephan Jay Gould, physicist Alan Guth, artist Peter Halley, anthropologist and shaman Michael Harner, computer scientist Danny Hillis, political activist (the late) Abbie Hoffman, software entrepreneur Mitch Kapor, novelist Ken Kesey, satirist Paul Krassner, energy experts Amory and Hunter Lovins, fractal mathematician Benoit Mandelbrot, biologist Lynn Margulis, biographer Paul Mariani, psychologist Rollo May, poet Michael McClure, religious historian Elaine Pagels, physicist (the late) Heinz Pagels, architect Witold Rybczynski, cognitive psychologist Roger Schank, art collector Eugene Schwartz, psychologist Robert Sternberg, historian William Irwin Thompson, sociologist Sherry Turkle, biologist Francisco Varela, biogerontologist Roy Walford, and architect James Wines.

Reality Club meetings are private, because membership is reserved for individuals who have been invited to speak before the Club. Speaker selection is a word-of-mouth enterprise among the membership. There is no selection committee. Among our members are best selling authors and individuals famous in the mass culture. Other members, though less well-known, are on the cutting edge of new ideas and disciplines. Together the members of The Reality Club constitute a community of people who think about new ideas and human possibilities for all of us.

The Reality Club encourages people who can take cultural materials from the arts, literature, and the sciences and put them together in their own unique way. We live in a largely mass-produced culture where many people, even many established cultural arbiters, limit themselves to secondhand ideas, thoughts, and opinions. The Reality Club fosters individuals who create their own reality and do not accept an ersatz, appropriated reality; Members are doers as much as they are thinkers.

Speculations is the first volume of a planned series of collections of essays by members of The Reality Club. The story behind this book series begins in 1986, when I accepted an invitation from *The Whole Earth Review* to be the guest editor of a "Reality Club Issue" of that publication. This in turn encouraged Mike Fine, who was starting a new publishing company, Lynx Books, to propose a four-book series of essays by Club members. Publication of *The Reality Club, no. 1* (Lynx Books, October 1988) was the result. Unfortunately, that series was discontinued as *no. 2* was about to be printed because of unanticipated problems affecting Lynx. Then John Thornton of Prentice Hall Press offered to publish a revamped series with a different plan of organization from its predecessors. Whereas "The Reality Club Issue" of *The Whole Earth Review* and Lynx's *The Reality Club no. 1* presented a potpourri of articles—more eclectic than thematic, more idiosyncratic and diverse than consistent in subject matter and style—each title in this new series of books will be devoted to a central theme. With some exceptions, I plan to include only new works not previously published, some of which will be prepublication excerpts from forthcoming books. (Because of the disturbance in the original publishing program, a few of the essays in this new series are excerpts from books already published. Moreover, in fairness, the essays originally published in *The Reality Club no. 1*, which was not widely distributed, will be made available again in various volumes of this new series.)

Our hope is that the individual titles in *The Reality Club* series will afford a regular opportunity for us to share the current thinking of some of our members with readers who cannot listen to or participate in our regular meetings. The essays in each volume are certainly representative of Reality Club talks, and are, in some cases, adaptations of such talks. In this inaugural volume I am pleased to present thirteen pieces on the subject of thinking. They include two essays by neurophysiologist William H. Calvin, one on trains of consciousness and the other on simulations of reality; neurobiologist Julius Korein on brain states of death, vegetation, and life; psychoanalyst Robert Langs on science and psychotherapy; psychologist Nicholas K. Humphrey on the uses of consciousness; philosopher Daniel C. Dennett on the evolution of consciousness; historian Morris Berman on creativity; biologist Lynn Margulis on speculation in the sciences; psychologist Dan Ogilvie on "the undesired self"; psychologist Robert Sternberg on the mysteries of human intelligence; psychologist Mihaly Csikszentmihalyi on cultural adaptation; artists Wim Coleman and Pat Perrin on a postmodern adventure in consciousness; and writer Dorion Sagan on the ecology of ideas.

The Reality Club is different from The Algonquin Roundtable, The Cambridge Apostles, The Bloomsbury Group, or The Club, but like them it offers intellectual adventure. The Reality Club is not just a group of people. I see it as the constant shifting of metaphors, the advancement of ideas, the agreement on, and the invention of, a new reality. To live the life of the mind is to belong to The Reality Club.

New York City
Winter 1990

The Trilogy of
Homo Seriatim

―――――――

WILLIAM H. CALVIN

We must face the fact that humans have a better claim on the title Homo seriatim *than on* Homo sapiens—*we're more consistently serial than wise.*

Three centuries ago, Leibnitz propounded what might now be called the *physiologist's premise*: "Everything that happens in man's body is as mechanical as what happens in a watch." Does that apply to the mind, too? Most people initially think it unlikely. But perhaps Spinoza suspected as much when he said, "The order and connection of ideas is the same as the order and connection of things." Earlier in the seventeenth century, Descartes was bold enough to conceive of a completely self-sufficient nervous mechanism able to perform complicated and apparently intelligent acts. Unfortunately, he still had a conceptual problem regarding followers and leaders, and so mired us even deeper in the dualistic body-and-soul metaphors of an earlier age.

But by the late nineteenth century, Thomas Henry Huxley had prophesied that "We shall, sooner or later, arrive at a mechanical equivalent of consciousness," and this is manifestly the premise of my fellow neurophysiologists. Huxley reflected not only the biologists' mood in the wake of Darwin's revolution; the physicist Ernst Mach summarized in 1895 what many psychologists and philosophers had also begun to say, about how mental mechanisms could use the potent variation-and-selection combination:

> [From] the teeming, swelling host of fancies which a free and high-flown imagination calls forth, suddenly that particular form arises to the light which harmonizes perfectly with the ruling idea, mood, or design. Then it is that which has resulted slowly as the result of a gradual selection, [that] appears as if it were the outcome of a deliberate act of creation. Thus are to be explained the statements of Newton, Mozart, Richard Wagner, and others, when they say that thoughts, melodies, and harmonies had poured in upon them, and that they had simply retained the right ones. [1]

And after this last century of spectacular progress in the brain sciences and evolutionary biology, we have arrived at the threshold of fulfilling Huxley's prophecy: *We are probably within a decade or two of creating consciousness.*

3

Our creations probably won't be full-fledged human mimics complete with our primate-style emotions and their overlay of Ice Age modifications. And undoubtedly not everyone will agree that they are "truly conscious" (we'll surely see escalating definitions, analogous to those of "true language," when animal studies started to turn up interesting abilities).

But our creations will be distinctive individuals *in silico* who can think much like our metaphorical "little person inside the head"— that which contemplates the past and forecasts the future, makes decisions about relative worth, plans what to do tomorrow, feels dismay when seeing a tragedy unfold, and narrates our life story as it unfolds. They will almost intuitively "speak our language." Because of that, conversations with such a "robot" (for lack of a better word) will be far more interesting than those we've attempted with our other animals—at least, once these robotic individuals have a few years experience observing the world and interacting with a potpourri of teachers. Most people will probably concede that they're conscious, and ethical considerations will arise (can one "pull the plug" on such an individual?).

What will make this possible? Two things, to my way of thinking: a mechanistic understanding of how brains chain things together, and a technological offshoot of massively parallel computers, which I call "massively serial computers" (which will be totally unlike today's rule-bound serial computers, more formally known as von Neumann machines). I propose to call the product of this marriage a Darwin Machine. It uses some emergent properties of the Law of Large Numbers—but basically, just think of it as mimicking biological evolution on a greatly accelerated time scale, creating new thoughts rather than new species.

▭

Mach's list of trial-and-error achievements, one notes, mostly involves Spinoza's "order and connection of ideas." We are always stringing things together: phonemes into words, words into sentences, concepts into scenarios, notes into melodies—and then fussing about getting them in the right order.

Chaining is most obvious for language: Our brain uses word-order rules to create a language with an infinite number of novel messages, rather than the several dozen standard interpretations associated with the several dozen cries and grunts in the repertoire of any other primate species. But we, too, only use a few dozen basic speech sounds: Though inflection rules may augment them, it isn't our mellifluous voices that constitute a significant advance but rather our arrangement rules, the meaningful order in which we chain our utterances. "Dick called Jane" means something very different from "Jane called Dick."

And talking-to-ourselves consciousness is, among other things, particularly concerned with creating scenarios, trying to chain together memory schemata to explain the past and forecast the future. As Peter Brooks recently observed in *Reading for the Plot*:

> Our lives are ceaselessly intertwined with narrative, with the stories we tell and hear told, those we dream or imagine or would like to tell, all of which are reworked in that story of our own lives that we narrate to ourselves in an episodic, sometimes semiconscious, but virtually uninterrupted monologue. We live immersed in narrative, recounting and reassessing the meaning of our past actions, anticipating the outcome of our future projects, situating ourselves at the intersection of several stories not yet completed. [2]

It is our ability to choose between such alternative scenarios that constitutes our free will—though, of course, our choices are only as good as our imagination in constructing a wide range of candidate scenarios.

Logical reasoning also seems dependent on the rules of reliable sequencing to create statements where one thing entails another. Our sophisticated projection abilities are very sequential: A chess master, for example, tends to see each board configuration, not just after the next move but a half dozen moves ahead, as one of several alternative scenarios.

Chaining things together isn't everything. Much of our imagination is pictorial; certainly our emotional judgments are similarly "right-brain," and we would be strikingly impoverished without them. But such "left-brain" sequential abilities are obviously a key development in post-ape brain evolution. Language, scenario-spinning consciousness, and music constitute a trilogy of sequential abilities for which we seek a better understanding. We must face the fact that humans have a better claim on the title *Homo seriatim* than on *Homo sapiens*—we're more consistently serial than wise.

And we do a lot of selecting from among choices we create and chain together—as if there were many planning tracks in the brain, something like the candelabra-shaped railroad marshaling yard where many trains are assembled but only one let loose on the "main track" of speech and consciousness. If we can understand such a process—how trains randomly vary, how their order is compared to memories of successful sequences of the past, what constitutes a "good enough" plan on which to act—we will have achieved an important step in understanding ourselves.

One can already envisage a class of possible computers which earlier I called Darwin Machines, because they would work like a greatly speeded-up version of biological evolution. They would shape up new thoughts in milliseconds rather than new species in millennia, using innocuous remembered environments rather than the real-life noxious ones, but in much the same way as Darwin's natural selection repeatedly edits the random genetic sequence variations in order to shape new body styles.

They, or something like them, may provide our second-generation mechanistic explanation of consciousness—the first generation belonging to the Darwin enthusiasts of the late nineteenth century and their many predecessors who overcame the seemingly natural tendency to treat mind as irretrievably different. As massively parallel computers develop, we will be better able to simulate such marshaling-yard arrangements—and such a massive serial computer may allow us our first conversations with an intelligent form of artificial life.

How we think is nowhere as clear as what we think about. Suppose, however, that we were to achieve such a general understanding of the mechanisms whereby we think—the way in which we analyze the world around us, arrive at new ideas and judge their usefulness, and so guide our actions? We might achieve some control over pathological thinking—*worry*, for example, is the unproductive repetition of a bothersome thought that prevents new ideas or concerns from rising to consciousness. How do we avoid "getting stuck"?

And an advanced understanding might create the potential for many of us to think in the creative ways that only a few geniuses now achieve. Personally, I'd like to be able to compose symphonies in my head, hear the combined instruments of the orchestra playing, and then write down the music, in the way that Mozart was reportedly able to do. I'd like to be able to think in four- or six-dimensional space, the way some mathematicians can. I'd like to be able to recall something that I read somewhere, complete with the sentences that preceded and followed it. I'd like to be able to run through in my head the next ten ploys of a labor negotiation or an important conversation, so as to better choose a good course of action.

Maybe, if we come to understand how the brain does such serial-order things, our children will be able to shape our education to match actual mental processes (rather than the Procrustean bed of guesswork education theories). And we will be able to craft artificial aids such as computers that will approximately match up with the mental processes inside our heads, providing a natural fit (rather than fitting someone's glorified idea of how logical rules structure the brain).

Our conception of what goes on inside our heads is central to the next step in evolution. That our present concepts are faulty can be seen by how awkwardly we wear the clothes crafted by the people who think our minds are some logical, rule-governed machine. The Artificial Intelligentsia have produced machines that do well what we naturally do poorly—such as solving mathematical theorems—but which are incredibly awkward at doing things that we do easily, such as navigating through a strange room or jumping to a correct conclusion on the basis of limited data. It is almost as if they were trying to appreciate things from the wrong viewpoint. Finding the right viewpoint can often effect an enormous simplification—remember what Copernicus's heliocentric vision did to Ptolemy's complicated epicycles?

No research areas are more troubled by the lack of a reliable viewpoint than psychology, cognitive sciences, artificial intelligence, and neurobiology. Though criticized for a century or more, most of us still fall back (albeit uncomfortably) on the lay view of what is inside the head. Most people, if questioned about what goes on inside their heads, will talk as if there were a little person there receiving reports from the eyes and ears and skin, and issuing the commands that run the muscles. We imagine an executive issuing orders to subservient departments; with the advent of computers and of the recognition of the importance of serial ordering, the executive became a "programmer" of equal omnipotence.

This old notion of hierarchies inside the brain led inevitably to the concept that somewhere there was a highest center, able to command all subservient centers. And we've actually found some. In fish, you can find two "command" neurons in the brain stem: If the right-hand Mauthner cell fires a single impulse, all of the muscles on the fish's left side twitch violently. This massive tail-flip is used to get the fish away from something that is starting to nibble on it. If one of those cells chooses to speak, it overrides all ordinary reflexes and the fish flips. Humans don't have Mauthner cells, but there are some single neurons that seem very important, that can get your attention so compellingly that all else seems irrelevant.

Where are they—perhaps in the pineal, where Descartes suggested the soul might reside? Or maybe in our all-important frontal lobes? (No. As romantics have postulated, this most important center is not even inside the brain; indeed, provided that you keep your head bowed, it is closer to the heart. These command neurons are in your teeth. A barrage of impulses from a few small nerve fibers inside a single tooth is quite sufficient to ruin your day. All other centers in the brain are seemingly rendered subservient to that tooth, when it chooses to speak.)

The ability to command is characteristic of the lowest, fire-alarm-like mechanisms in our nervous systems—but not, it seems, of the highest mental processes. The obligatory response is handy for military commands, but in seeking the basis of higher mental processes, we are looking for something more like policy-making and diplomacy, with a lot of give and take, and with consensus as an arbiter. We shall have to be concerned with creativity—where we get our ideas. And choice—how we evaluate candidates and judge if any one of them is good enough to try implementing.

Yes, even mentioning the "little person inside the head" sometimes

promotes a fallacy—that there is a "seat of the soul," a cave somewhere inside the brain where "the *real* me" homunculus resides as a
voyeur and puppeteer, watching our senses and pulling our strings.
And yes, we need to explain why that is an oversimplification with a
lot of excess baggage from body-and-soul days. But we need not throw
out our *enfant terrible* with the bathwater: The narrator of our conscious experience can emerge from a committee of brain regions just as
the pattern of a snowflake emerges from a cooling committee of water
molecules. It doesn't even require a snowflakelike center to form: The
unity of consciousness can result from a virtual center, just as physicists can treat all of the molecules constituting the earth as if they
were all concentrated in the center of the earth when computing
gravitational attractions. Virtual centers are much handier concep-
tually and computationally, and it is not surprising that our brains
often make use of a virtual center as we decide what to do next.

Understanding thought is not without its hazards. I suppose that
there is always the danger of someone's inventing a human version of
the hog-tie: Cowboys have a way of trussing up a cow or a pugnacious
bronco that fixes the brute so that it can neither move nor think
(someone could argue that religious and political leaders invented the
human hog-tie long ago).

But I don't share Gregory Bateson's apprehension; he argued in
Angels Fear that "if we were aware of the processes whereby we form
mental images, we would no longer be able to trust them as a basis for
action. They say the centipede always knew how to walk until somebody asked it which leg it would move first."[3] Getting stuck,
whether from incessant worry or Hamlet-like indecision, is always a
potential problem—but for many people, an understanding of how to
utilize more effectively the mental processes would be liberating
rather than hazardous. While motivations affect the biases and so the
judgments (I do worry about a super-cocaine being concocted as we
better understand the neurochemistry of motivational systems), what
we are talking about here is thought itself: in particular, the mechanisms by which we generate new ideas, compare them to past experience, and then choose between them.

Even there, we can see some potential problems. I have come to suspect that some of the multiple meanings of the word *consciousness* are grounded in fear; that there is intentional obfuscation as well as befuddlement. We use *conscious* for one extreme of a sleep–wakefulness spectrum, as in *unconscious*. We often use it as a synonym for aware-ness, as when we say, "I was *conscious of* a breeze touching my face." As Ralph Barton Perry said in 1904:

> There is no term [consciousness] at once so popular and so devoid of standard meaning. How can a term mean anything when it is em-ployed to connote anything and everything, including its own nega-tion? One hears of the object of consciousness and the subject of consciousness, and the union of the two in self-consciousness; of the private consciousness, the social consciousness, and the transcendental consciousness; the inner and the outer, the higher and the lower, the temporal and the eternal consciousness; the activity and the state of consciousness. Then there is consciousness-stuff, and unconscious con-sciousness. . . . The list is not complete, but sufficiently amazing. Consciousness comprises everything that is, and indefinitely much more. It is small wonder that the definition of it is little attempted.[4]

With such a list (and it has only expanded during the present cen-tury), we must ask whether consciousness confusion is not being intentionally compounded, whether fear of understanding has domi-nated curiosity. Julian Jaynes usefully pruned down this laundry list in the introduction to his 1976 book *The Origin of Consciousness in the Breakdown of the Bicameral Mind* and tried to refocus attention on the narrator of our conscious experience as the most important of the many things we call consciousness. Though I see little reason to accept Jaynes's conclusion that this narrator emerged in evolution as recently as three thousand years ago, I do agree with Jaynes that the narrator is the name of the game. And that it is one of the most interesting games in town. We must not only answer "when?" ques-tions but mechanistic "how?" questions and evolutionary "what for?" questions about narrator-dominated consciousness.

Yet we must not forget the many other aspects of consciousness when focusing on the narrator issues, just because they are less susceptible to a mechanistic analysis—though, for the present pur-poses, I am indeed setting them aside temporarily. I am not redefining consciousness to mean exactly what I want it to mean, neither more nor less (shades of *Alice in Wonderland*), but rather exploiting one handle on a multifaceted problem, casting about, trying to find a Copernican improvement in viewpoint.

⊏⊐

Consciousness is undeniably useful. Again we find the most succinct statement coming from the late nineteenth century, this time from the physicist Heinrich Hertz: "The most important problem which our conscious knowledge should enable us to solve is the anticipation of future events, so that we may arrange our present affairs in accordance with such anticipation."

Richard Alexander expanded on this in *The Biology of Moral Systems*:

> Consciousness and related aspects of the human psyche (self-awareness, self-reflection, foresight, planning, purpose, conscience, free will, etc.) . . . represent a system for competing with other humans for status, resources, and eventually reproductive success. [They are] a means of seeing ourselves and our life situations as others see us . . . so as to outguess, outmaneuver, outdo those others—most particularly in ways that will cause . . . them to continue to interact with us in fashions that will benefit us and seem to benefit them. Consciousness, then, is a game of life in which the participants are trying to comprehend what is in one another's minds before, and more effectively than, it can be done in reverse.[5]

This illuminates one of the potential hazards of understanding how we think (as opposed to understanding motivation *per se*): As Alexander points out, if others understand how we think, they might somehow take advantage of it. Of course, one could say that modern pseudo-scientific advertising has already done this, and that charlatans have traditionally done it. But Alexander also points out one cure: "I have suggested that consciousness is a way of making our social behavior so unpredictable as to allow us to outmaneuver others. . . ." By creating lots of choices, we have so many avenues open to us that we are hard to predict, too wily to trap. And an understanding of how to generate even more of Mach's "teeming, swelling host of fancies" can only make each of us more unique, not more predictable and manipulatable.

―

But why sequencing? And how did an elaborated sequencing committee arise in evolution? While often useful, command queues for detailed preplanning are seldom essential: Goal-plus-feedback usually suffices, as when raising a cup to one's lips and getting progress reports from the joints and muscles, using them to adjust the path.

Where planned chains become essential, and thus likely to evolve rapidly, is where feedback becomes impossible, yet a linked series of moves must be precisely executed. Reaction time becomes a problem for brief ballistic movements such as hammering, throwing, clubbing, or kicking: For example, a dart throw takes 119 milliseconds until the fingers let loose the dart, but the round-trip reaction time from arm to spinal cord and back to arm takes 110 milliseconds. The progress reports will mostly arrive too late for path corrections to be made. For organisms that need to be both large (meters of conduction distance) and fast, one often needs the neural equivalent of an old-fashioned roll for a player piano. We carefully plan during "get set" to act without feedback.

Humans often hunt with projectiles; faster and farther throws are always better, provided accuracy can be maintained. My 1983 biophysical model for throwing emphasized the need for submillisecond timing precision in letting loose the projectile. Such timing precision is far in excess of what one can expect from even the best of neurons (they are always pretty jittery, not merely after too many cups of coffee), and the jitter remains troublesome when many are chained together in a single command buffer. This suggests that the precision of the release of a projectile must arise from the Law of Large Numbers (the same rationale for why, in order to halve a standard deviation, one averages four times as much data).

Thus there must be many sequencers that, at least temporarily, can be ganged in parallel (imagine multiple columns of horses pulling a single wagon) during the occasions demanding peak performance in one-shot timing. To reliably hit a rabbit-sized target from twice the distance requires that the jitter in rock release time be narrowed by a factor of eight, and the only known way of accomplishing this feat is, as one gets set to throw each time, to assign sixty-four times as many noisy neurons to the task and then average their recommendations for the release time. To triple throwing distance requires a 729-fold increase in neurons assigned to the task. "Concentrating" as we get set to throw probably involves recruiting a lot of nervous neighbors to help out, all "pushing" together—not unlike when a dozen bystanders heave together to push an automobile out of a ditch. But it's not just a dozen, in the case of neurons—since faster and farther throws are always better, throwing has a prodigious appetite for more and more sequencing neurons.

This gives one a very different perspective of randomness. Technology treats noise as an unwanted impediment, Darwinism as a means of exploring new avenues, but here we see it as a stimulus to evolve redundant machinery—whose secondary uses may be revolutionary. I have proposed (in *The Throwing Madonna* and more elaborately in *The River That Flows Uphill*) that hand movements may have a lot to do with the evolution of our brain's greatly improved abilities to handle sequence. As Jacob Bronowski said: "The hand is a cutting edge of the mind." And, indeed, various cognitive scientists have suggested that the hand shapes up our conceptual abilities via tool-making.

But I am suggesting something that is mechanistically rather different from the proposal of the cognitive cognoscenti, proposing instead that the brain's sequencer machinery can be used for shaping up sentences, scenarios, and listening to arpeggios when not required for planning a complicated hand movement. This says that spare-time "co-opting" may have been all-important. So even if evolution shaped up our sequencing machinery via our success in rock throwing, we would get some "free" improvements in other chaining-dependent abilities such as language and planning—at least, during the times when we were not busy getting set to throw.

———

Darwin Machines aren't just some future class of massively serial computers that simulate Darwinism: Darwin Machines could be biological as well. Where in the brain does our Darwin Machine live? It may involve much of the left cerebral hemisphere in mammals. This is not to say that the right brain is uninvolved, only that even in monkeys, the left hemisphere is best at deciphering rapid sound sequences—and so it apparently became a natural home for many language-related abilities.

Indeed, the core of human language in the cortex is a sequencing area for both incoming sounds and outgoing movements—just what grammar needs. Comparison of grammars shows that the typical subject-verb-object word order of an English sentence is not biologically determined: Japanese syntax uses subject-object-verb, while classical Arabic puts the verb first. What the biology may provide is the serial buffer to hold the phrase while it is analyzed according to the learned rules (though more subtle grammatical linkages are perhaps constrained by buffer branchings, corresponding to Chomsky's deep structure). There are some suggestions that the capacity of one important serial buffer is about a half dozen items, judging from phenomena such as chunking of memory.

Precisely timed hand movements are probably controlled out of the cerebral cortex, mostly the frontal lobe's motor strip, about an inch above your ear. But, along with the cerebellum, most of the rest of the frontal lobe gets in the act, too. Just in front of the motor strip is the so-called premotor cortex (a term that here includes the supplementary motor area), and it has a reputation for chaining together fluent sequences of action, such as you might use to insert a key into a lock, turn a doorknob, and push open a door. When we practice playing a musical instrument, we are likely tuning up the premotor cortex; injuries to it do not result in weakness or paralysis (as do injuries to the motor strip) but merely diminish one's ability to carry out a chained series of motions quickly, what the neuropsychologist Aleksandr Romanovitch Luria liked to call a "kinetic melody."

And the rest of the frontal lobe, that which is in front of both the motor strip and the premotor cortex (and known as the "prefrontal cortex"), has a lot to do with planning a novel sequence. A patient with a prefrontal tumor can raise his arm on command if the arm is lying atop the bedcovers—but might get stuck if asked to raise his arm if he first has to extract it from under the covers and then raise it. If you ask the patient to remove his arm from under the covers, he can do it. If he is then asked to raise it, he can. But he may not be able to plan out this novel sequence and then execute it.

Detailed knowledge of movement programs is still a goal rather than an accomplishment; I would share the assessment of J. Z. Young: "I must stress how little is yet known about the programs of the brain. The code has not yet been properly broken; but we begin to see the units of it. . . . We can see that the code is somehow a matter of sequences of neural activities, providing expectancies of what to do next."[6]

So large areas of the frontal lobe are involved in sequencing, and also the temporal and parietal lobe areas associated with language. But they might not have arisen for their usefulness in talking and planning—sequencing machinery might have grown extensive simply because so much of it is occasionally needed for accurate throwing. It's a very different view of our origins from the usual bigger-is-smarter-is-better notions. As I said in *The River That Flows Uphill*:

> From such an evolutionary ratchet jacking up brain size, there arose unbidden our own brain of unbounded potential. From basketball to tennis, this mosaic brain expresses its ancient pleasure in precisely timing a sequence. Transcending its origins, our brain can now create novel sequences using grammar and music. Blind to our foundations, we nonetheless created poetry and reason; with a clearer footing, we can perhaps contemplate how our enlarged consciousness evolved and is evolving.[7]

Musical forms may yet have much to teach us about our brains. Not only do we string muscle commands together to make unique movements, words together to make never-heard-before sentences, and concepts together to make innovative scenarios, but we make melodies as well. The folk singer Bill Crowfoot observes that children in many cultures, speaking many languages, still all use the musical interval known as a minor third to harass their siblings: *Na-na na na-na na*. The more elaborate forms of the Magnificat may not be as universal—but, still, they resonate. Why?

If we come to understand why Bach's brain still speaks so compellingly to our brains today, we will have bridged the gap between primary evolutionary adaptations and the magnificent secondary uses that can be made of the same brain machinery. Music is an emergent property, unless someone can figure out how a lilting aria and a choral fugue and a rippling arpeggio were shaped up by survival-sensitive adaptations. Senza Sordino's notes for the Mass in F and the Magnificat demonstrate some of the musical features that tickle our brains:

. . . the final "kyrie eleison" is composed as a counterfugue—that is, each thematic entry is answered by its inversion. In the further course of the movement, Bach makes use of the contrapuntal techniques of stretto, parallel voice-leading, and mirror inversions of themes. As the fugal chorus builds to a climax, each voice enters one note higher than its predecessor; and the repetition of this device gives the impression of an endless succession of voices. . . .

The phrase *mente cordis sui* calls forth an astounding harmonic progression, suggesting, in the course of some nine measures, D-major, F-sharp-minor, F-sharp-major, B-minor, D-minor, and, finally, D-major, the first trumpet bringing everyone back to the home key with a descending scale passage and trill that haunts the dreams of every trumpeter.

What is it about our brains that so disposes them to the minor third and the trill, despite the lack of evolutionary adaptations for such musical patterns? Natural selection conceivably might have shaped up our response to the drumbeat—but hardly four-part harmony. Though this question is seldom asked, I am sure that the standard answer would be the tie with language: both are sequences of sound where recognizing patterns is all-important. And so natural selection for language abilities would, *pari passu*, gain us musical abilities as a secondary use of the same neural machinery. Maybe so. But the many parallel planning tracks as the key element of "get set" in ballistic movements suggests that both language and music are potentially secondary uses of the neural machinery for ballistic skills, that music might have more to do with modern-day baseball than modern-day prose. Sordino's notes end with:

> *Gloria Patri, gloria Filio, gloria et Spiritui sancto! Sicut erat in principio et nunc et semper in saeculorum. Amen.* ("Glory to the Father, and to the Son, and to the Holy Ghost! As it was in the beginning, is now and ever shall be, world without end. Amen.")
>
> . . . Bach cannot resist the musical symbolism of triplets in the three invocations, to represent the tripartite nature of the Trinity, and a return of the opening music at the end, taking his cue from, "As it was in the beginning. . . ." But the musical return serves aesthetics as well as theology, making a perfectly satisfying close to one of the most perfect and satisfying works of the choral literature.

There are many aspects of human brains that would vie for a trilogy if anyone tried to pick the three focal *mechanistic* aspects of our humanity. Surely if one's criteria were traits whose improvements would help us survive the next century, the mental machinery controlling *cooperation*, *conflict resolution*, and *family size* would undoubtedly rank high (all are likely to be strongly shared with our primate cousins—yet researchers in those areas operate on shoestring budgets). But if we focus on the three primary traits via which we differ from the apes in an order-of-magnitude way, we can wind up with a curious trio: *language*, *scenario-spinning consciousness*, and *music*—three aspects of sequential patterns in our brains. Their beginnings are still dimly seen but in their elaboration may lie the higher humanity. And possibly the artificial humanity.

NOTES

[1] T. H. Huxley, *Methods and Results* (New York: Appleton, 1897), p. 191.

[2] P. Brooks, *Reading for the Plot* (New York: Knopf, 1984): p. 3.

[3] Gregory Bateson and Mary Catherine Bateson, *Angels Fear* (Macmillan, 1987), p. 88.

[4] Ralph Barton Perry, "Conceptions and Misconceptions of Consciousness," *Psychological Review*, (1904) vol. 11. pp. 282–296.

[5] Richard D. Alexander, *The Biology of Moral Systems* (New York: Aldine de Gruyter, 1987), pp. 112–113.

[6] J. Z. Young, *Philosophy and the Brain* (Oxford: Oxford University Press, 1987).

[7] W. H. Calvin, *The River That Flows Uphill: A Journey from the Big Bang to the Big Brain* (New York: Macmillan, 1986), p. 365.

Reality and the Brain: The Beginnings and Endings of the Human Being

JULIUS KOREIN, M.D.

Being conservative, we could estimate the onset of the life of a human being—as reflected by the organizational structure of the critical system of the brain and its incipient function—to be after twenty weeks; a person begins to emerge.

We may philosophize about reality and discuss its relative or absolute nature—the underlying invariance or the limitations and distortions of our sensory neural apparatus—but when faced with an individual in extreme pain or one who is bleeding massively, reality becomes a very simple, immediate problem. In the emergency situation one does not contemplate the brain as the organ that perceives itself, and naïve reality predominates. When we study the brain through psychophysiological experiments or consider experiments of nature such as patients with strokes, seizures, or dementia, we begin to learn about structural and functional aspects of what the brain does and how it works. Sophistication in experimental paradigms and advances in a variety of technologies allow us to delve deeper into what the brain does and how it does it. Although we are far from a solution that clarifies brain function in a succinct and total manner, enough knowledge has been amassed so that the brain has a fairly good idea of what the brain does. Certainly, we know enough to make a diagnosis of brain dysfunction with good localization of the abnormality and its probable cause. Complex tests may be performed to gain information about multiple levels of structure and function; these include tests relating to behavioral responses, electrophysiology, and imaging techniques that reveal biochemical and physical architecture of the brain. Ultimately, when an autopsy is performed on a patient who dies with central nervous system disease, the gelatinous brain is placed in a fixative such as Formalin to allow hardening for subsequent microscopic examination. Many other structural and chemical tests and examinations may be performed on the tissue. By correlating the pathology found with the clinical and laboratory evaluations performed on the patient, one confirms or refutes the diagnosis and gains further insight into how the brain perceives reality.

However, the reality discussed in this essay relates to the functioning of the human organism as a whole—as a person and as an individual entity. This approach is, or should be, that of the physician in his interaction with the patient.

The patient may be considered as an information generator describing his complaints and symptoms to the physician, who receives and processes the information. The patient is then examined, and more information is obtained. Based on his previous knowledge and experience, the physician attempts to categorize the clinical findings and formulates a differential diagnosis. This set of localizations and probable causes is a hypothesis to explain the patient's problem. This may then be confirmed by further tests. In this manner medicine appears to be a science. Thus, if a forty-two-year-old man has a sudden onset of headache followed by some weakness of his right face and upper extremity and difficulty with speech comprehension, confirmed by examination, a neurologist would include in his differential diagnosis localization of the dysfunction to the left cerebral hemisphere, since the functions of speech and right-sided motor activity reside in the left hemisphere. A second part of his diagnosis would suggest a cause or etiology, which, because of sudden onset of the headache, might be a small hemorrhage, possibly from an aneurysm. In order to substantiate or refute the diagnosis, computerized axial tomography might be performed, which might show a hemorrhage. Further tests might reveal the aneurysm. Of course, all medicine is not so straightforward.

Let us contrast this patient with one suffering intermittent, severe, pulsating headaches occasionally preceded by minor visual disturbances. The headache may be described in greater detail as to its characteristics, onset, duration, locus, intensity, and periodicity. Physical examination and laboratory findings are negative. It is not uncommon for a physician to come to a primary diagnosis of atypical migraine—the patient does not have the scintillating aura, nausea, or vomiting often associated with classical migraine. Here we clearly see a problem in definition of the disease state depending on how one defines migraine. It may be a narrow filter through which only patients with a highly specific set of findings can be classified, or it may be broadened to include a huge percentage of headache syndromes. The diagnosis, therefore, depends upon the definitions as well as observations, and subsequently on the therapeutic response. There is no clear-cut observation that may be used to refute the diagnosis, since the fuzziness of the concept is related to imprecise definitions. The field of psychiatry and mental illness is a prime example. Thus, a diagnosis is not identical to a hypothesis. We attempt to diagnose specific clinical states of the human being, but these may be imprecise, preventing the performance of tests that will confirm or refute a diagnosis.

We may imagine a multidimensional space of n variables, each representing the value of a clinical observation at a given time. Every individual can be represented at a given moment in time in this n-space by n-coordinates. As time passes the variables may change. The trajectory of "normal" states will be a path that would be well defined with some blurring at the edges. As different patients become ill, the trajectories will deviate from normal but will vary from one another depending on the illness—a patient with a brain tumor would go in one "direction," while patients with multiple sclerosis will traverse another path. Similar diagnostic entities would cluster in grouped trajectories. The trajectory of patients with a diagnosis of intracerebral hemorrhage would be well delineated, while that of schizophrenia will be much less clearly demarcated. Diagnoses can be considered a symbol or shorthand for the complex of findings that deviate from the normal. If the patient improves, he will tend to return to the normal group.[1]

In the above-described multidimensional space there will be terminations of trajectories depending on how the patient dies, but all will die and ultimately collect in one invariant group. Similarly, we may expect these variables to have some specific onset or beginning. It is toward these diagnostic states involving the beginning and termination of the human being that we will address ourselves.

The problem of seeing the world in terms of a naïve reality (accepting the world at the face value of our "senses") is that this does not permit one to take into account changes, and their deeper consequences. Modern technology has been applied to medicine with a vengeance. The advent of resuscitative and life-support systems in the intensive-care unit are only modest innovations heralding an age exemplified by chemotherapy, organ transplantation, artificial organs, *in vitro* fertilization, storage and implantation of embryos, and genetic engineering, among others. The thrust in this direction of improving medical care has been backed by enormous effort, time, and money.

Consider the deep reasons for this effort—certainly, the quest for truth and the betterment of humankind, and many other noble ideals may be invoked. On a more primitive level, a large segment of the population of Western civilization equates death with evil, and people have given the government the mandate to push the barriers of death as far away as possible. A "life at any price" ethic has saturated medicine. This does not say that all modern technology is monstrous or misused, but it does set the stage for misuse at levels heretofore unimagined. The dilemma of the physician is to curb himself and respond appropriately to the demands of the variety of groups in our culture. The technological response to the reality of disease must be tempered with parallel behavior that considers the reality of the individual's dignity, feelings, and overall well-being. A particular set of practical and ethical problems arising from the new technology relates to brain death and "brain life."

Traditionally, in medicine, death has been defined as irreversible cessation of cardio-respiratory function. We will start from this classical definition and essentially ignore any definitions pertaining to loss of the soul or other concepts related to religion or myth. Practically, when the physician makes the diagnosis of death he can test the state of the patient by checking pulse, blood pressure, respiration, responsivity, spontaneous movements, and the like. If the diagnosis is not obvious, further examination may include cutting a blood vessel to see if pulsatile bleeding occurs; or, laboratory tests such as an electrocardiogram may be performed to verify absence of cardiac activity. It has been said in the more ancient literature that the only unequivocal finding in death is putrefaction. But considering the state of some patients when they arrive at, say, Bellevue Hospital in New York City, this is not entirely reliable. Errors have been made despite precautions, and patients have been pronounced dead under a variety of circumstances when they are in fact comatose and still alive. This occurs rarely in the patient's home and virtually never in a hospital setting. Many physicians have anecdotal stories of a patient who is pronounced dead and wakes up in the morgue. The patient is then sent to the hospital, usually to be pronounced dead again within a relatively short period of time. Even Vesalius had the misfortune to attempt to dissect a cadaver that proved to be alive, ultimately resulting in the patient's death and the dissector's inquisition.[2] Consider that the real purpose of modern embalming techniques is to prevent patients from being buried alive. Yet the possibility of this happening is extremely slight with any degree of sound medical judgment on the part of the physician.

In 1957[3] a group of anesthesiologists presented to Pope Pius XII the question, whether it was appropriate to keep the corpus or body "alive" when irreparable destruction of the brain was present. The response was a papal allocution entitled "The Prolongation of Life," from which two relevant pronouncements will be stressed. The first was that the pronouncement of death was not the province of the Church but the responsibility of the physician: "It remains for the doctor . . . to give a clear and precise definition of 'death' and the 'moment of death' of a patient who passes away in a state of unconsciousness." The second point was that there came a time in the course of a patient's disease where the situation was hopeless and death should not be opposed by extraordinary means. The definitions of the words *hopeless* and *extraordinary* were not precisely stated in medical terminology, but it was clear that in hopeless cases resuscitative measures could be discontinued and death be unopposed. This papal allocution historically may be considered the point of departure for the reevaluation of death in terms of brain death.

In 1959 three groups of French physiologists did clinical studies on patients in the deepest state of unresponsive coma who were being maintained on a respirator.[4] They had no spontaneous respiration, movement, or responsiveness, and electrodes placed deep in their brains showed no evidence of electrical activity. The condition was described as *coma dépassé*, literally translated as "beyond coma" or "ultra-coma." Later it was demonstrated that these patients had no intracranial blood flow. This situation remained a clinical idiosyncrasy associated with the intensive-care unit until the need for organ donors began to increase with the inexorable advance of technology. The initial impetus for redefining death was clearly present prior to the era of organ transplantation. But once organ transplants became therapeutically reliable, the pressure to redefine death in relation to irreversible brain dysfunction increased exponentially. During the period from 1968 to 1981 there was a marked increase in research and studies at an international level to redefine death appropriately. The definition became inextricably intertwined with the ever-increasing demands for kidneys, livers, hearts, and other organs for purposes of transplantation. For example, the treatment of choice for permanent renal failure is transplantation, and dialysis was considered as a temporizing treatment that would be used until the patient could be matched for a kidney.

The Harvard Criteria are most quoted and were published in 1968.[5] The terminology was imprecise, but the diagnosis of brain death was considered established if the patient had none of the following: cerebral responsiveness, movements, respirations (non–respirator-dependent), and reflexes. Additionally, there was to be no evidence of drug intoxication or hypothermia (reversible conditions), the presence of a flat EEG, and persistence of the entire clinical state for twenty-four hours. During the same year at a medical meeting the Declaration of Sydney was made. This statement reaffirmed death as a process rather than an event and, more important, indicated that the pronouncement of death should involve two physicians unrelated to any transplant procedure. Variations, refinement, and greater precision in the definition and diagnosis of death were developed over the next decade by research performed in Scandinavia, Japan, and the United States. The conclusions of these studies may be summarized as follows:

> A prerequisite required establishment of a diagnosis with the performance of all appropriate diagnostic and therapeutic procedures.
>
> Criteria after the onset of apnea and coma included coma with cerebral unresponsivity, absolute apnea (specific test for respirator dependence), absent cephalic (brain-stem) reflexes with fixed dilated pupils, and EEG with electrocerebral silence. The duration of the findings was to be at least six hours from the onset.
>
> A confirmatory test for absence of intracranial circulation, if necessary, was also required.

The redefinition of death, despite the pressures of secondary gain via organ transplantation, has a rational basis. Classical cardiorespiratory death resulted in the diagnosed brain state. This may be looked upon as a causal coincidence in that in the human organism the cessation of respiration and circulation results in central nervous system destruction. It may be argued that it is only with the destruction of *the critical system of the human organism* that death of the individual occurs. We may define the critical system as that system which cannot be replaced by any biological, chemical, or electromechanical device. The critical system must subserve the essential behavioral characteristics of the individual human being. Virtually all organ systems are replaceable in humans, with the exception of the brain. The heart can be replaced by a pump, the kidneys by an appropriate dialysis unit, the endocrine glands by hormonal replacement therapy, and so on. A limb may be artificial, but when it comes to the neuronal cells that comprise the central nervous system, soon after birth an individual has a set of these elements that does not reproduce or regenerate. A neuron may grow by increasing its dendritic tree and interconnections with changes in the production of neurotransmitters. The soma may support growth of a crushed axon, but if the soma is destroyed, the process is irreversible. The brain depends on the neurons for its function, and the organism depends on the brain. If the brain is destroyed, or becomes irreversibly nonfunctional, the critical system is destroyed, and despite all other systems being maintained by any manner whatsoever, the human organism as an individual functioning entity can no longer be considered to exist. Neuronal "brain" transplants may alter brain function but do not replace the entire critical system. If the brain as a whole or the head could be transplanted, the *donor* would be the *recipient*. The basis of the individual organism—the person who is the member of the human species—resides in his or her brain.

Brain death, then, is death. This is not to be construed as two definitions of death, since both the classic definition and brain-death criteria are based on irreversible cessation of brain function. The argument may be illustrated both experimentally and clinically. If a dog's head is experimentally severed from the body and kept alive by an appropriate life-support system and the same is done to the dog's body, the essence of the animal's "personality" is in the head, not the corpus. The head in such an experiment will eat, salivate, blink, sleep, and respond to stimuli to which it has previously been conditioned—for example, when its name is called. The body can also be kept "alive," but it in no way has the dog's essential being. If a human is quadriplegic because of a cervical spinal cord transection but has a normal brain, he or she may be kept alive by a life-support system; unquestionably, he or she is a person who is aware and responds meaningfully to external stimuli. However, if a person's cerebral hemispheres were destroyed by a shotgun blast, with subsequent deterioration of the brain stem, the temporary maintenance of the body by modern scientific methods does not mean that a human life is being maintained. To press the analogy to an extreme, we may culture skin cells from a person and keep them growing in artificial media for months. If we destroy these cultured cells, however, this does not constitute the killing of a person, although we are obliterating DNA molecules that potentially may be used to construct a human organism. The pitfall of considering words such as *potential* or *imminent* is that they result in ambiguity and confusion—potential death is not death. The critical system of the human organism is composed of the cerebral hemispheres, deep structures, the brain stem, and cerebellum. It does not include the spinal cord. The functions subserved by the cerebrum are sentience, cognitive behavior, awareness, learning, memory, voluntary movement, speech, ideation, reasoning, and mentation, as well as emotional and goal-directed activity. In contrast, functions subserving the brain-stem mechanisms include complex, stereotyped reflex patterns, respiration, and extraocular movements. The stem also contributes by means of the ascending reticular formation to aspects of consciousness. The cerebellum is involved with coordination and movement patterns. It is the irreversible dysfunction of all these structures that must occur in order to diagnose the death of the human being.

If we accept the definition that death of the human being can be diagnosed when the brain, as the critical system, is dead, we must establish appropriate tests to determine when the brain is irreversibly nonfunctional. These tests must be completely reliable insofar as an error in diagnosis is only permissible in calling a dead person, live. One must never under any circumstances diagnose a living person as dead.

Studies and research efforts carried out after 1968 to establish an appropriate battery of clinical and laboratory tests, then, have been concerned with evaluating and codifying those observations and tests required to diagnose unequivocally brain death. In 1981 the President's Commission for the Study of Ethical Problems in Medicine and Biomedical and Behavioral Research established guidelines for a uniform determination-of-death act, defined as follows:

An individual who has sustained either (1) irreversible cessation of circulatory and respiratory functions or (2) irreversible cessation of all functions of the entire brain, including the brain stem, is dead. A determination of death must be made in accordance with accepted medical standards.[6]

In essence, this statement gives parity to the determination of death by either irreversible cessation of circulation and respiration or irreversible cessation of brain function. One should reiterate that condition (1) is actually based on condition (2) both diagnoses devolve on brain death. Clinical observations and tests must unequivocably establish the cessation of all brain function and the irreversibility of that cessation. History and clinical examination of laboratory studies are all considered, and while no specific tests are excluded, it will become evident that clinical judgment is required to determine the extent and duration of tests performed. We will illustrate the application of these tests in two clinical examples.

The first patient is a thirty-seven-year-old man who was involved in an automobile accident and sustained head trauma. He is stuporous, with blood trickling from his left ear. The patient is found to be responsive to painful stimuli with some spontaneous movement and spontaneous respiration. Cephalic reflexes reveal some disconjugate eye movements and sluggish response of the pupils to light. Radiological imaging by computerized tomography (CT scan) reveals an intracranial hemorrhage involving both cerebral hemispheres. Within several hours the patient's condition deteriorates. He is in unresponsive coma. Respirations cease, and he has to be maintained by artificial ventilation. All brain-stem (cephalic) reflexes are absent, including pupillary response to light, and eye movements. Pupils are fixed and dilated. There are no spontaneous movements. However, deep tendon reflexes are elicited from the lower extremities. Tests reveal the absence of toxic agents, and the patient is appropriately evaluated to ensure that he is, in fact, respirator-dependent. If it is observed by repeated examinations that the patient remains in this condition for six hours he will fulfill the *clinical* criteria for brain death despite normal heartbeat and blood pressure. However, the clinical judgment of the physician requires that he determine unequivocally that the patient is, in fact, brain dead, and an electroencephalogram (EEG) is performed, which is isoelectric—no activity even with maximal amplification and inter-electrode distances. A second physician evaluates the patient. The clinical findings, their duration, and the EEG results are confirmed.

This leads to the diagnosis of brain death—which is death—of this patient. The diagnosis and the time it is made are documented. Subsequently, relatives donate the patient's kidneys, which were removed prior to discontinuation of the respirator. The moment of death occurred at the time the tests were completed and the diagnosis was established. The time of removal of the respirator and kidneys is irrelevant.

The second patient is a twenty-eight-year-old woman who was found in her bed with an empty bottle of sleeping pills (barbiturates) and a suicide note on the night table. She is brought into the hospital by ambulance and is found to be in deep coma, unresponsive, with shallow respirations. She is areflexive, with small, equal, unreactive pupils and no cephalic reflexes. Respirations cease soon after admission and she requires a respirator. Barbiturate level is markedly elevated in the blood, and tests indicate absolute respirator dependence. EEG is isoelectric. CT scan is normal. The patient does not meet the clinical criteria of brain death since the probable cause of her condition is barbiturate intoxication, which is known to be reversible despite the isoelectric EEG. Dialysis is instituted for a period of thirty-six hours, after which the patient has return of spontaneous movements, cephalic reflexes, pupillary activity, and EEG activity. Her barbiturate level has decreased significantly. Patient recovers uneventfully, she is cleared by psychiatry, and on the day she is to be discharged she hangs herself in the bathroom. She is discovered, cut down, and found to be in deep coma, unresponsive to painful stimulation, with absent cephalic reflexes. Respiration has ceased, and the patient is immediately placed on artificial ventilation. Cardiac arrest occurs, but heartbeat is reestablished by appropriate resuscitative methods. Tests reveal minimal barbiturates in the blood and the patient is respirator-dependent. Cephalic reflexes are absent. EEG is isoelectric. CT scan is consistent with brain edema (swelling). The patient is again in a clinical state compatible with brain death. However, the likely etiology of her condition—cerebral anoxia—may be completely irreversible, but there is a remote possibility that the small amount of barbiturates present could contribute to her condition. The physician elects to do four-vessel angiography, which reveals absent intracranial blood flow, thus confirming the diagnosis of brain death.[7]

In both of these patients the clinical criteria of unresponsive coma, absolute apnea, and absent cephalic reflexes were present. These are required for the diagnosis of brain death. Reflexes below the neck may be related to a living spinal cord, and they are not significant. The absence of intoxicants is important, since they can cause reversible coma. In the first case, the EEG was confirmatory and supported the clinical picture allowing the clinician to make his diagnosis. In the second case, despite isoelectric EEG, the initial episode was reversible due to the presence of barbiturates. The etiology of the coma in the final episode—anoxia—resulted in minimal uncertainties in contrast to the first patient with the massive, demonstrable intracranial hemorrhage. Therefore, an additional test of intracranial blood flow was performed to confirm the diagnosis.

▭

There are conditions, such as the *persistent vegetative state* (PVS), which are not brain death but which result in irreversible termination of the human being as a thinking, mentating, emotional, aware entity. Consciousness level can be anywhere from impaired to absent. While some patients in this state are arousable or even awake, there is an absence of mental content—there is no sentience. Complex stereotyped reflexes and respirations commonly occur. In this situation patients may have irreversible damage to portions of their brain rather than to their entire brain due to a variety of etiologies. They do not meet the clinical or laboratory criteria of brain death patients but have lost all that capacity that we consider fundamental to the human being.

We will illustrate this by the classic patient Karen Ann Quinlan, whom I examined in 1975, approximately six months after the onset of her condition. The patient was a twenty-one-year-old woman who was celebrating a birthday with three other friends. She drank gin-and-tonics, became ill, vomited, and aspirated vomitus into her lungs. After the aspiration she became blue, comatose, and pulseless. She was given mouth-to-mouth resuscitation. The ambulance that was called arrived in approximately fifteen to thirty minutes. She was given oxygen by mask and her color improved, and spontaneous movements were noted. Her pulse and blood pressure were normal. Upon arriving at the hospital she was found to be responsive to painful stimuli, and moved all limbs and head spontaneously. Cephalic reflexes were all present with some minor abnormalities of eye movements. Breathing became impaired and she was placed on a respirator.

She had some decorticate posturing, with her legs rigid and extended, but arms flexed and drawn up below her chin. She did not respond to verbal stimuli and no communication could be established. Laboratory studies immediately after admission revealed a less-than-therapeutic dose of Valium in her blood, but there were no barbiturates, opiates, or "hard" drugs found (she had two Valium pills in her purse). Quinine was present in the blood (from the tonic mixer) and no test for alcohol was performed. Within several days she had clinical and radiological evidence of an aspiration pneumonia, which was treated. Subsequently, her EEGs revealed normal to moderate diffusely abnormal activity. A CT scan was normal, as were tests for intracranial blood flow.

The patient's condition over the next six months stabilized, with decorticate posturing, four-limb flexion contractures, and abnormal hyper-reflexia. Attempts to remove her from the respirator resulted in episodes of prolonged apnea. Although the patient moved spontaneously and had sleep/wake cycles, there was no evidence of ability to communicate or demonstration of awareness of her surroundings. The clinical syndrome the patient manifested was diagnosed as *persistent vegetative state* (PVS). At the time of my examination she clearly responded to painful stimuli with altered respiratory patterns while on the respirator. But all movements were stereotyped and related to complex brain-stem reflexes. There was no evidence of awareness, cognition, or goal-directed movements. She was successfully weaned from the respirator within a year of being in coma and could breathe on her own. The patient was then kept on supportive therapy, including tube feeding and turning every two hours, as well as antibiotics for infection for ten years until her death. Her mental status never reached the level of sentience. CT performed prior to her death revealed massive cerebral atrophy.

This condition—the persistent vegetative state, or irreversible noncognitive state—may become chronic. Case reports indicate that with appropriate care patients can live as long as thirty-seven years. At a 1977 New York Academy of Sciences meeting,[8] some health-care professionals wished to include persistent vegetative state as a form of human death, especially insofar as these patients are incapable of mental function other than that described. However, it was decided that vegetative states could not be considered death, for two reasons.

The first is that the certainty of diagnosis is less accurate than that of brain death. Second, and more important, if such a patient were pronounced dead, what does the physician do after the pronouncement? He has a breathing, heartbeating cadaver on his hands. In order to terminate the situation he may withdraw all treatment and feeding, but the time between the pronouncement of death and the cessation of cardiopulmonary function might still be considerable. An active measure, such as injecting the patient with an intoxicant to stop cardiopulmonary function, was considered identical to shooting the patient and, therefore, reprehensible and unethical. The specter of a Nazi medical ethics was raised. Even though one is not killing a human being—since the humanity, if the diagnosis is correct, is irreversibly gone—the act of killing is contrary to the tenets of medicine. Further, this vegetating husk is a shell of a human being and carries with it to friends, relatives, and society and culture as a whole, the aura of what that individual was. This very real, emotional problem and the requirement to terminate actively are crucial to understanding why brain death was defined as it was to exclude persistent vegetative states.

The *critical system of the brain* is irreversibly nonfunctional in these vegetative patients, in contrast to the *critical system of the human being*, which is irreversibly nonfunctional in brain death. In these clinical entities described under the umbrella of irreversible noncognitive or persistent vegetative state, several clearly defined structures or systems within the brain may be identified with sentience. Without these structures, the brain, and hence the individual, can no longer function in a manner that we may describe as human. This pathological state is devoid of sentience, mentation, emotion, and awareness, although arousal may alter with sleep/wake cycles present. Although the lighting of the stage may fluctuate according to the script of the play, no actors are onstage. Complex stereotyped reflexes related to brain-stem and spinal function persist, but this repertoire of activity has no cognitive or emotional mental content. The critical structures include the cerebral cortex, and/or thalamus, and basal ganglia, bilaterally (destruction of the basal ganglia alone may not result in PVS). Bilateral destruction or irreversible dysfunction of any set or combination of these structures will result in an irreversible noncognitive state. In addition, a single lesion destroying the midline upper brain-stem ascending reticular formation prior to its splitting into two parts in the thalamus can also cause a persistent vegetative state in and of itself. Most often patients with PVS who are autopsied show a multiplicity of lesions with severe involvement and atrophy of the above-described structures. The brain of one patient in persistent vegetative state for seventeen years was reduced to 20 percent of the normal weight of three pounds.

We will consider the cerebral hemispheres in their entirety and the ascending reticular portion of the midbrain to comprise the critical system of the human brain. This excludes the cerebellum and most of the brain stem. Thus, on clinical and pathological grounds we have defined the critical system required for the functioning of the essence of a human brain.

In anencephalic malformations we have the unusual situation in which the critical system of the brain has never developed. The more typical case history is that the mother, usually prior to term, delivers this pathological specimen (I do not believe it is accurate to use the term "infant"), which may have the appearance of a troll, with no forehead or skull, and most if not all of the cerebral hemispheres missing. Fortunately, most of these pathological entities are stillborn and those that survive and have spontaneous respirations rarely live for any significant period. However, some cases may breathe for pro-longed periods—from weeks to months. The disorder usually can be diagnosed early in pregnancy by special tests, including amniocentesis and sonography, and therapeutic abortion may be undertaken. Even more rarely, the birth of what appears to be a normal infant occurs at term. The repertoire of behavior at birth and in the first week of life includes breathing, sucking, withdrawal from pain, and random eye movements, all derived from the brain stem. Only after several weeks is the behavioral lag noted, with lack of attention, absence of awareness or eye contact, and other forms of inappropriate behavior becoming obvious. If the child is held up to a light bulb the skull transilluminates, revealing the absence or marked diminution of cerebral contents. In one such case, when a flashlight was placed at the back of the head two beams of light shone, one from each pupil. The skull is essentially full of cerebral spinal fluid, and the disorder is called hydroanencephaly. These specimens may live for an unspecified period if they are carefully cared for or treated. They will never attain sentience. A colleague of mine knew of a case that was maintained to the age of seventeen years—tied to a chair, diapered, and lovingly fed by his mother in the backwoods of Kentucky. The importance of these anencephalics is twofold; first is the classification of their problem, and second is that they may be used for organ transplants. They cannot be considered brain dead, since they may have a living brain stem that maintains them. They are essentially analogous to the persistent vegetative state, with one significant exception: They never develop even the beginnings of a person. It is our thesis that they were never alive as a human being, since they never developed an operational critical system of the brain.

From this point we may consider the definition and diagnosis of the onset of the individual—the earliest beginnings not of human life but of the human being as an entity—a "person."

Utilizing the constructs previously defined in relation to brain death and persistent vegetative state (PVS), we will attempt to define and diagnose the onset of the life of a human being. The focus will be on the critical system of the brain rather than the entire brain (the critical system of the organism). For the practical and ethical reasons discussed above, PVS cannot be used to define brain death as a diagnostic entity. However, it is clear that the termination of the life of the human being in every sense occurs in the PVS. It is for this reason that the reciprocal, inverse, or opposite of PVS (rather than brain death) will be used to approximate the emergence of the human being. In order to determine when the life of the human being begins, we will review the *ontogenesis of the human brain*—more specifically, that of the cerebral hemispheres along with the ascending reticular formation. The period when human life begins will be defined as corresponding to the construction of these systems and the development of their functional capacity. We wish to establish the earliest limits relating to the completion of major construction and the incipient onset of function.

In order to make the diagnostic statement that a human life has begun, we must have available tests and measurements to use as indicators of the state of development and functional capability of the critical system of the brain. Others have chosen to link the emergence of the life of a human being to events or processes such as fertilization or conception, embryonic segmentation, electrical activity of any neurons in the fetal brain, quickening, viability, or the moment of birth. Although each of these has proponents, and some of these events, such as the moment of birth and the time of conception, are clearly demarcated, none is consistent with definitions relating to the termination of human life. One problem is that from the time of conception through the time of birth, adolescence, and adulthood, the human organism is always alive, although it has not yet become a human being in its earliest stages. What we must include in our definition relates to a set of characteristics that are invariant and define a human being from its earliest stages until its termination. We will assume that diagnosed states are "real" states-of-being in transition, but not potential ones. Thus, the process is considered as the set of states observed during the period of transition.

Fetal development will be analyzed to derive a period that can be considered as a transition state marking the emergence of the critical system of the brain of the human being—the construction of the cerebral reticular complex. All embryological and fetal ages will refer to age from onset of fertilization. Although structure and function are inextricably interwoven, the nature of the research and data available forces us to separate them into different aspects of fetal ontogenesis. This simplified description will be modified and revised depending on new knowledge.

———

The fusion of the sperm and egg results in a zygote with a new mixture of DNA. This single cell is triggered for action by fertilization. There is an impetus for rapid and massive reproduction of cells. The underlying mechanism of reproduction in each cell requires nucleic acids— DNA as the recipe and RNA as the translator of the recipe into operational components—such as proteins. The first step is replication of DNA—producing more and more copies of the required recipe for the organism. In each cell transcription of DNA to RNA follows. This step results in the creation of the components for and assembly of the necessary parts for cell function. This translation of RNA to protein using amino acids leads to the production of parts for the dynamic operation of all aspects of cell metabolism and function, even feeding back to maintain the DNA and RNA. On the multicellular level, gross parts of the organism are being created, but we do not yet have the semblance of a human being.

As cell reproduction proceeds they form a ball, which becomes hollow and invaginates—the blastula-gastrula stage. Chemical gradients and structural forces form a "morphogenetic field," which results in a sculpturing of this embryonic organism from within and without. It is impossible for the DNA to specify the development of the entire organism. Rather, the DNA sets in motion other (epigenetic) mechanisms, such as protein enzymes, which, through competition and interaction with the local environment, specify the building of the organism within restricted limits. Thus, the development of an invaginated, cylindrical, three-layered structure in three dimensions begins. The dimensional aspects are along head–tail and back–front axes with right–left symmetry. The layers from inside to out are called endoderm, mesoderm, and ectoderm, respectively.

The indentation that occurs from head to tail on the back surface of the embryo forms the beginnings of the nervous system. From the ectoderm the neural groove becomes a neural tube, finally expanding and segmenting to develop the early structures that are antecedents to the brain and spinal cord. At three weeks after fertilization the embryo is about one-eighth of an inch long. This period, called neurulation, lasts until six weeks, ending with the cleavage of the cerebral hemispheres and deep structures. Neuronal development has occurred in the spinal cord and brain stem to a significant degree but lags markedly in the cerebrum. At about eight weeks there is a transition from the embryonic to the fetal stage. Significant features of the embryo at this stage include head, eyes, limbs, fingers—all in a one-and-one-quarter-inch organism. The minuscule brain at this time is composed of a well-developed brain stem with a smooth cerebrum of the same size. While the fetus more than doubles its weight at thirteen weeks, the cerebral hemispheres become dominant, overshadowing the brain stem and cerebellar structures. The cerebral hemispheres are still smooth, undifferentiated, without convolutions, and microscopically neuronal development is just beginning. There is thickening of the cortical wall with the beginning of a neuronal stratification: synaptic organization (neuronal interconnections) is nonexistent.

During the period from ten to twenty weeks the major event of *neural proliferation* occurs, and *neural migration* begins in the cerebrum.[9] The construction of the cerebral hemispheres from primitive neuroblasts, the precursors of neurons, occurs by the utilization of a process described as *interkinetic nuclear migration.* This phrase attempts to describe the reproductive ritual dance of neurons. The primitive cells lie deep within the cerebrum on the surface of the ventricle (a natural cavity within the brain). Some of these primitive cells proliferate, dividing by mitosis. The daughter cells then migrate toward the cortical plate by entwining themselves around the elongated process of a radical glial cell (a nonneuronal component of the nervous system involving supportive functions) and ascends much like a snake climbing up a vine. Some neurons will climb to a predetermined level and remain there, beginning the layering of the cortex. These have been *determined* and will subsequently *differentiate* into a specific neuron. Other daughter cells will return, descending to the ventricular surface only to reproduce again and repeat the cycle. This dance of reproduction, migration, and return continues to oscillate until the cortical layers are saturated. In this manner, at an estimated rate of 250,000 neurons per minute,[10] the stratification of the cortex is virtually complete in terms of its neuronal complement at twenty weeks.

There is marked overproduction of neurons in virtually all cell assemblies of the developing nervous system. This occurs in the spinal cord and in the neuronal groups of the brain stem, thalamus, and cerebral cortex. This overproduction is a normal, ubiquitous occurrence in ontogenesis of the central nervous system and is later followed by massive neuronal death. The reasons for this unusual phenomenon in ontogenesis are directly related to the interconnecting of groups of neurons with one another. After neurons have developed and differentiated, short processes called dendrites and long ones called axons begin to grow. Bundles of axons form tracts from one neuronal group (cell assembly or nucleus) to another, where they interconnect on their cell bodies and dendrites. These connections are termed *synapses.* The processes underlying the mapping of connections among different neuronal groups are elaborate, dynamic, and competitive. Part of the process involves neuronal overproduction. In order to have sufficient neurons to match one group with another, an extra reproductive cycle occurs to ensure that there will be no deficiency in the number of cells required. This results in doubling the number of neurons needed. After the competition for synaptic connections, a large mass of un-matched cells—the losers of the competition—dies. The final stages of synapse formation and cell-assembly matching involve modifica-tion and retraction of the synaptic connections. The crux of the function of the nervous system is keyed into the (synaptic) connec-tivity among individual neurons and neuronal cell assemblies. It is this crucial stage of development that begins the separation of ana-tomical structure from functioning systems. Consider the analogy of a computer system before and after its components are wired together—it is totally inoperable prior to there being connections between parts.

We are primarily interested in connections within the cerebrum and from the cerebrum to the brain stem and spinal cord in fetal development. These represent a measure of structural completion of the critical system of the brain and its proximity to onset of function. By twenty weeks of fetal age the complement of cerebral neurons is virtually complete, but migration continues. The essential migration of cortical neurons is complete at about twenty-one weeks. The cortical-spinal tract, which descends to superimpose its control over spinal reflex mechanisms, reaches the spinal cord during the fifteenth to nineteenth week. Within the cerebrum, thalamo-cortical fiber connections—which relay sensory information—are present at about seventeen weeks, while the corpus callosum, which interconnects the two cerebral hemispheres, approaches completion at eighteen weeks. Tract development and interconnections of neurons continue for longer periods. There is a significant delay between projection of pioneer fibers to a target and the onset of function. These data represent the beginnings of the cerebral structural substrate for infor-mation input, processing, and output.

What probably occurs toward the end of this twenty-week period is the projection of the neurons of the cerebrum to and from infracere-bral structures, with modification due to information input at this time. The significance of synaptic development relates to the ability of neurons to process information essential for the operation of the critical system of the brain. We are not focusing on when this process is complete; it may in fact go on for the entire life of the individual.

Rather, we wish to delimit the beginnings of this process in the cerebrum. Synaptic development of the spinal cord occurs at a much earlier time, occurring in phases from six to fourteen weeks. The brain stem likewise has evidence of synaptic activity at an early stage in fetal development—the development of the trigeminal nucleus (subserving sensation from the face), for example, has been traced from its inception at about six weeks to up to twenty-two weeks, when significant maturation has occurred. The cerebrum, on the other hand, matures late, and synaptogenesis begins after nineteen to twenty-three weeks in the cortical plate, continuing through the postnatal period and probably through the preadolescent period.

Thus, the structural substrate for function exists quite early in the spinal cord but only begins to develop at about twenty weeks in the cerebrum, from which time it becomes progressively more elaborate in terms of intracerebral and extracerebral projections (to the brain stem and spinal cord). It should be clear that as the cerebral structures superimpose their effects on the brain stem and spinal cord by tract growth, changes occur in these infracerebral structures. The dynamism and competition of the changes are significant in that they represent the instability of the earlier developmental neural states in relation to their transition to the more mature operational state. This flux is the major indicator that we are dealing with only a partial system prior to the establishment of the major outlines of brain structure. We wish to ascertain the range of the lower limit—or rather the initial boundary conditions that reflect the earliest structural and incipient operational phases of the critical system of the brain.

The invariant anatomical substrate is composed of the structures and connections of the ascending reticular system and the cerebral hemispheres. These structures change with development, but the beginning of the invariance occurs when the structure is first being built and is in the process of becoming operational. This functional state is characterized by its ability to be modified by informational input. The earliest time at which the cerebrum may be significantly modified by informational input via the neuronal route on the synaptic level in a manner remotely similar to that of the adult organism occurs at about twenty weeks.

Neurotransmitters are molecules, produced at synapses, allowing them to function as a conduit for information. They transmit information through excitation or inhibition across the synapses. Quantitative studies in the human fetus have been performed on several of these neurotransmitters.[11] Although minuscule amounts of these agents may be present in the fetal nervous system prior to eighteen weeks, significant increases occur in the last half of fetal life and continue to increase exponentially after birth. This exponential rise, starting at about eighteen weeks, indicates the onset of cerebral neurotransmitter function related to synaptic activity. Detailed analysis of neurotransmitter-related enzymes indicates that the picture above is an oversimplification; but it serves as a first approximation. The findings are compatible with the timing of the impact of the developing cerebrum on the remainder of the nervous system after the twentieth week.

▭

The nature of the electrophysiological activity of the fetal brain is of paramount importance in evaluating the presence and function of neuronal activity and synaptic transmission. Neural tissue is most appropriately studied by evaluating spontaneous electrical activity (the electroencephalogram, or EEG), changes in such spontaneous activity related to altered neural states (sleep/wake cycles). Induced electrical activity (evoked potentials) in response to a variety of sensory stimuli (somatosensory, auditory, and visual) also represents an important technique in evaluating the activity of neuronal interaction.

The first evidence of electrophysiological activity has been described variously between six and one-half and eight and one-half weeks of fetal age. EEG activity has also been described during the third and fourth month of fetal life. In reviewing these studies it becomes apparent that the size of the fetal brain is so minute and the recording techniques so gross that we are obtaining electrical activity from infracerebral structures. The most well defined of these studies were recorded from within the structures of the brain of the human fetus with needle electrodes.[12] Evidence indicated that low-voltage electrical activity could be recorded from the brain stem at eight and one-half weeks of fetal age. EEG activity arising from the cerebral hemispheres rather than brain-stem structures has been reliably described to begin at between twenty and twenty-two weeks.[13] The studies on premature neonates indicate a gradual development of EEG activity. Initially, at about twenty weeks, there is none; but as the fetus grows, there are bursts of activity, with long quiescent intervals. At twenty-nine to thirty weeks, more continuous electrical activity is observed. Sleep/wake cycles can also be more clearly distinguished at this time in contrast to the fragmentary episodes seen at twenty-four to twenty-six weeks. Sleep/wake cycles include the stage of rapid eye movements (REM) and concomitant low-voltage EEG activity and suppression of electromyographic (EMG-muscle) activity. These cycles have their source in the cerebral hemispheres, with contributions from infracerebral structures. Ascending reticular activity as demonstrated by EEG arousal and some cortical function begins at about twenty weeks. Evoked potentials have been identified between twenty-two and twenty-five weeks from the cortex but may start somewhat earlier.[14] Prior to this period, electrical activity is derived from subcortical structures in the brain stem. Some activity may arise in the limbic system (primitive cortex subserving survival of individual and species—oral-genital behavior) at about nineteen weeks.

The cerebral hemispheres and the ascending reticular formation are the critical system of the human brain—the electrical activity of these structures reflects the invariant that is the requisite of the onset of the life of the human being as an entity. This period is concurrent with the termination of a major construction phase of the cerebrum—internal components and connections as well as major input and output tracts. Thus, this transition stage occurs at about twenty weeks of fetal life based on the onset of cerebral electrical activity. The next step is to consider fetal behavior itself.

Fetal behavior will be discussed in relation to three modes of experimental observation. The first will be related to those studies in the analysis of direct fetal response outside the uterus. These include observations of spontaneous movements of the fetus and those that occur in response to stimulation of the fetus itself. The second set of studies relates to sonography and the indirect observation of the fetus within the mother's uterus. Although some of these studies attempt to stress input-output relationships, they are almost entirely related to spontaneous movements. The third and perhaps most interesting approach relates to conditioning and learning of the fetus *in utero*.

Movements in response to direct stimuli begin during the seventh week of fetal life.[15] Over the next ten weeks a progressively more complex repertoire of patterned movements is observed, including specific focal reflex patterns relating to the head and limbs. Mass reflexes of the entire body are also elicited. These are more generalized responses to localized stimuli. These stimuli are usually produced by tickling the face or extremity of the fetus with a fine hair. Both input (sensory) and output (motor) activity develop in a sequence beginning at the head and ending at the lower extremities. Immature sensory receptors in the skin and muscle develop during early periods of fetal life to form reflex arcs within the brain stem and spinal cord. By the sixteenth week the generalized patterns are more difficult to produce and focal responses are the rule. There is an increased variety in face, limb, and trunk movement.

Spontaneous movements generally occur slightly later than induced movements. These include sucking, swallowing, grasping, grimacing, and squirming, as well as spontaneous thrusting and jerking. The mother may feel these quickening at about the sixteenth week, but they can occur as early as the thirteenth week.

The neural circuitry underlying these movements is completely infracerebral, involving those components of the spinal cord and brain stem that control simple and complex reflex involuntary behavior patterns. The cerebral structures are still undergoing developmental structural changes at this time and do not contain a functioning structural apparatus.

From the seventeenth to the twenty-second week of fetal life a period of relative *behavioral quiescence* occurs. The fetus, outside the uterus, has decreased, sluggish responses to stimuli. Long periods of inactivity occur and bursts of spontaneous activity are more difficult to evoke. This period terminates at about twenty-three weeks, when self-sustained respirations occur and movement patterns reappear, starting at the head and ending at the feet. We may conjecture that the quiescence is related to superimposition of cerebral on infracerebral structures. The movements occurring after this period are often described as more complex and less stereotyped; they include conjugate lateral eye movements, and indeed, these movements blend into those of the earliest viable premature infant.

In summary, responsivity to stimuli in these fetal experiments progresses from localized to generalized mass reflex response, changing gradually to more highly specific and less generalized reflex patterns as the receptive region to sensory stimuli increases. By the seventeenth week this repertoire of stereotyped movements is punctuated by quiescence and sluggish responsivity to stimuli; and the cycle is reestablished after the twenty-second week, with more complex, less stereotyped response patterns and spontaneous respirations. From here on the progression of behavior complexity increases.

Sonography allows visualization of the fetus *in utero* by means of sound waves and has been used for longitudinal studies of the development and evolution of spontaneous movements. Breathing movements are first noted at about fourteen weeks and become frequent at twenty-four weeks. Startle reactions decrease in frequency during the same period. From the twentieth to the thirtieth week responses to external stimuli are noted, such as increased heart rate to sound; habituation to this response occurs with repeated auditory stimuli. Responses to touch and light are extremely simple reactions but herald more complex ones, to be discussed under fetal learning. Additionally, at about thirty weeks sleep/wake patterns with eye-movement changes are noted. These states apparently can be observed in a premature infant as well as in the fetus at the same age. Sonography has additional clinical importance in that fetal age estimates may be made with considerable accuracy by measurement of the biparietal diameter of the skull or, in early stages, crown-to-rump measurements. [16]

In summary, what sonography has revealed is that there are apparently complex patterns that do change after twenty weeks, and that patterned cyclic changes evolve into sleep/wake cycles after thirty weeks. Additionally, the fetus, *in utero*, appears to be responsive to external stimuli such as sound, with capability of habituation after twenty weeks.

Recent studies on fetal learning by DeCasper and colleagues [17] will be detailed here briefly. In the first experiment a group of pregnant mothers read aloud a paragraph from Dr. Seuss's *The Cat in the Hat* twice a day for the last six weeks of pregnancy. After birth the infant was tested for preferential sucking in response to two different stimuli. The first was the reading of the same *The Cat in the Hat* paragraph, and the second was the reading of a matched paragraph from another story (matched for phonemes and duration). The infant clearly responded with increased preferential sucking to the Seuss story. The second experiment, similar but more elaborate, used two groups of mothers from their thirty-second to thirty-eighth week, each hearing one of two different matched stories. These were taped and played to their respective group twice a day. Fetal heart rate was measured at the end of thirty-eight weeks with both recordings played to each mother—each group acted as the other's control. In both groups the fetal heart rate slowed significantly when the story it was exposed to was played, and increased in rate in response to the story that was played for the first time. The conclusion is inescapable. The fetal nervous system at this stage has captured, stored, and retrieved complex patterned information to which it now can respond (this does not infer understanding of meaning in any manner).

The logical experiment would be to utilize this technique to find the earliest state at which the fetus could respond to an incorporated complex signal.

▭

In view of these data on behavior, movement, and learning of the fetus, it appears clear that until the twentieth week of fetal life there is no evidence that the structure of the critical system of the brain is either complete or operational. In contrast, during the twenty-to-thirty-week period there is ample evidence that the reticular cerebral complex has some level of completeness in its structure and has begun incipient function. After thirty weeks there is no question that the cerebral-reticular complex, although immature, is structurally operational, certainly in terms of sleep/wake patterns, eye movements, and the ability to learn and respond to complex environmental stimuli. Being conservative, we could estimate the onset of the life of a human being—as reflected by the organizational structure of the critical system of the brain and its incipient function—to be after twenty weeks; a person begins to emerge.

Evidence has been presented to support the hypothesis that the life of a human being begins with the onset of the structural organization and incipient function of the critical system of the brain—the reticulo-cerebral complex. The utility of this hypothesis is that it conforms with a large body of biological and scientific data as well as current concepts of brain death and vegetative states. The hypothesis does not depend on conception or birth; nor is it rooted in a biological function that may be altered by advancing technology. It is possible that modern technology may lead to the construction of an artificial uterus, and the entire reproductive cycle from fertilization to birth may be performed outside the woman's body. In this case a practical statement of when the life of the human being begins becomes more significant, dependent only on the invariance of the critical system of the brain.

If we accept the hypothesis, many problems may be resolved, but new and different ones will take their place. For example, the problem of organ transplants from anencephalics is resolved by considering that this partial or incomplete system is not a human being as an entity. It is not, and never was, and never will be a person. Therefore, it does not have the rights we grant to a human being and does not have to be pronounced dead. The organs may be used with the approval of the mother; if the placenta turned out to have therapeutic utility, one would require the mother's approval for its use. Current attempts at declaring anencephalics brain dead is logically incorrect and unnecessary.

Applications to the problem of abortion are also relevant. Utilizing the present concepts, abortion prior to twenty weeks does not affect a human being, since the fetus has not yet developed to this level. Sometime after twenty weeks the rights of the fetus as a human being require consideration. In obstetrical nomenclature, a fetus of less than twenty weeks is termed a spontaneous abortion, while one of more than twenty weeks is called a stillbirth. This leads to problems that relate to fetal rights. When does the fetus have rights, and what are those rights in juxtaposition to the rights of the woman carrying the fetus?

More complex problems arise in considering organ transplantation from the fetus; already, transplantation of parts of the brain have been made in the treatment of Parkinson's disease. Research indicates that portions of the fetal brain might be successfully used to treat a variety of neurological disorders—possibly the dementia of Alzheimer's disease. The primitive neurons required are to be derived from the brain of a fetus of about sixteen weeks, well within the period before which the life of the human being begins. The results of an abortion now become a product for treatment. Issues to be addressed range from the enormous benefits that may be derived for individuals who are seriously ill with brain dysfunction to the specter of harvesting fetuses for profit. How society and individuals will handle the ethical aspects of these problems will determine in part the moral shape of the world to come.

NOTES

[1] Julius Korein and T. J. Hefferman, "On the Use of Computers in Medicine: Personal Experiences and Critique," *The Jewish Memorial Hospital Bulletin,* (1972), vol. 16, pp. 1–27.

[2] J. J. Bruhier d' Albaincourt, *The Uncertainty of the Signs of Death* (London: Globe in Paterson-Row, 1746), pp. 221.

[3] Pius XII, "The Prolongation of Life" (an address by Pope Pius XII to the International Congress of Anesthesiologists, November 24, 1957) in *The Pope Speaks* (1958), pp. 393–398.

[4] Julius Korein, "The Diagnosis of Brain Death," *Seminars in Neurology* (1984), vol. 4, pp. 52–72.

[5] "Definition of Irreversible Coma: Report of Ad Hoc Committee (Chairman, H. K. Beecher) of Harvard Medical School to Examine Definition of Brain Death," *JAMA,* (1968), vol. 205, pp. 85–88.

[6] "Guidelines for the Determination of Death: Report of the Medical Consultants on the Diagnosis of Death to the President's Commission for the Study of Ethical Problems in Medicine and Biomedical and Behavioral Research," Special Communication, *JAMA,* (1981), vol. 246, pp. 2184–2185.

[7] Julius Korein, "Brain States: Death, Vegetation and Life," in J. E. Cottrell and H. Turndorf, eds., *Anesthesia and Neurosurgery,* 2nd ed. (St. Louis: The C. V. Mosby Co, 1986), pp. 293–351.

[8] Julius Korein, ed., "Brain Death: Interrelated Medical and Social Issues," *Annals of New York Academy of Sciences* (1978), vol. 315, pp. 1–454.

[9] J. J. Volpe, *Neurology of the Newborn,* 2nd ed. (Philadelphia: W. B. Saunders Co., 1987), pp. 1–68.

[10] W. M. Cowan, "The Development of the Brain," *Scientific American* (1979) vol. 241, pp. 112–133.

[11] M. V. Johnston, and J. T. Coyle, "Development of Central Neurotransmitter System," in C. Elliot and J. Whelan, eds., *The Fetus and Independent Life*, CIBA Foundation (London: Pitman Publishing Ltd., 1981), pp. 251–270.

[12] R. M. Bergstrom, "Electrical Parameters of the Brain During Ontogeny," in R. J. Robinson, ed., *Brain and Early Behavior, Development in the Fetus and Infant* (London: Academic Press, Ltd., 1969), pp. 15–37.

[13] J. R. Hughes, *EEG in Clinical Practice* (Woburn, Massachusetts: Butterworth Publishers, 1982), p. 235.

[14] D. P. Purpura, "Morphogenesis of Visual Cortex in the Preterm Infant," in M. A. B. Brazier, ed., *Growth and Development of the Brain* (New York: Raven Press, 1975), pp. 33–49.

[15] D. Hooker, "The Prenatal Origin of Behavior," Porter Lectures, Series 18, (Lawrence, Kansas: University of Kansas Press, 1952) pp. 54–85 and 123–136.

[16] A. Inniruberto and E. Tajani, "Ultrasonographic Study of Fetal Movements," *Seminars in Perinatology*, (1981), vol. 5, pp. 175–181.

[17] A. J. DeCasper and M. J. Spence, "Prenatal Maternal Speech Influences Newborns' Perception of Speech Sounds," *Infant Behavior and Development*, (1986), vol. 9, pp. 133–150. (Cf. A. J. DeCasper, *et al*, "Familiar and Unfamiliar Speech Elicit Different Cardiac Responses in Human Fetuses," a paper presented at The International Society of Developmental Psychobiology, Annapolis, Maryland, 1986.)

Psychotherapy Systems and Science

ROBERT LANGS, M.D.

I mean something different by the term unconscious. *I don't understand the word to designate a repository for emotional blueprints that make of every new situation the same old defensive fortress. I understand the term to designate a process whereby emotionally charged information is systematically screened out of awareness, essentially for the purpose of survival.*

The status of psychotherapy, whatever forms it may take, should be of concern to virtually everyone within its sphere of influence. And few of us today in Western culture operate outside that influence. Psychotherapy encompasses multitudes of practitioners with myriad aims and tactics; it also encompasses research into the means by which we store and process emotionally charged information. In a culture avidly interested in formulas that will ensure both personal and professional fulfillment, every line of research is a potential pop-psych article on achieving self-worth and a satisfying relationship. At stake here are basic insights into the nature of human functioning. Yet psychotherapy often seems to function less as a science of human emotional processing than as a kind of parascience, inferring "laws" from commonsense observations and assumptions, and expressing them by way of metaphors that have no measurable analogues.

It would be nearly impossible to imagine a hydroelectric plant being built and operating before the existence of physics and engineering; yet Freudian psychoanalysis has spawned a vast and complex network of therapeutic systems that stand suspended, as it were, in midair, having no substantial scientific foundation. Even the nineteenth-century ideas that informed Freud's theory functioned as analogies rather than hypotheses proper. One is reminded of the Chinese proverb, "Theory without observation is like a bird without feet." The fundamentals of psychotherapy stand as theoretical postulates, figments of the imagination of formulating psychotherapists rather than outgrowths of solid scientific observation.

Why, then, have we—lay public and mental-health professionals alike—so easily tolerated this anachronism in our midst? Are there ways of conceptualizing the transactions of psychotherapy and the processing of emotionally charged information that can both help us to understand this state of affairs and to move ahead? As physicists and biologists become more concerned with the role of consciousness in their own domain of research and theorizing, what might psycho-

Note: I am particularly grateful to Lenore Thomson for her work on this essay.

analysis contribute that would be useful to them in their work with the complex issues raised by mental phenomena?

These are but a few of the pressing questions that need our attention. I intend here, without extensive attempts at documentation, to develop perspectives that will help to answer these questions as they bear on the state of psychotherapy both as a science and as a treatment technique, and on our understanding of ourselves as interactive human beings.

▭

Rather than begin from the vantage point of the field or process of psychotherapy as such, I would like to focus for the moment on the inner domain that we have called, for the most part, "unconscious." Most forms of psychotherapy are based on the idea that an individual's behavior may be influenced by feelings and reactions that are not immediately accessible to awareness. Those forms of psychotherapy that are closely allied to the basic concepts of classic psychoanalysis understand this to mean that the individual will strive to gratify unconscious instinctual desires, or that the individual will accommodate his or her immediate perceptions to archaic patterns of defensive behavior learned in childhood. I mean something different by the term *unconscious*. I don't understand the word to designate a repository for emotional blueprints that make of every new situation the same old defensive fortress. I understand the term to designate a process whereby emotionally charged information is systematically screened out of awareness, essentially for the purpose of survival. This screened-out information is subsequently "worked over" outside of awareness, freeing the conscious mind for situations that require immediate and direct action.

All of us have different thresholds for the direct realization of emotional pain. And, of course, beyond our own inclinations, certain traumas cannot be avoided, at least in terms of perceiving the fact of their existence—the so-called acts of God: fire, flood, and social disaster, the death of a loved one. Nonetheless, we are inclined to detach ourselves from even these irrepressible emotional assaults, and to screen out many of the implications and ramifications of this type of terrible experience. We know that these implications and ramifications have registered because of the way in which we also tend to minimize direct communications in response to such incidents, resorting instead to communications that are indirect; that is, instead of talking about the charged event that has set us off, we talk about something else, using that secondary topic as a vehicle for the feelings we haven't yet recognized in response to the incident proper.

Thus, for example, a young man who lost his father in an airplane crash spoke for some fifteen minutes in a psychotherapy session of his grief, of the suddenness of the loss, of his anger at his father for needing to travel, and of other additional, direct, undisguised, manifest, and conscious responses to the event. The therapist, himself inclined toward probing experiences of this kind, responded with intense questions that did indeed elicit reactions in the young man not previously disclosed—for example, a small sense of relief over the death of his father, who had been unsympathetic and at times even brutal toward his son. This was a feeling that had occasioned a sense of guilt, which the patient had not previously brought into focus.

The young man was grateful to the therapist for this illumination of his feelings, then went on to speak of an uncle who had been at his father's funeral and barraged his nephew with a series of infuriating questions. It was the young man's opinion that the uncle was enraged by his brother's death because he had relied on him for important business connections, and that he had chosen to take out his fury on the nephew. Besides, the patient said, this uncle was a dishonest businessman; in fact, he wished that his uncle had died instead of his father.

In this instance, we see an individual processing a series of conscious reactions to a sudden and terrible loss. With probing, additional conscious responses are elicited, and they manifest themselves as direct reactions to the trauma. Granted, this kind of direct processing of emotionally charged information is difficult and painful; however, I would contend that its manifestation as direct information is an *a priori* confirmation of its nature as consciously perceived information.

When emotionally charged information cannot be tolerated and processed in awareness, it is screened out and processed unconsciously. When something is processed unconsciously, we are simply unaware of what has been perceived. If these emotionally charged perceptions reach consciousness at all, they do so only indirectly. In the example I just gave, the young man was talking about a painful situation directly, and then he shifted away from the immediate trauma and talked about something else that was related, but less disturbing. Consciously, the patient was no longer thinking about the initial hurt; he was thinking over and working over something else. *Yet, all the while, he was still processing the first trauma, albeit without awareness.* Because unconscious working over is displaced and often disguised or symbolized, we say that the mental processing is silent, and that the communication is indirect or encoded.

The young man in question was actually working over two traumas that were represented by one set of images. This is a process that Freud first recognized as a property of dream imagery; he called it *condensation*. Although the young man consciously shifted topics and began to talk about his uncle, unconsciously he was still talking about his reactions to the sudden death of his father. As the father's brother, the uncle handily lent himself to this displacement of themes, but it is important to understand that the uncle's assaultive behavior was a factor as well. The uncle's behavior provided the young man with a ready vehicle to express the extent to which he had experienced his father's death as a personal attack. The young man also knew that his father had been involved in a number of dishonest business dealings that had jeopardized the entire family. Thus, the patient's painful feelings and thoughts—his sense of rage and indignation and his feeling that his father deserved to die—which could not be expressed or directly experienced after his father's death, found a ready means of displaced or encoded expression in his comments and feelings about his father's brother.

My hypothesis, then, is that emotionally charged situations in everyday life will set off both conscious and unconscious processes and communications. Broadly speaking, one might say that these traumatic experiences are first cousins to Freud's "day residues" in dreams, given the fact that dreams were Freud's particular model of inner mental processing and communication. I say "first cousins" simply because Freud's idea was that day residues were commandeered by instinctual desires for disguised gratification in dreams. My idea is that emotionally charged situations are stimuli that "trigger" unconscious processing of the perceptions involved. Triggers, then, are traumatic stimuli containing information that sets off parallel processing and two-level communicative responses.

I should explain here that the conscious mind screens out a surprising amount of information, simply because the situations perceived will not admit of a direct or immediate course of action. Most of the reactions that we express indirectly, once recognized consciously, are ordinary enough; but they are guilt-evoking or reveal emotional ambivalence that is difficult to resolve. As human beings, we are exquisitely sensitive to ambiguity and feelings of guilt and rejection; a particular thought or feeling that seems not especially terrible to an outside observer can be unconsciously experienced as shattering and intolerable by the person involved. It would be difficult to overestimate the enormous vulnerability we feel at times of emotional stress. And once we have unconsciously elected to divert a particular set of perceptions and reactions to unconscious processing, we will do virtually anything we can to keep the information unconscious. In fact, as already noted, direct access to this information is possible only by recognizing that some other direct expression has been serving indirectly as its vehicle. That is, we need to decode unconscious messages before we can understand them consciously.

Again, Freud discussed this type of decoding procedure as early as 1900 in *The Interpretation of Dreams*; but I would maintain that encoded communication exists in every human context, not just in dreams. We are constantly using displaced images to work over painful trigger situations indirectly. What we can tolerate knowing, we allow immediately out into the open; but what we feel we cannot tolerate knowing, we keep buried at all costs. This becomes particularly relevant in the psychotherapeutic process, where the intimacy of relationship and the yearning expectations of the patient for acceptance and a sense of well-being make for a highly charged atmosphere. But without a sense of how unconscious processing works, this particular level of experience goes unrecognized. The psychotherapeutic process, ironically, can function as a defense against the unconscious material it claims to unearth and interpret.

This point can be brought home clearly by returning to the example of the young man who lost his father. I said this patient was working over two unconscious traumas by way of one set of conscious images. We saw how the first trigger for his associations to his uncle was his perception of his father's death as a personal attack and his sense that his father actually deserved to die. The second trigger for his associations to the uncle was more immediate—his experience of the therapist's interventions. As described, the therapist had decided to ask the patient a series of probing questions. The patient accepted these questions, responded to them directly, and was grateful for the insight they afforded him. This was the young man's conscious perception of and response to the situation. But the patient also had an unconscious view of the therapist's probing style of operation. The young man's feelings about his uncle's behavior at the funeral served as a vehicle for that unconscious view as well as for his unconscious view of his father's death.

Note, again, that the unconscious view of the therapist, which was displaced onto the story about the uncle, is not an old tape loop out of childhood that has encouraged the patient to distort the therapist's behavior. Neither animals nor human beings distort at the level of initial perception; indeed, perception, conscious and unconscious, is essential to survival. The story of the uncle reflects a valid displaced perception of the ramifications of the information contained in the therapist's effort. And clearly, these displaced images are rather different from the young man's conscious view of and response to that effort. The story of the uncle indicates that the therapist's questions were unconsciously perceived as an assaultive barrage. And if we extend the connection of the story about the uncle to the young man's unconscious perceptions of the therapist, we get a view of the therapist as a dishonest person, a destructive person, someone venting his rage on a substitute party, someone who deserves to die. Small wonder, sitting there in the presence of the psychotherapist, that the patient found such emotionally charged perceptions intolerable and unutterable directly—though he stated them amply in encoded expressions.

We can see, too, that the truths of unconscious perception are intolerable for both patient and therapist. Rare, indeed, is the psychotherapist who can bear the reflection of himself in his or her patient's associations as inadvertently assaultive, dishonest, and even criminal in his or her manner of analytic conduct. And equally rare, though we might expect otherwise, is the patient who can tolerate knowing that he or she has validly perceived the implications of a hurtful or dishonest intervention. In the long run, an exploitative or dishonest therapist can reassure a patient that his or her own defenses and denial will not be subjected to therapeutic scrutiny.

[========]

The small vignette that we have been examining has many ramifications. Perhaps most fundamental is the postulate that we process information in two different ways. I think of these as separate systems, and I realize that I am resorting to metaphor in order to describe the processing involved. One system is conscious, and it processes information directly—particularly practical information that issues in direct action. Of course, we are not aware at all times of every piece of information that we process directly. The conscious system encompasses a kind of storage house, a subsystem, for information that was perceived directly but is not currently the focus of our awareness—memories, recent and old impressions, thoughts, feelings, all of which are directly accessible to awareness again. If we want to retrieve a memory—say, the name of that restaurant someone recommended, or the date of someone's birthday—we perform an act of recollection, or we may let our mind wander until the relevant information comes into focus. This sort of direct processing is the hallmark of the conscious system and its component subsystem.

The second system is the deep unconscious system. This system is not equivalent to Freud's original definition of an unconscious domain. Freud believed this domain to be rather like a large garbage bin that functioned as a repository for anything the conscious mind disowned; he assumed that the conscious mind had perceived phenomena that triggered shameful fears and desires and had repressed awareness of those perceptions or disguised them before the perceptions could register. He believed that under the right conditions one could be led to admit those perceptions back into consciousness and deal with their ramifications consciously. My idea is that the deep unconscious system is a parallel system; whatever its storage capacity, it has been designed specifically to process emotionally charged information outside of awareness. This information entirely bypasses the conscious system. The conscious system has no way to retrieve it. And the conscious system has no access to the information unless it is expressed indirectly, by way of something that is already conscious and does not carry the same degree of emotional trauma.

I do not wish to imply that the deep unconscious system is making some kind of decision about which perceptions to divert from conscious awareness. When I say parallel systems, I mean that the two systems work simultaneously, and they are essentially perceiving different things about the same phenomena. The conscious system is perceiving directly accessible and observational phenomena; it is noticing that the traffic light has changed, that a man two cars back is honking his horn. One becomes directly aware of the need to move. The deep unconscious system is perceiving the same set of elements, but it is registering another set of meanings; some of them are only indirectly evident or implied. For example, this second system may register the feeling of humiliation attending one's lack of attention to that traffic situation. It may register the peripheral impression that the man honking the horn resembled a colleague at work. The deep unconscious system also perceives encoded messages from others. For example, the therapist in the vignette is unconsciously perceiving his patient's unconscious criticism of him via the story about the assaultive uncle.

We enter here, to some extent, the familiar world of subliminal perceptions, though with a more elaborate conceptualization. That is, the deep unconscious system is capable of processing information that is unconscious to the sender as well as to the receiver. Indeed, this deep unconscious system receives the very information that the conscious mind prefers to do without, and it works over this information with intelligence, sensitivity, and perceptivity well beyond the capacity of conscious processing. (One of my students calls this capacity the mind's UQ, as opposed to the mind's IQ.) It is actually a distinct disadvantage to be consciously aware of emotionally charged information; the unconscious system is better equipped to deal with it. On the other hand, it is our misfortune that the work of the deep unconscious system is not directly available to the conscious system, where its conclusions could be used as a tool for coping.

As I once explained to a business friend, the situation is something like having a computer that can store and process every conceivable fact known about IBM, but being unable to use that information to predict the company's future because the printout is encoded. It follows from this analogy that we can make use of our unconscious intelligence only by decoding the indirect messages that convey its perceptions and reactions.

I started this discussion with the idea that psychotherapy operates without the support of a scientific foundation. One of the reasons for this state of affairs is the fact that psychotherapy has not been based on verifiable phenomena. Of course, there are many levels of truth in life, but in the realm of emotionally charged information processing, there are only two: conscious and unconscious. And, as our little example suggests, the truth of one system is often diametrically opposed to the truth of the other. Most of our psychotherapies today are based on the truth of the conscious system and its subsystem of directly perceived information.

In general, the conscious system is designed for utility, immediate reactions, matters of survival, self-protection, and, where possible, companionship and perpetuation of the species. The language of desire, which Freud invented in terms of his ideas about instinctual striving for gratification, is well suited to the designs and stratagems of the conscious system, which measures out success in terms of the distance between wanting and having. But there is little room here for the kinds of emotional issues processed by the unconscious system, which do not admit of quick solutions, and whose realizations initially make for anxiety rather than relief.

The problem, of course, is the fact that the information perceived by the deep unconscious system is legitimately unconscious. Thus, we are in the paradoxical position of facing the truth of our emotional lives when we don't know that we are doing so, and avoiding the truth when we give the subject our undivided, conscious attention. Unconscious perceptions are revealed only indirectly; so we must know what has triggered them before we can recognize them in disguise.

Much of psychotherapy is conducted in a way that avoids the indirect language of the deep unconscious system. Take another look at our vignette: A conventional therapist might have recognized the young man's displacement of anger toward his father onto his father's brother; but the recognition of his own contribution to the unconsciously displaced perceptions is unlikely. This is because much of psychotherapy is still operating on the assumption that the therapist can essentially observe the patient empathically and infer from his or her own feelings and associations what the patient must be feeling. This is to ignore one of the most important elements of a modern scientific worldview—the fact that the patient and therapist together create a system that functions *as a system*. The patient-therapist system is surrounded by a psychophysical boundary created mainly by the physical space and the ground rules of the treatment situation. Both parties are perceiving the situation consciously and unconsciously. Unless both levels of truth are taken into account, the therapy is based on a lie, however empathic the therapist, however well-intentioned the patient, however lasting the relief a lie may admittedly bring.

This is an important issue—the fact that we offer a service to our patients. A patient comes into therapy because he or she is unhappy and wants to feel better. By accepting this patient as a client, we are implying a contract whose ultimate aim is in concert with the patient's. But this service is not the foundation for a scientific pursuit of the truth about emotional functioning in human beings. It can't be.

And, ultimately, a lie cannot be the foundation for psychological growth, even if it does stop the pain of an ill-lived life. Nor can a lie foster an expanding conception of the therapeutic interaction.

There is much to be said on the interplay between psychotherapy, psychoanalysis, and science. Elsewhere, I have written extensively on the proposition that psychoanalysis, defined as the investigation of the processing of emotionally charged information, has not yet become a science because it is mired in an Aristotelian paradigm of "what things are." A Galilean science would ask, "How do things work?" A post-Galilean science would ask, "How do the systems that contain and define things work?"

In order to move—at the very least—from an Aristotelian framework into a Galilean mode of thinking, psychoanalysis requires a systemic and quantitative foundation. As I said earlier in this discussion, psychoanalysis is based instead on common-sense impressions that are enormously vulnerable to self-deception. One of those impressions is the concept of "transference," which holds that distorted archaic needs and the defenses against them that were acquired during childhood will emerge in the therapeutic interaction in relationship with the therapist. In the vignette that we've been discussing, a classically oriented therapist might suggest that the young man had experienced his therapist as assaultive and dishonest because he had reestablished in the analytic situation a pattern of relationship whose source was the archaic parental imago. This suggestion seems to contain both insight and validity, but it is hardly a fact that can be proved; nor can the establishment of transference be measured or predicted, because it is assumed to emanate from the patient's expectations for the relationship.

Transference is actually a proposition masquerading as a fact, and it largely serves to protect a therapist from being charged with ill-considered behaviors and interventions. Attention to unconscious communication suggests, rather, that patients tend to perceive quite accurately the implications of their therapists' behaviors; they do not distort what they have perceived. They very naturally respond to those perceptions in keeping with their early life experiences. That is what we all do when we perceive emotionally charged situations. We may cast about in life, looking for hooks on which to hang our unresolved emotional issues, but that's the point: The hook is a real component of the situation. The therapist described in the vignette did barrage his patient with intrusive and assaultive questions, and the patient responded quite validly, albeit unconsciously. And he naturally associated the therapist's methods with the already admitted and recognized brutality of his father.

Unfortunately, psychoanalysis has grown in upon itself and become an esoteric enterprise, isolated from interaction with the scientific community. For this reason, the field has failed to benefit from the remarkable developments in most other sciences, and in many important respects has remained unchanged in its first hundred years of existence.

As is true of all Aristotelian sciences, psychoanalysis does have its scientific researchers. But much of this work is statistical, assuming that the average situation is paradigmatic, whereas a Galilean science does not traffic in situations at all but in the laws that govern situations. Many years ago, a well-known Gestalt psychologist, Kurt Lewin, contrasted the methods of Aristotelian and Galilean thinkers.

For an Aristotelian thinker, he said, a ball rolling down an inclined path has an ultimate goal: The approach to that goal can either be facilitated or impeded by some external force. This is how a conventional psychotherapist understands a patient: as a self whose life's plan may be encouraged to unfold or robbed of its impetus. For a Galilean thinker, the rolling ball is not understood to have a "goal" independent of its surroundings or context. Galileo was interested in the course of the ball, given the angle of the inclined plane. In other words, the ball and its surface constitute a single system, a unity.

On the basis of the idea of parallel processing of information, I have developed a research instrument that treats the psychoanalytic dyad as a system. (It is here that certain aspects of Aristotelian teleology reenter the picture.) I am looking at this system as a structural entity that has specific operational laws. In the service of this research project, carried out in collaboration with Lenore Thomson, I am working with a scoring system of sixty items (a sixty-dimensional space). Videotaped psychotherapy sessions are transcribed and then scored for every two lines of recorded dialogue on such items as: Who is talking? For how long? What is the sphere of reference? Is there continuity of theme? Is the material narrative or intellectualization? These items are scored for patient and therapist alike. In this work we are quantifying, among other dimensions, the intensity of the themes, along with their positive and negative valences, and we have just begun to track the interplay of these dimensions from moment to moment, using dynamical, mathematical models as our guide. There are suggestions of characteristic trajectories for each patient-therapist system, a finding all the more striking since it has proven possible to obtain consultation sessions in which a single patient is seen by three different psychotherapists.

The fundamental conception of this work is that the patient and therapist constitute the basic therapeutic system, as influenced by the boundary conditions—for example, in this particular instance, the conditions of the videotaping of the consultation.

In one initial study, using special, educational consultation sessions, the gender material—family interactions, sexuality, concern with sexual identity, and the like—was rated for one particular unmarried female patient who was seen in consultation by each of three male psychotherapists. The first therapist evoked little in the way of gender material from this young woman, and the second responded only to allusions to family interactions. In marked contrast, the third therapist pressured the patient intensely about her sexual feelings and even suggested that there was sexual involvement between the patient and her present treating psychotherapist. When the patient tried to move away from themes of sexuality, the therapist repeatedly brought her back to this particular line of exploration.

An analysis of the complexity of the information being exchanged between this patient and her three consultant therapists also proved feasible. Working closely with a mathematician-physicist, Dr. Paul Rapp, of the Medical College of Pennsylvania, and using a program designed by mathematician Dr. Miguel A. Jimenez-Montano, of the Universidad Veracruzana, Mexico, it proved possible to show that the first therapist in general created an interaction with the patient that was rather simple and uncomplicated, with repetitive rather than distinctive patterns of exchange—a finding that also suggests a low level of meaning in the information the two exchanged. The second interviewer, the one interested in the patient's family, shifted about in these areas of gender and identity and created a pattern of information exchange that was especially rich and complex. This high level of complexity suggests either a relatively chaotic or disordered system or one that is richly and elaborately structured with multiple layers of organized meaning. (Inspection of the consultation hour seemed to favor the latter formulation.) Finally, with the third therapist, the one interested in the patient's sexuality, the exchanges between patient and analyst were intermediately complex, falling between the other two. This level of complexity was largely the result of the patient's attempting for much of the session to change the subject and remain on safer ground.

Although this research is too new to anticipate specific conclusions, it has raised fresh issues with respect to our view of the psychotherapeutic experience. This particular data, and other data on the richness of imagery and themes, suggests that there are two broad ways in which therapists bring relief to their patients. In the first, virtually all levels of information and meaning, conscious and unconscious, are reduced to a minimum. The resulting system is highly predictable, well organized, ordered, and constrained, relatively low in complexity and information content, and relatively low in entropy (*i.e.*, in the degree of disorder or randomness that characterizes this system)—if the concept can be applied there. To the extent that patients obtain relief within such systems, they do so through the avoidance and destruction of emotionally relevant meanings.

In contrast, other therapists produce with their patients systems of great complexity, great richness of information, a sense of disorder and uncertainty, and perhaps a high degree of entropy. Such systems are either enormously chaotic or extremely and richly complex, suggesting two possible avenues of emotional change. In the first instance, order might emerge out of chaos, a possibility that has of late gained much attention. On the other hand, systems rich in conscious and especially unconscious meaning lend themselves readily to interpretations that take unconscious perception and response into account, and they may well produce a cure in this particular way.

I personally believe that psychotherapy is on the brink of a renaissance; but we are still in the dark ages. I hear myself use such words with some discomfort, but I do understand this research as a kind of "quest"—as a search for enlightenment, together with other seriously concerned researchers who worry about the field and its practices and are working to give psychotherapeutic techniques the kind of foundation and basis for growth and evolution that supports every worthy scientific discipline today.

The Uses of Consciousness

NICHOLAS K. HUMPHREY

The problem of self-observation's producing an infinite regression is phony. No one would say that a person cannot use his own eyes to observe his own feet. No one would say, moreover, he cannot use his own eyes, with the aid of a mirror, to observe his own eyes. Then why should anyone say a person cannot, at least in principle, use his own brain to observe his own brain? All that is required is that nature should have given him the equivalent of an inner mirror *and an* inner eye.

Denis Diderot—philosopher, novelist, esthetician, social historian, political theorist, and editor of the *Encyclopédie française*—wrote in the 1770s a treatise called the *Elements of Physiology*. Tucked into that surprising work is this remark:

> If the union of a soul to a machine is impossible, let someone prove it to me. If it is possible, let someone tell me what would be the effects of this union.[1]

Replace the word "soul" with "consciousness," and Diderot's two riddles about *conscious mechanisms* remain the central questions in the science of mind. Diderot was appalled by the dualistic philosophy of Descartes:

> A tolerably clever man began his book with these words: "Man, like all animals, is composed of two distinct substances, the soul and the body." . . . I nearly shut the book. O! ridiculous writer, if I once admit these two distinct substances, you have nothing more to teach me. For you do not know what it is that you call soul, less still how they are united, nor how they act reciprocally on one another.[2]

Two hundred years later, the issue of the *union* of a soul to a machine no longer looms so large. First has come the realization that there is no need to believe in two distinct "substances." Rather, consciousness should be regarded as a "surface feature" of the brain, an emergent property that arises out of the combined action of its parts. Second has come the realization that the human brain itself *is* a machine. The question now is not, *Could* a machine be conscious or have a soul?— clearly it could: I am such a machine, and so are you—but rather, What *kind* of machine could be conscious? How much more and how much less would a conscious machine have to resemble the human brain—nerve cells, chemicals, and all? The dispute has become one

This article is based on my James Arthur Lecture on the Evolution of the Human Brain, presented at the American Museum of Natural History on April 7, 1987 and published 1987 by the American Museum of Natural History.

between those who argue that it's simply a matter of having the appropriate "computer programs" and those who say it's a matter of the "hardware," too.

Daniel C. Dennett, the philosopher, is all for programs. Nothing about nerve cells, Dennett maintains, is so especially special. If a human brain can carry out the logical functions that, when translated into behavior, persuade us that it's conscious, then so too—at least in theory—could an artificial brain. I say "persuade us that it's conscious," because that—in Dennett's view—is precisely what human brains do: We do not *know* that other human beings are conscious, we simply are led to believe that they are by their behavior.[3] John Searle, by contrast, finds the idea of artificial consciousness deeply troubling. For him, a fundamental distinction exists between a human, who is "genuinely" conscious, and a machine that merely behaves as if it were conscious.[4] But this is precisely the distinction that Dennett says is philosophically invalid. And so the argument goes on—at the level, so far as I can read it, of " 'Tis . . . 'Tisn't."

This is not a dispute on which I want to dwell—partly because I am not sure that it will ever be resolved, but chiefly because it seems to me to jump the gun. It may be all very well to discuss whether a machine that fulfilled in every respect our expectations of how a conscious being ought to behave would actually be conscious. But what, exactly, are our expectations, and how might we account for them? In short, what do we think consciousness produces? If a machine could be united to a soul, what effects—if any—would the union have?

When Diderot asked this crucial question, I suspect he was asking rhetorically for the answer "None." A machine, he was prepared to imagine, might have a soul—and yet for all practical purposes, it would be indistinguishable from a machine without one:

> What difference between a sensitive and living pocket watch and a watch of gold, of iron, of silver and of copper? If a soul were joined to the latter, what would it produce therein?[5]

Presumably, as a timekeeper—and that, after all, is what a watch is—the watch would be just the same as it was before. The soul would be of no *use* to it; it wouldn't *show*.

I would not pin on Diderot himself the authorship of the idea of the functional impotence of souls. But the realization that *human* consciousness itself might actually be useless—whenever it came, and whether or not it came first to Diderot—was something of a breakthrough. I remember my own surprise and pleasure at this naughty idea, when I first came across it in the writings of the behaviorist psychologists. J. B. Watson, in 1928, argued that the science of psychology need make no reference to consciousness:

> The behaviorist sweeps aside all medieval conceptions. He drops from his scientific vocabulary all subjective terms such as sensation, perception, image, desire, and even thinking and emotion.[6]

As philosophical backup, I could adduce Wittgenstein's argument that concepts referring to internal states of mind have no place in the "language game."[7] If nothing else, it was an idea to tease one's school friends with. "How do I know that what I experience as the color red isn't what you experience as green? How do I know that you experience anything at all? You might be an unconscious zombie."

A naughty idea is, however, all that this notion amounts to: an idea that has had a good run and now can surely be dismissed. I shall give two reasons for dismissing it. One is a kind of Panglossian argument, to the effect that whatever exists as a consequence of evolution must have a function. The other is simply an appeal to common sense. Before I give either, let me say what I am *not* dismissing: I am not dismissing the idea that consciousness is a second-order and in some ways inessential process. In certain respects the behaviorists may have been right.

Diderot gives a nice example of unconscious behavior:

> A musician is at the harpsichord; he is chatting with his neighbor, he forgets that he is playing a piece of concerted music with others; however, his eyes, his ear, his fingers are not the less in accord with them because of it; not a false note, not a misplaced harmony, not a rest forgotten, not the least fault in time, taste or measure. Now, the conversation ceases, our musician returns to his part, loses his head and does not know where he has got to. If the distraction of the conscious man had continued for a few more minutes, the unconscious

animal in him would have played the piece to the end without his
having been aware of it.[8]

The musician, if Diderot is right, sees without being aware of seeing,
hears without being aware of hearing. Experimental psychologists
have studied similar examples under controlled laboratory conditions
and confirmed that the phenomenon is just as Diderot described:
While consciousness takes off in one direction, behavior may sometimes go in quite another. Indeed, consciousness may be absent
altogether. A sleepwalker, for example, may carry out elaborate actions and even hold a simple conversation without waking up.
Stranger things still can happen after brain injury. A person with
damage to the visual cortex may lack all visual sensation, be consciously quite blind, and nonetheless be capable of guessing what he
would be seeing *if* he could see.[9] I have met such a case: a young man
who maintained that he could see nothing at all to the left of his nose,
and yet could drive a car through busy traffic without knowing how he
did it. This is what I am *not* dismissing: the possibility that the brain
can carry on at least part of its job without the presence of consciousness. What I *am* dismissing is the possibility that when consciousness
is present, it isn't making any difference. Let me now give the two
reasons.

First the evolutionary reason. When Diderot posed his question, he
knew nothing about Darwinian evolution. He believed, certainly, in
evolution of the most radical kind:

> The plant kingdom might well be and have been the first source of the
> animal kingdom, and have had its own source in the mineral king-
> dom; and the latter have originated from universal heterogeneous
> matter.[10]

What is more, Diderot had his own theory of selection, based on the
idea of "contradiction":

> Contradictory beings are those whose organization does not conform to
> the rest of the universe. Blind nature, which produces them, extermi-
> nates them; she lets only those exist which can co-exist tolerably with
> the general order.[11]

Surprising stuff, considering that it was written in the late eighteenth century; but note that, compared with Darwin's theory eighty years later, something is missing. Diderot's is a theory of *extinction*. According to him, the condition for a biological trait's survival is merely that it should not contradict the general order, that it should not get in the way. Darwin's theory, on the other hand, is a theory of adaptation. For Darwin, the condition for a given trait's surviving *and spreading through the population* is much stricter: It is not enough that the trait be simply noncontradictory or neutral; it must be beneficial in promoting reproduction.

This may seem a small difference of emphasis, but it is crucial. For it means that when Diderot asked, of consciousness or anything else in nature, "What difference does it make?" he could reasonably answer, "None." But when a modern Darwinian biologist asks the same question, he cannot reasonably give the same answer. The Darwinian has to say that a given biological phenomenon has evolved because and only because it is serving some useful biological function.

You may wonder, however, whether we can still expect consciousness to have a function if we accept the idea that it is a "mere surface feature" of the brain. Let us not be misled by the word "mere." We might say that the colors of a peacock's tail were a mere surface feature of the pigments, or that the insulating properties of fur were a mere surface feature of a furry skin. But it is, of course, precisely on such surface features that natural selection acts: The color or the warmth matters to the animal's survival. Philosophers have sometimes drawn a parallel between consciousness as a surface feature of the brain and wetness as a surface feature of water. Suppose we found an animal made entirely out of water. Its wetness would surely be the first thing for which an evolutionary biologist would seek to find a function.

Nonetheless, we clearly have a problem—and that is to escape from a definition of consciousness that renders it self-evidently useless and irrelevant. Here the philosophy of mind has been less than helpful. Too often we have been offered definitions of consciousness that effectively hamstring the inquiry before it has begun: for example, that consciousness consists in private states of mind of which the subject alone is aware, which can be neither confirmed nor contradicted, and so on. Wittgenstein's words, at the end of his *Tractatus*, have haunted philosophical discussion: "Whereof we cannot speak, thereof we must be silent".

All I can say is that neither biologically nor psychologically does that feel right. Such definitions, at their limit (and they are meant, of course, to impose limits), would suggest that statements about consciousness can have no information content—technically, that they can do nothing to reduce anyone's uncertainty about what's going on. I find that counterintuitive and wholly unconvincing. This brings me to my second reason for dismissing the idea that consciousness is of no use to human beings, which is that this notion is contrary to common sense.

Suppose I am a dentist, and I am uncertain whether the patient in the chair is feeling pain: I ask, "Does it hurt?" And the patient says, "Yes . . . I'm not the kind of person to show it, but it feels awful." Am I to believe that such an answer—as a description of a conscious state—contains no information? Common sense tells me that when a person describes his states of mind, either to me or to himself (not something one need be able to do, but something one often can do), he is making a revealing self-report. If he says, for example, "I'm in pain," or "I'm in love," or "I'm having a green sensation," or "I'm looking forward to my supper," I reckon that I actually know more about him; but, more important, *through being conscious* he knows more about himself.

Still, the question remains, What sort of information is this? What is it about? And the difficulty seems to be that whatever it is about is, at least in the first place, private and subjective—something going on inside the subject to which no one else can have direct access. This difficulty has been greatly overplayed. I'd suggest that the question of what conscious descriptions are about has an obvious answer—namely, they are about what is happening inside the subject's brain. To be sure, such information is "private," but it is private for the good reason that it happens to be *his* brain, hidden within his skull, and he is naturally in a position to observe it, in which the rest of us are not. Privacy is no doubt an issue of great biological and social significance, but it is not philosophically all that remarkable.

The suggestion that consciousness is a "description of the brain" may nonetheless seem rather odd. Suppose someone says, "I'm not feeling myself today." That certainly doesn't sound like a description of a brain state. True enough, it does not *sound* like one; and, no doubt, I'd have trouble persuading most people that it was so. Few people, if any, naturally make any connection between mind states and brain states. For one thing, almost no one except a brain scientist is likely to be interested in brains as such. For another, clearly a huge gulf separates brain states, as they are in fact described by brain scientists, from mind states, as described by conscious human beings. That gulf is practically—and, some would argue, logically—unbridgeable.

Yet is that really such a problem? Surely we are used to the idea that the same thing can be described in completely different ways. Light, for example, can be described either as particles or as waves; water can be described either as an aggregation of H_2O molecules or as a wet fluid; Ronald Reagan can be described either as an aging movie actor or as a former president of the United States. The particular description we come up with depends on what measuring techniques we use and what our interests are. In that case, why should not the activity of the brain be described either as the electrical activity of nerve cells or as a conscious state of mind, depending on who is doing the describing? One thing is certain: Brain scientists have different techniques and different interests from ordinary human beings.

I admit, however, that I am guilty of some sleight of hand here. It is all very well to suggest that consciousness is "a description" of the brain's activity, by a subject with appropriate techniques and interests; but what I have not done is to locate this conscious subject anywhere. "To describe" is a transitive verb. It requires an object as well as a subject, and they cannot, in principle, be one and the same entity. A brain, surely, cannot describe its own activity, any more than a bucket of water can describe itself as wet. In the case of the water, it takes an observer outside the bucket to recognize the water's wetness, and to do so requires employing certain observational procedures—the individual has to stick a hand into it, swish it around, watch how it flows. Who, then, is the observer of the brain? Are we stuck with an infinite regress? Do we need to postulate another brain to describe the first one, and then another brain to describe that? Diderot would have laughed:

If nature offers us a difficult knot to unravel, do not let us introduce in order to unravel it the hand of a being who then becomes an even more difficult knot to untie than the first one. Ask an Indian why the world stays suspended in space, and he will tell you that it is carried on the back of an elephant . . . and the elephant on a tortoise. And what supports the tortoise? . . . Confess your ignorance and spare me your elephant and your tortoise.[12]

I can hardly be expected, halfway through this essay, to confess my ignorance, and, in fact, I shall do just the opposite. The problem of self-observation's producing an infinite regression is phony. No one would say that a person cannot use his own eyes to observe his own feet. No one would say, moreover, he cannot use his own eyes, with the aid of a mirror, to observe his own eyes. Then why should anyone say a person cannot, at least in principle, use his own brain to observe his own brain? All that is required is that nature should have given him the equivalent of an *inner mirror* and an *inner eye*. And that is precisely what she has done. Nature has, in short, given to human beings the remarkable gift of *self-reflexive insight*. I propose to take this metaphor of "insight" seriously. What is more, I propose to draw a picture of it.

Imagine first the situation of an unconscious animal or a machine that does not possess this faculty of insight (see figure below). It has a brain, which receives inputs from conventional sense organs, sends outputs to motor systems, and in between runs a highly sophisticated computer and decision maker. The animal may be highly

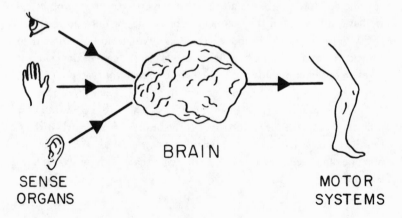

BRAIN

SENSE
ORGANS

MOTOR
SYSTEMS

intelligent and complexly motivated; it is by no means a purely reflexive mechanism. Nonetheless, it has no picture of what this brain-computer is doing or how it works. The animal is in effect an unconscious Cartesian automaton.

Now imagine that a new form of sense organ has evolved, an "inner eye" (see figure below) whose field of view is not the outside world but the brain itself, as reflected via this loop. Like other sense organs, the inner eye provides a picture of its information field—the brain—which is partial and selective. Like other sense organs, it has been designed by natural selection so that this picture is a useful one—in current jargon, a user-friendly description, designed to tell the subject as much as he requires to know in a form that he is predisposed to understand. Thus it allows him, from a position of extraordinary privilege, to see his own brain states as conscious states of mind. Now every intelligent action is accompanied by the awareness of the thought processes involved, every perception by an accompanying sensation, every emotion by a conscious feeling.

Suppose this is what consciousness amounts to. I have written of consciousness as a surface feature of the brain, and so I think it is; but now I am suggesting that it is a very special sort of surface feature. For

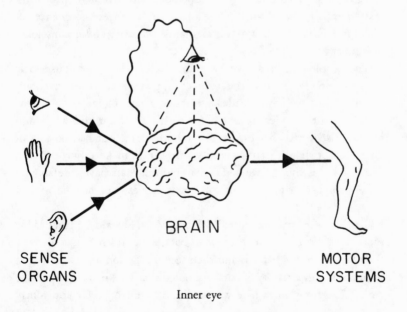

SENSE
ORGANS

BRAIN

MOTOR
SYSTEMS

Inner eye

consciousness actually is a feature not of the whole brain but of this added self-reflexive loop. Why this particular arrangement should have what we might call the "transcendent," "otherworldly" qualities of consciousness, I do not know. But I have allowed here for one curious feature: *The output of the inner eye is part of its own input.* A self-referential system of this sort may well have strange and paradoxical properties—not least that so-called truth functions go awry.[13]

To recapitulate; We have seen that the brain can do much of its work without the presence of consciousness; it is fair to assume therefore that consciousness is a second-order property of brains. We have seen that Darwin's theory suggests that consciousness evolved by natural selection; it is fair to assume therefore that consciousness helps its possessor to survive and reproduce. We have seen that common sense coupled with self-analysis suggests that consciousness is a source of information, and that this information is very likely about brain states. To make the point that immediately follows, it is fair to assume that access to this kind of second-order information about one's own brain states helps a person to survive and reproduce.

Although the weightier part of my argument is now complete, the reader may still feel dissatisfied. I set out to ask what difference consciousness makes, and have concluded that through providing insight into the workings of the brain, it enhances the chances of biological survival. The question remains, however, of *how* consciousness functions.

The problem is this. We have an idea of what consciousness is doing—namely, giving the subject a picture of his own brain activity—but we have no idea yet about what biological good that does him in the wider context of his daily life. It is rather as though we had discovered that fur keeps a rabbit warm, but had no idea of why a rabbit should want to keep warm. Or, to make a more relevant analogy, it's as though we had discovered that bats have an elaborate system for gathering information about echoes, but had no idea of why they should want such information.

The bat case provides a useful lesson. When Donald Griffin did his pioneering work on echolocation in bats,[14] he did not first discover the echolocating apparatus and then seek a function for it. He began with the natural history of bats. He noted that bats live largely in the dark, and that their whole way of life depends on their apparently mysterious capacity to see without the use of eyes. Hence, when Griffin began his investigation of bats' ears, faces, and brains, he knew exactly what he was looking for: a mechanism within the bat that would allow it to "listen in the dark." When he discovered such a mechanism, he had no problem in deciding what its function was.

This is precisely the tactic we should adopt in examining consciousness in human beings. Having gotten this far, we should turn to natural history and ask whether anything about the specifically human way of life suggests that people, quite as much as bats, possess a mysterious capacity for understanding their natural environment, for which consciousness could provide the mechanism.

I shall cut a long story short (the substance of two books I have written on this issue.[15]) When the question is what a natural historian would notice as being special about human life, I'd say the answer must be this: Human beings are extraordinarily sociable creatures. The environment to which they are adapted is before all else the environment of the family, the working group, the clan. Interpersonal relationships have a depth, a complexity, and a biological importance that far exceed those of any other animal. Indeed, without the ability to *understand, predict, and manipulate the behavior* of other members of his own species, a person could hardly survive from day to day.

Now, that being so, every individual has to be, in effect, a "psychologist" just to stay alive, let alone to negotiate the maze of social interactions on which success in mating and breeding will ultimately rest. Not a psychologist in the ordinary sense, but what I have called a "natural psychologist." Just as a blind bat develops quite naturally the ability to find its way around a cave, so every human being must develop a set of natural skills for penetrating the twilight world of interpersonal psychology—the world of loves, hates, jealousies; a world where so little is revealed on the surface and so much has to be surmised.

This seems, upon reflection, rather mysterious. For psychological understanding is immensely difficult; and understanding at the level that most people clearly have it would not, I suspect, be possible at all unless each individual had access to some kind of "black box" model of the human mind—a way of imagining what might be happening inside another person's head. In short, psychological understanding becomes possible because and only because people naturally conceive of other people as beings with minds. They attribute to them mental states—moods, thoughts, sensations, and so on—and claim to understand them on that basis: "She's *sad* because she *thinks* he doesn't *love* her"; "He's *angry* because he *suspects* she's *telling lies*"; and so on across the range of human interaction.

I shall not, of course, pretend that this is news. If it were, it clearly would not be correct. But what we ought to ask is where this ordinary, everyday, taken-for-granted psychological model of other human beings originates. How is it that people latch on so quickly and with so little apparent effort to seeing other people in this way? It is, I suggest, because that is first of all *the way each individual sees himself.* And why is that? Because nature has given him an *inner eye.*

Here, at last, is a worthy function for self-reflexive insight. What consciousness does is provide human beings with an extraordinarily effective tool for natural psychology. Each person can look in his own mind, observe and analyze his own past and present mental states, and on that basis make inspired guesses about the minds of others.

As an experiment, we may try this, for example, with a "picture" of other human beings. A painting by Ilya Repin, entitled *They Did Not Expect Him*, hangs in the Tretyakov Gallery in Moscow. Imagine yourself looking at this picture with me (and note how successfully you "reconstruct" it):

A man wearing a coat and dirty boots enters a drawing room. The maid could close the door behind her, but she doesn't—she waits to see how he's received. An old woman stands, alarmed, as though she's seen a ghost. A younger woman—eyes wide—registers delighted disbelief. A little girl is suddenly shy. Only a young boy shows open pleasure.

Who is the man? Perhaps the father of the family. They thought he'd been taken away, and now he's walked in, as if from the dead. His mother can't believe it; his wife didn't dare hope; his daughter is confused by the grown-ups' response; his son had been secretly confident that he'd return.

Where has he been? The maid's face shows a degree of disapproval, the son's, excited pride. The man's eyes, tired and staring, tell of a nightmare from which he himself is only beginning to emerge.

The painting represents, as it happens, a Russian political prisoner, who has been released from the Czar's jails and returned home. We may not catch every nuance—more information is needed. But if we try to construct or interpret a scene such as this *without* reference to consciousness, to what *we know* of human feelings—and the depth, its human depth, completely disappears.

I give this example to illustrate just how clever we all are. Consider those psychological concepts we've just "called to mind": apprehension, disbelief, disapproval, weariness, and so on. They are concepts of such subtlety, I doubt that any of us could explain them. Yet, in analyzing this scene—or any other human situation—we wield them with remarkable authority. We do so because we have first experienced their meaning in ourselves. It works. However, a problem remains as to why it works. Perhaps we do, as I just said, wield these mental concepts "with remarkable authority." Yet, who or what gives us this authority to put ourselves in other people's shoes? By what philosophical license do we trespass so nonchalantly upon the territory of "other minds"?

I am reminded of the following story. During a dock strike in London, enormous trucks were going in and out across the picket lines with impressive notices: By the Authority of H. M. Government, By the Permission of the Trades Union Congress, By the Authority of the Ministry of War. Among them appeared a tiny donkey cart, driven by a little old man in a bashed-in bowler, and on the cart was a banner: By My Own Bloody Authority.

That is a good, plain answer to the problem. Nonetheless, I will not pretend that it will do. Tell a philosopher that ordinary people bridge this gap from self to other "by their own bloody authority," and it will only confirm his worst suspicions that the whole business of natural psychology is flawed. Back will come Wittgenstein's objection that in the matter of mental states, one's own authority is no authority at all:

> Suppose that everyone has a box with something in it; we call this thing a "beetle." No one can look into anyone else's box, and everyone says he knows what a beetle is only by looking at *his* beetle . . . it would be quite possible for everyone to have something different in his box . . . the box might even be empty.[16]

The problem, of course, is not entirely trivial. Strictly speaking, it is true we can never be sure that any of our guesses about the inner life of other people are correct. In a worst-case scenario, it is even possible that nature played a dreadful trick on us and built every human being according to a different plan. Not just the phenomenology of inner experience might differ from one person to another, the whole functional meaning of the experience might be different. Suppose, for example, that when I feel pain, I do my best to stop it; but when you feel pain, you want more of it. In that case my mental model would be useless as a guide to your behavior.

This scenario is, however, one that as biologists we can totally discount. For it is a biological fact—and philosophers ought sometimes to pay more attention than they do to biology—that human beings are all members of the same biological species: all descended within recent history from common stock, all still having more than 99.9 percent of their genes in common, and all with brains that—at birth, at least—could be interchanged without anyone's being much the wiser. It is no more likely that two people will differ radically in the way their brains work than that they will differ radically in the way their kidneys work. Indeed, in one way it is—if I am right— even less likely. For while it is of no interest to a person to have the same kind of kidney as another person, it is of interest to him to have the same kind of mind: otherwise as a natural psychologist he'd be in trouble. Kidney transplants occur very rarely in nature, but something very much like mind transplants occurs all the time—we have just undergone such an operation with those people in the painting. I think we can be sure that if the possibility of, shall we call it, "radical mental polymorphism" had ever actually arisen in the course of human evolution, it would quickly have been quashed.

The first and simplest reason why this method of doing psychology can work is the fact of the structural similarity of human brains, but it is not the only reason, nor the most interesting one. Suppose that all human beings actually had identical brains, so that literally everything a particular individual could know about his own brain would be true of other people's: his picture of his own brain might still be of no help in reading other people's behavior. Why? Because it might just be the wrong kind of picture; it might be psychologically irrelevant. Suppose that when an individual looked in on his brain, he were to discover that the mechanism for speech lay in his left hemisphere, or that his memories are stored as changes in RNA molecules, or that when he sees a red light there's a nerve cell that fires at 100 cycles per second. All these things would very likely be true of other people, too; but of how much use would this kind of inner picture be as a basis for human understanding?

To return to my diagram of the inner eye: When I described what the inner eye does, I said that it provides a picture of its information field that has been designed by natural selection to be a "useful" one, "a user-friendly description, designed to tell the subject as much as he requires to know." But I was vague about what exactly was implied by the crucial words "useful," "user-friendly," and "requires to know." I had to be vague, because I had still to define the nature of the user, and his specific requirements. However, we now know exactly the nature of the user: The user of the inner eye is a natural psychologist. His requirement is that he build up a model of the behavior of other human beings.

That is where the natural selection of the inner eye has almost certainly been crucial. For we can assume that throughout a long history of evolution, all sorts of ways of describing the brain's activity have in fact been experimented with—including, quite possibly, a straightforward physiological description in terms of nerve cells, RNA, and so on. What has happened, however, is that only those descriptions most suited to doing psychology have been preserved. Thus, the particular picture of our inner selves that human beings do in fact have—the picture we know as "us" and cannot imagine being of any different kind—is neither a necessary description nor merely any description of the brain; it is the one that has proved most suited to our needs as social beings.

That is why it works. Not only can we count on other people's brains to be very much like ours, we can count on our particular conception of what it's like to have a brain to provide us with a tailor-made psychological model of other human beings. Consciousness is a sociobiological product, in the best sense of "social" and "biological."

Therefore, in the end, what difference does it make? It makes, I suspect, nothing less than the difference between being a human and being a monkey: the difference between human beings, *who know what it is like to be ourselves*, and other creatures, which essentially have no idea. "One day," Diderot wrote, "it will be shown that consciousness is a characteristic of all beings."[17] I am sorry to say that I think he was wrong. I recognize, of course, that human beings are not the only social animals on earth; and I recognize that many other animals require at least a primitive ability to do psychology. But how many animals require anything like the level of psychological understanding that we humans have? How many can be said to require, as a biological necessity, a picture of what is happening inside their brains? And if they do not require it, why ever should they have it? What would a frog, or even a cow, lose if it were unable to look in on itself and observe its own mind at work?

I have imagined a discussion of this matter with my dog, which goes like this:

DOG: Nick, you and your friends seem to be awfully interested in this thing you call consciousness. You're always talking about it instead of going for walks.

NICK: Yes. Well, it is interesting—don't you think so?

DOG: You ask *me* that! You're not even sure I've got it.

NICK: That's why it's interesting.

DOG: Rabbits! Seriously, though, *do* you think I've got it? What could I do to convince you?

NICK: Try me.

DOG: Suppose I stood on my back legs like a person? Would that convince you?

NICK: No.

DOG: Suppose I did something cleverer. Suppose I beat you at chess.

NICK: You might be a chess-playing computer. I'm very fond of you, but how do I know you're not just a furry, soft automaton?

DOG: Don't get personal.

NICK: I'm not getting personal. Just the opposite, in fact.

DOG: (gloomily) I don't know why I started this conversation. You're just trying to hurt my feelings.

NICK: (startled) What's that you said?

DOG: Nothing. I'm just a soft automaton. It's all right for you. You don't have to go around *wishing* you were conscious. You don't have to feel *jealous* of people all the time, in case they've got something that you haven't. And don't pretend you don't know what it feels like.

NICK: Yes, *I* know what it feels like. The question is, Do *you*?

That, I think, remains the question. I need hardly say that dogs, as a matter of fact, do not think (or talk) like this. Do any animals? Yes, there is some evidence that the great apes do: chimpanzees are capable of self-reference to their internal states, and they can use what they know to interpret what others may be thinking.[18] Dogs, I suspect, are on the edge of it—although the evidence is not too strong. For the vast majority of other less socially sophisticated animals, however, not only is there no evidence that they have this kind of conscious insight, there is every reason to think that consciousness would be a waste of time for them.

For human beings, however, so far from being a waste of time, it was the crucial adaptation—the sine qua non of our advancement to the human state. Imagine the biological benefits to the first of our ancestors who developed the capacity to read the minds of others by reading their own—to picture, as if from the inside, what other members of their social group were thinking about and planning to do next. The way was open to a new form of social relationships, to sympathy, compassion, trust, deviousness, double-crossing, belief and disbelief in others' motives . . . the very things that make us human.

The way was also open to something else that makes us human (and which my dog was quite right to pick up on): an abiding interest in the problem of what consciousness *is* and *why* we have it—sufficient, perhaps, to have diverted you from anything else for the past hour.

NOTES

1 Denis Diderot, *Elements of Physiology* (1774–80), in Jonathan Kemp, ed., *Diderot: Interpreter of Nature*, trans. Kemp and Jean Stewart (London: Lawrence & Wishart, 1937), p. 136. (All page numbers refer to Kemp's edition.)

2 *Elements of Physiology*, p. 139.

3 Daniel Dennett, *The Intentional Stance* (Cambridge, Massachusetts: Bradford Books, 1987).

4 John Searle, *Minds, Brains, and Science* (Cambridge, Massachusetts: Harvard University Press, 1984).

5 *Elements of Physiology*, p. 136.

6 J. B. Watson, *Behaviorism* (London: Routledge & Kegan Paul, 1928), p. 6.

7 Ludwig Wittgenstein, *Philosophical Investigations* (Oxford: Blackwell, 1958).

8 *Elements of Physiology*, p. 139.

9 L. Weiskrantz, *Blindsight* (Oxford: Oxford University Press, 1986).

10 *Elements of Physiology*, p. 136.

11 *Elements of Physiology*, p. 134.

12 Denis Diderot, *Promenade of a Skeptic* (1747), p. 28.

13 Douglas R. Hofstadter, *Gödel, Escher, Bach* (New York: Basic Books, 1979).

14 Donald R. Griffin, *Listening in the Dark* (New Haven: Yale University Press, 1958).

15 Nicholas Humphrey, *Consciousness Regained* (Oxford: Oxford University Press, 1983); and Nicholas Humphrey, *The Inner Eye* (London: Faber and Faber, 1986).

16 Ludwig Wittgenstein, *Philosophical Investigations* (Oxford: Blackwell, 1958), p. 100.

17 *Elements of Physiology*, p. 138.

18 David Premack and Ann Premack, *The Mind of an Ape* (New York: W. W. Norton, 1983).

The Evolution of Consciousness

DANIEL C. DENNETT

It is now possible, for the first time, to formulate testable hypotheses about how activities in the brain can add up to the phenomena of consciousness.

How is human consciousness situated in the natural world? This is a great, ancient problem of philosophy, but also one of the most perplexing unanswered questions of science. There is no longer any serious doubt that the seat of consciousness is the brain, and nothing but the brain. In the last few decades, the explosive growth of our knowledge of the brain—and of some of the mechanisms, processes, and principles of cognition—has brought us tantalizingly within range of the big question. It is now possible, for the first time, to formulate testable hypotheses about how activities in the brain can *add up to* the phenomena of consciousness.

Some philosophers are offended by the suggestion that science could solve *our* problem, the philosophical mystery of the mind, but this proprietary attitude, which never made good sense, is particularly out of place now. Today the philosophical problem is everybody's problem. Scientists have made great progress on the mechanisms of vision and the other senses, motor control, memory, and attention; nevertheless, as they close in on the remaining big question of how all these mechanisms contribute to consciousness, they find themselves beset by deep conceptual (or philosophical) puzzles. For instance, we now understand how very complex and even apparently intelligent phenomena, such as genetic coding, the immune system, and low-level visual processing, can be accomplished without a trace of consciousness. But this seems to uncover an enormous puzzle of just what, if anything, consciousness is for. Can a conscious entity do anything for itself that an unconscious (but cleverly wired up) simulation of that entity couldn't do for itself? This is just one of the philosophical illusions that are now starting to bedevil the scientists.

It is true that most of the progress has been made by scientists resolutely ignoring the philosophical issues and concentrating on questions that they know how to answer, but this backlog of postponed puzzles is beginning to get in the way of further progress. As Darwin observed in 1838, "Experience shows that the problem of the mind cannot be solved by attacking the citadel itself."[1] However enough indirect progress has been made since Darwin for us to prepare realistically for a final assault on the citadel.

Darwin is, in fact, one of the two heroes of this essay; the other is another brilliant Englishman, Alan Turing, the mathematician who could justly be called the inventor of the computer. The subject here is the philosophical offspring created by the union of their great ideas: an answer to the question with which I began.

How is human consciousness situated in the natural world? Human consciousness is a "virtual machine" (something rather like a computer program) implemented by the brain; it is the product of three distinct but interacting processes of evolution by natural selection.

Comparisons between brains and computers, and between minds and software, have become hackneyed. The media called the first computers, those heroic monstrosities of Turing's day, "giant electronic brains"; ever since then the comparisons have been irresistible, for reasons good and bad. I will try to show that if we invert some of the standard points of comparison, and refresh our sense of the biological processes that have created human minds, we can rediscover the analogy; it is deeper, and more fruitful, than the threadbare slogans.

Three processes of evolution conspire to create consciousness:

1. *The evolution of species with genetic transmission.* Standard neo-Darwinian evolution by natural selection
2. *The evolution of neural patterns.* Patterns of activity within individual brains, in processes of learning and training
3. *The evolution of "memes"** Ideas available in the cultural environment, culturally transmitted and "implanted" in individual brains by social interactions

In each process the mechanism is classically Darwinian. The process consists of

---

* A term coined by Richard Dawkins.

1. A wellspring of variation
2. Heritability or transmission of traits
3. Differential replication due to blind, mechanical factors that are nevertheless often noncoincidentally linked (probabilistically) to *reasons*

Thus, in all three processes, there is not just natural selection, but natural selection *for* features that have some discernible raison d' être. The three distinct processes are listed in order of their antiquity. First came species evolution; one of its discoveries was the plasticity that provided the medium for neural evolution. That process, in turn, yielded a "technology" of learning and transmission that provided the medium for cultural evolution; the latter eventually created the virtual machine of human consciousness, which, when it was reflected back onto all three processes, rendered them all swifter and more efficient.

Let us start with the first process, and remind ourselves that nervous systems are for controlling the activities in time and space of organisms that have taken the strategic path of locomotion. (The juvenile sea squirt wanders through the sea searching for a suitable rock or hunk of coral to cling to and make its home for life. It has a rudimentary nervous system. When it finds its spot and takes root, it doesn't need its brain anymore—so it eats it! This puts one in mind of a similar effect among tenured professors.*

The key to control is the ability to track, or even anticipate, the important features of the environment; all brains are, in essence, "anticipation machines." The clam's shell is fine armor, but it cannot always be in place; the hard-wired reflex that snaps the shell shut is a crude but effective harm anticipator-avoider. Brains that have some plasticity are better than fixed reflex links; they are capable not just of stereotypic anticipation, but also of adjusting to trends. Even the lowly toad has some small degree of freedom in how it responds to novelty, gradually altering its patterns of activity to track—with a considerable time lag—those features of its environment that matter

---

* The analogy between the sea squirt and the associate professor was first pointed out, I think, by Rodolfo Llinas. Patricia Churchland has helped to spread this most infectious meme through the academisphere.

most to its well-being.[2] But for more high-powered control, what you want is an anticipation machine that will think ahead, avoid ruts in its own activity, solve problems before encountering them, recognize novel harbingers of good and ill, and in general stay more than just one step ahead of the environment. For all our foolishness, we human beings are vastly better equipped for that task than any other self-controllers, and there can be little doubt that it is our enormous brains that make this possible. But how?

Our brains differ dramatically from those of our nearest ancestors among the hominids and other primates, but primarily in size, rather than in structure. Just why our ancestors' brains should have grown so large so fast (in the evolutionary time scale, their development was more an explosion than a blossoming) is a matter of some controversy, but little controversy surrounds the nature of the product: an enormously complex brain of unrivaled plasticity. That is to say, while its gross architecture is genetically fixed, its microstructure of trillions of connections is remarkably unfixed. Some of this variability is required simply to provide a medium for the moment-to-moment transient patterns of brain activity that somehow register, or represent, or at any rate track, the important, variable features of the environment— the bird that flies by, the drop in air temperature—and of the organism's own states—the drop in blood sugar, the increase of carbon dioxide in the lungs. Thus, some of the brain's variability is used to hold on to the fleeting data about current events that should matter to any self-controller. But much of it is available for relatively permanent fixing by events and features of that environment, and this is the job of our second evolutionary process.

While the first process of evolution "hard-wires" the nervous systems of lower organisms, in our case (more than in any other organism), it provides incompletely designed nervous systems, which postpones the completion of the design until after birth. Then specific, highly variable features of the environment can be counted on to provoke further appropriate fixings of microconnections, turning the basic brain into, say, an English speaker's brain rather than a Japanese or Swahili speaker's, to take the best-known example of postnatal design.

The processes of postnatal design fixing appear to be various, giving rise to incessant and largely unnecessary controversy: How much is innate and how much is learned? Does one really *learn* one's mother tongue, or is this process best seen as one of differential switch setting that is continuous with embryological development? (Birds don't *learn* to grow feathers; do they really *learn* to fly? Babies don't *learn* to shed their baby teeth; do they really *learn* to walk or to speak?) One can blandly rise above the fray and make the following point: Some things come quite effortlessly to us all (such as acquiring a mother tongue, or learning that we cannot walk on water) and others require focused practice or rehearsal (such as playing the violin, doing long division, or mastering a second language in adulthood). A good theory must explain all the varieties of postnatal design fixing; while some variations are apparently due to processes that are simply continuous with the gene-directed construction of the phenotype, others can be fruitfully viewed as arising from a distinct evolutionary process, on a much faster time scale (measured in seconds, not generations), and with suitable surrogates for offspring and the selective effect of the grim reaper. In short, as many have argued, the brain is itself a "Darwin Machine," (to borrow William H. Calvin's term) in which novel structures evolve and are revised, extinguished, propagated, co-opted for novel tasks, and so on.[3]

I will not say any more here about the presumed details of those evolutionary processes. Instead, I will turn to the relationship between that second process and the third: cultural evolution. Plasticity, as we have seen, is a good thing, for it makes learning possible. It is all the better if somewhere in the environment there is something to learn that is itself the product of a prior design process, so that each of us does not have to reinvent the wheel. We human beings have used our plasticity not just to learn, but to learn how to learn better, and then we've learned better how to learn better how to learn better, and so forth. We have also learned how to make the fruits of this learning available to novices. We somehow install an already invented and largely "debugged" *system* of activity habits in the partly unstructured brain.

This particularly sophisticated process of postnatal design can be best understood if we contrast it with a similar process, invented by Alan Turing: the process of creating virtual machines on computers. A computer has a basic fixed, or hard-wired, architecture. However, it also has huge amounts of plasticity thanks to its memory, which can store both programs (software) and data (the merely transient patterns that are made to track whatever is to be represented). Computers, too, are thus incompletely designed "at birth," with flexibility that can be used as a medium to create more specifically disciplined architectures, special-purpose machines, each with a strikingly individual way of responding (via the CRT screen or other output devices) to the environment's stimulation (via the keyboard or other input devices).

These temporary structures are made of rules rather than wires, you might say, and computer scientists call them virtual machines. A virtual machine is what results when a particular pattern of rules (or dispositions, or transition regularities) is imposed on all that plasticity. Anyone who is familiar with a word processor is acquainted with at least one virtual machine. If you have used more than one word-processing program, or used a spreadsheet or played a game on the very same computer you use for word processing, you are acquainted with several virtual machines, which take turns existing on a particular real machine.

Everybody knows that different programs endow computers with different powers, but not everybody knows how a computer works. A few of the details are important to our story, so I must beg your indulgence and provide a brief, elementary account of the marvelous process invented by Alan Turing.

Turing was not trying to invent the word processor or the video game when he made his beautiful discoveries; he was thinking, self-consciously and introspectively, about just how he, a mathematician, went about solving mathematical problems (or performing computations), and he took the important step of trying to break down the sequence of his mental acts into a sequence of primitive components. He was an extraordinarily well-organized thinker, but his stream of consciousness, like yours or mine or James Joyce's, was a variegated jumble of images, decisions, hunches, reminders, and so forth, from which he tried to distill the mathematical essence: the bare-bones, minimal sequence of operations that could accomplish the goals he accomplished in the florid and meandering activities of his conscious mind. The result was the specification of what we now call a Turing machine, a brilliant idealization and simplification of a hyperrational, hyperintellectual phenomenon: a mathematician performing a rigorous computation. The basic idea had five components: (1) a *serial process*, occurring in (2) a severely restricted *work space*, to which (3) *data* and *instructions*, are brought from (4) an inert but superreliable *memory*, to be operated on by (5) a finite set of *primitive operations*.

The set of primitives (the acts "atomic to introspection," if you like) was deliberately impoverished, so that there could be no question of their mechanical realizability. In other words, it was essential to Turing's mathematical purposes that each step in the processes he was studying be, without doubt, so simple, so stupid, that it could be performed by a simpleton—by someone who could be replaced by a machine.

Turing saw, of course, that his ideal specification could serve, indirectly, as the blueprint for an actual computing machine. Others saw this as well, in particular, the mathematician John von Neumann, who modified Turing's basic ideas to create the abstract architecture for the first realistically realizable digital computer. That architecture, the von Neumann machine, is illustrated in the figure below.

Briefly, the machine operates as follows. The memory is just a very large array of identical pigeonholes, or registers, each with an address, and each capable of having a number as its "contents." The CPU, or

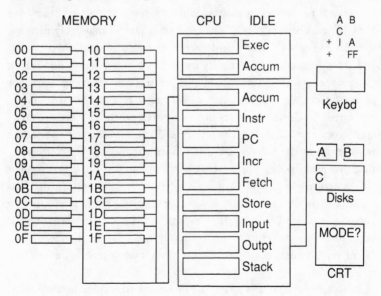

A von Neumann machine

central processing unit, is where all the action takes place. Here instructions (coded in numbers) are brought, one at a time, to the instruction register (Instr), where they are decoded and executed; the results appear in the accumulator (Accum). The instruction register and accumulator together are the famous "von Neumann bottleneck"; only one instruction at a time can be executed, and only one result at a time can appear in the accumulator. For instance, one such instruction would be to subtract the contents of register 12 from the number already in the accumulator (leaving the result in the accumulator). The next instruction could be to see if this result was greater than zero and, depending on the outcome, to fetch as the next instruction the contents of either register 25 or register 48.

All digital computers are direct descendants of the von Neumann design; and while they carry many modifications and improvements, they share (like all vertebrates) a fundamental underlying architecture. It is a considerable historical irony that the popular press misdescribed this architecture from the moment it was created. These fascinating new von Neumann machines were called, as I remarked earlier, "giant electronic brains," but they were, in fact, giant electronic *minds*, electronic imitations of the Joycean stream of consciousness: serial processors in which a single operation occurred at any one time. The architecture of the brain, in contrast, is massively parallel, with millions of simultaneously active channels of operation.

Is this difference theoretically important? In one sense, no. Turing had proven—and this is probably his greatest contribution—that one of his machines (called today a universal Turing machine) could compute any function that any computer, with any architecture, could compute. In effect, the universal Turing machine is the perfect mathematical chameleon, capable of imitating any other computing machine and doing, during that period of imitation, exactly what that machine does. You have only to feed the universal Turing machine a suitable description of another machine, and it produces a perfect imitation based on that description; it becomes, virtually, the other machine. A computer program can thus be seen either as a list of primitive instructions to be followed or as a description of a machine to be imitated.

In fact, once you have a von Neumann machine on which to build, you can nest virtual machines like Chinese boxes. For instance, you

can first turn your von Neumann machine into a Unix machine (the
Unix operating system) and then implement a Lisp machine in the
Unix machine—along with WordStar, Lotus 1-2-3, and a host of
other virtual machines. Each virtual machine is recognizable by its
user interface—the way it appears on the screen of the CRT and the
way it responds to input. This self-presentation is often called the user
illusion, since a user cannot tell—and does not care—how the particular virtual machine he is using is implemented in the hardware. It
doesn't matter to him whether the virtual machine is one, two, three,
or ten layers away from the hardware.[4] (For instance, WordStar users
can recognize, and interact with, the WordStar virtual machine wher-
ever they find it, no matter what variation exists in the underlying
hardware.)

Now, since any computing machine at all can be imitated by a
virtual machine on a von Neumann machine, it follows that if the
brain is a massive parallel processing machine, it can be imitated by a
von Neumann machine. It is easy enough to see how this is done: by a
process analogous to knitting. Suppose the parallel processor being
simulated is ten channels wide, as in the figure below. The von
Neumann machine is instructed to perform the operations handled by
the first node of the first channel, saving the output in a buffer
memory, and then the operations of the second node, and so forth,
until the outputs of all the first row of nodes have been calculated and
saved; these then become the inputs to the second row of nodes, whose
operations are calculated one at a time, "knitting back" and forth,
trading off time against space. A ten-channel machine will take at
least ten times as long to simulate as a one-channel machine, and a

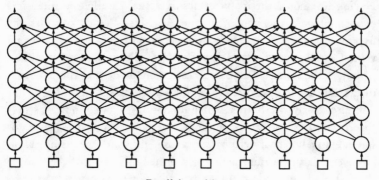

Parallel machine

million-channel machine (like the brain) will take at least a million times as long to simulate. Turing's proof says nothing about the speed with which the imitation will be accomplished, and for some architectures, even the blinding speed of modern digital computers is overwhelmed by the task. That is why artificial intelligence researchers interested in exploring the powers of parallel architectures are today turning to *real* parallel machines—artifacts that really perform thousands or millions of operations at the same time, and thus might with more justice be called "giant electronic brains"—on which to compose their simulations.

The trouble with merely virtual parallel machines running on real von Neumann machines is that they are terribly inefficient and wasteful. Von Neumann machines were not designed to perform this sort of work. Of course, von Neumann machines were also not meant to be word processors! Nothing in the design of their central processing units and memories (as opposed to their peripheral organs—the keyboard, for instance) was designed with an eye to making word processing possible; but now, probably the most common activity of these architectures is word processing. And here we can see a familiar evolutionary principle applied to human technology: An organ or tool that was initially designed for one purpose or set of purposes comes to be valued more for a new purpose, and is appropriated, inefficiencies and all, for that new purpose.[5]

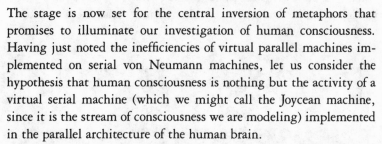

The stage is now set for the central inversion of metaphors that promises to illuminate our investigation of human consciousness. Having just noted the inefficiencies of virtual parallel machines implemented on serial von Neumann machines, let us consider the hypothesis that human consciousness is nothing but the activity of a virtual serial machine (which we might call the Joycean machine, since it is the stream of consciousness we are modeling) implemented in the parallel architecture of the human brain.

Quite clearly, our brains (which do not differ much in basic structure from those of other mammals) weren't designed—except for some relatively recent peripheral organs—for word processing. Now, however, a large portion, perhaps even the lion's share, of the activity that takes place in adult human brains is involved in a sort of word processing, namely, speech production and comprehension, and the serial rehearsal and rearrangement of linguistic items or, better, their neural surrogates.

Language, then, is one of the most important innovations in the environment that provoked the development of this virtual machine. But it is not only words that we process in our streams of consciousness: There are images, diagrams, and other wordless mental items that defy both novelists' and phenomenologists' efforts at direct description. We might do better, in fact, to leave the citadel of consciousness, turn our backs temporarily on the beguiling and ineffable items that swim by in the stream, and see if we can discover something useful by the indirect method of trying to answer the standard questions one would raise about such an evolutionary novelty:

1. How did this virtual machine, to Joycean machine of consciousness, arise?
2. What alternatives are there in the "gene pool" of virtual machines?
3. How is it transmitted?
4. How is it implemented in the brain?
5. What—if anything—is it good for?

If I could answer any of these questions definitively at this time, it would be a sure sign that I hadn't come up with a very fruitful idea. I present the idea as a guide to future empirical research, not as an a priori truth deduced from first principles, so I certainly do not want to be understood as claiming to have proved anything about this virtual machine. I will offer some speculations and suggestions, however, which I hope will eventually lead to confirmed answers to all these questions.

1. How did this virtual machine arise? Since, *ex hypothesi*, the human beings who discovered this technology were not already conscious (in the way we are), we shall have to suppose that it had its beginnings in unconscious invention. This is no paradox; all the inventions and discoveries of species evolution have been unconscious, and all but the most recent innovations in the behavior of individual phenotypes (the novel actions of animals, human and otherwise) must have arisen unconsciously. When Julian Jaynes speculates that the date of this unconscious invention was less than ten thousand years ago, he might be off by an order of magnitude (though I suspect he is close to the mark). In any case, there undoubtedly was a time before which our ancestors lacked our sort of consciousness and after which they had it. The intervening processes must have been unconscious, and calling them inventions is just honoring them as appreciated innovations. But what sort of processes were they? I have speculated that they were various modes of relatively undirected self-exploration (stimulating oneself over and over and seeing what happened). Because of the brain's plasticity, coupled with the no doubt innate restlessness and curiosity that motivates us to explore every nook and cranny of our environment (of which our own bodies are such an important and ubiquitous element), it is not surprising, in retrospect, that we hit upon strategies of self-stimulation, or self-manipulation, that led to the inculcation of habits and dispositions that radically altered the internal communicative structure of our brains.[6] For instance, if some subsystem of the brain had information that would be valuable to another, but genetic evolution had provided no hard-wired communication links between the subsystems, it would be immensely useful to develop a behavior (such as talking out loud to oneself) that "broadcast" the relevant information, making it available to any system that had access to auditory input. Once this became habitual, it would create a "virtual wire" linking the subsystems informationally. That is just one instance of the sort of role I suppose virtual machine elements to play in restructuring the functional architecture of the brain.

2. *What alternatives are there in the "gene pool" of virtual machines?* First of all, many varieties of self-stimulation and self-manipulation that presumably have no clearly valuable effect on cognition or control, and hence do not lead to the creation of new virtual machine elements, fail to be extinguished, for standard Darwinian reasons, and may even drift to fixation in certain subpopulations. Likely candidates are painting yourself blue, beating yourself with birch boughs, cutting patterns in your skin, starving yourself, saying a "magical" formula to yourself over and over again, and staring at your navel. In our own culture we should not overlook such apparently "noisy" but possibly quite functional activities as scratching one's head, biting one's fingernails, twisting one's hair, and doo-

dling. One man's mere fidget may be another's brilliant mnemonic crutch.

More dramatically, we can note the current population explosion of a clear rival to the standard Joycean operating system: multiple personality disorder (MPD). In 1944 approximately one hundred cases of MPD were reported (that is, in books and periodicals of some general accessibility in research libraries). By 1980, about a thousand cases were reported in the literature—again, the clinical literature, but also in the popular press. (Over the years, MPD cases have been the subjects of such popular books, and films, as *The Three Faces of Eve*, *Sybil*, and *The Minds of Billy Milligan*.) Four years later, more than two thousand cases were reportedly in professional therapy in the United States; a back-of-the-envelope calculation of one knowledgeable observer suggests that in 1988 more than four thousand cases were in therapy and perhaps another twelve thousand existed in the United States alone. (The disorder is almost unknown in other contemporary cultures.)

If we think of MPD as (whatever else it is) an alternative operating system—a different way of organizing all the "files" and "subroutines" and "applications programs"—then we can begin to trace the production and reproduction of this software, and its elaboration and transmission through the culture.[7] (We might well compare it to the software "viruses" of which we have heard so much.) As usual, looking at pathology is a good way of getting hints about the normal case.

3. How is the normal, Joycean virtual machine transmitted? This machine is not, of course, transmitted in sequences of zeroes and ones (like von Neumann software), on diskettes, or over networks. It is important to acknowledge this fundamental *disanalogy* between the virtual machines of computer science and the virtual machines of psychobiology. A von Neumann machine has a random access memory (RAM) that is extremely demanding about the form of whatever it stores (chunks of eight, sixteen, or thirty-two bits, for instance), and a central processing unit (CPU), that is even more rigid in the way it responds to those bit-strings, treated as instructions in its entirely proprietary and fixed machine language. These characteristics are definitive of the stored-program digital computer, and a human brain is no such thing. For one thing, the plasticity that somehow subserves its memory is not isolated as a passive storehouse; and, for another, there is nothing that could plausibly serve as the machine language of the brain—if by that we mean some uniform, generative, systematically compositional way of building larger processing dispositions out of smaller ones.

The methods of transmission that guarantee a fairly uniform virtual machine operating throughout the culture must be social, highly context-sensitive, and to some degree self-organizing and self-correcting. Getting different computers—say, a MacIntosh and an IBM-PC—to "talk to each other" is a matter of intricate, fussy engineering that depends on precise information about the internal machinery of the two systems. Insofar as human beings can "share software" without anyone's having such knowledge, it must be thanks to a high degree of system lability and format tolerance. A variety of methods are plausible: learning by imitation, learning as a by-product of subtle reinforcement (encouragement, disapproval, threat) in the course of communicative encounters, and even learning as the result of explicit instruction in a natural language that has already been learned via the first two methods.[8]

4. How is this virtual machine implemented in the brain? I suspect that some of the most puzzling features of human consciousness can be explained only if we go back and consider how this virtual machine may exploit features of the human nervous system designed long ago with different purposes in mind.

One of the yawning chasms in current cognitive theories of the conscious mind is the absence of any clear role for what is somewhat lamely called "affect" or "emotion," or even just "the way things feel" or (in philosophers' jargon) "qualia." Concentrating as we do these days on cognition, we have tended to incorporate its all but forgotten twin, conation, the "faculty of volition and desire," into the colorless ranks of information-bearing states; We thus tend to ignore as unacknowledged implementational noise all the zest, aversion, joy, and anguish that so typically accompany the information-bearing states of our cognitive apparatus. "What could their role be?" we ask ourselves, and, drawing a blank, we divert our attention from them. But perhaps we can make sense of their presence as a vestige of an earlier internal economy.[9]

Back in the early days of nervous systems, before the development of advanced locomotion and its concomitant need for long-range, or distal, perception, stimuli more or less wore their meanings on their sleeves: bad things triggered alarms by directly contacting—perhaps even injuring—the receptors or transducers designed to signal their presence, while the harbingers of good were stimulated by the very presence, in or adjacent to the organism, of the things they informed about. There was no such thing as a value-free, purely objective, informing "report" from a sense organ to an inner executive. Rather, every report had imperative connotations: *Grab me!* or *Flee me!* or some variation on those themes—*Look out!* or *Yummy!* or *Yuck!* As behavior became more devious, though, nervous systems came to need more dispassionate, detached sorts of signals to guide the control of behavior. But perhaps all these new armies of "reporters" were recruited from the ranks of "warners" and "applauders," and hence carried with them, now for no particular reason, a leftover trace of the positive or negative. That is, the price the organism paid for being informed about this or that was being irritated somewhat, in a particularly informing way, or, on other occasions, soothed or encouraged by the very process of being informed. All this need mean, non-metaphorically, is that some information-providing states would happen to cause the creature to strive to get out of them (intrinsically annoying or irritating states, one might call them, but it would all be just a matter of how they were wired in), while others would happen to cause the creature to strive to stay in them (intrinsically pleasant states—*other things being equal*). Suppose, however, other things weren't equal; suppose the value of staying informed about these various "irritating" matters was greater than the original disvalue that had underwritten the avoidance link, and suppose that the disvalue of lingering in the "intrinsically pleasant" information-providing states on occasion outweighed the value that had made them pleasing in the first place. In any system that began to track these higher-order values and disvalues, a host of tensions would arise, played off against each other, and keeping the whole system in a more or less incessant struggle of countervailing reactions to its own internal states. In lower creatures, this all might play itself out with no spectators and no partisans, but once the loops of self-monitoring began to feed back recognitions of these patterns, a logical space would be created for the first time in which enjoyment and disgust and their paler kin could find some room to play. (This does begin to sound more like home, doesn't it?)[10]

One shouldn't suppose that this imposition of the new cognitive economy on top of the older conative economy was simply a matter of tolerating the anachronistic pressures and vibrations and whatnot thereby created. It could very well be that the new virtual machinery opportunistically harnessed these ancient features. This could explain a great deal. As Jacob Bronowski once said, "The most powerful drive in the ascent of man is his pleasure in his own skill. He loves to do what he does well and, having done it well, he loves to do it better."[11] The meme that unlocked this storehouse of creative, exploratory energy was bound to pay for itself in both the short and the long term.

5. *What—if anything—is this virtual machine good for?* The upshot of my account is that all this self-stimulation creates a much more powerful virtual architecture, one that disposes the brain to ever more effective self-stimulation. It creates an architecture that is incessantly reorganizing itself, trying out novel combinations, sometimes idly, sometimes with great purpose casting about through the huge search space for a good—pleasing—new combination. And what is all this good for? It seems to be good for the sorts of self-monitoring that can protect a flawed system from being victimized by its own failures. Nicholas Humphrey has also seen it as providing a means for exploiting what might be called social simulations—using introspection to guide one's hunches about what others are thinking and feeling.[12] Julian Jaynes has argued, persuasively, that its capacities for self-exhortation and self-reminding are a prerequisite for the sorts of elaborated and long-term bouts of self-control without which agriculture, building projects, and other civilized and civilizing activities could not be organized.

These are all very plausible claims, and I am sure other good and essential uses for the architecture of consciousness can also be found.[13] As good Darwinians, however, we should remember that an innovation such as this does not *have* to be good for anything except self-replication.[14] The Joycean machine *might* just be a parasitical meme, an irresistible fad that happens to thrive in the medium provided by our huge and plastic brains, while not paying its keep with any great advantage to the creatures it infests. [15]

━━━

Still, you may object, all this has little or nothing to do with consciousness. After all, a von Neumann machine is entirely unconscious. Why should implementing it, or something like it (a Joycean machine), make the brain any more conscious? I do have an answer: the von Neumann machine, by being wired from the outset as a serial machine with maximally efficient informational links, didn't have to become the object of its own elaborate perceptual systems. The workings of the Joycean machine, on the other hand, are just as "visible" and "audible" to it as any of the things in the external world that it is designed to perceive—for the simple reason that they have much of the same perceptual machinery focused on them. [16]

Now, this appears to be a trick with mirrors, I know. And it certainly is counterintuitive, hard to swallow, initially outrageous—just what one would expect of an idea that could break through centuries of mystery, controversy, and confusion. If the key to the mystery of consciousness were obvious, we would have settled on it long ago.

Let me try to make the idea a little clearer, at least, and perhaps a little more plausible. A little earlier, I mentioned the user illusion by which different machines are rendered perceptible. I am suggesting that human consciousness is a virtual machine in the brain—but *who is the user?* We seem to need selves, or egos, or subjects, to be the "victims" (or beneficiaries) of this user illusion. If this is so, we are right back where we started: at the mystery of the conscious mind and how it is situated in the natural world.

But this is not so. The user illusion is defined relative to a user, to be sure, but not necessarily to a *conscious* user. All we need posit in order to make sense of the concept of a user illusion is an information-gathering agent of some sort (it might be a robot, or even just another sedentary computer), with a limited access to features of the entity that presents the user illusion. Suppose, for instance, we make a robot—as unconscious as you please, but equipped with a televisual "eye" that provides it with "visual" information—and train it to type

letters for us, using WordStar. What it will "know" (in its unconscious way) about WordStar is only what it "sees," only those aspects
of WordStar that are presented to it on the CRT or that it can
manipulate from the keyboard. The rest of WordStar is all backstage
and invisible—and irrelevant. (That, remember, is the chief beauty of
virtual machines.) Such a user is external to the system in question—
adopting a third-person point of view toward it—and there are
indeed similarly placed agents relative to each of us: namely, the
people with whom we interact socially. For whom is *my* Joycean
machine a user illusion? Among others, for you.

The potency of this third-person role is revealed with particular
clarity when one is confronted with a living human body that runs a
different operating system: the MPD user illusion. I quote a few
passages from the user's manual:[17]

> Treat all alters with equal respect and address the patient as he or she
> wishes to be addressed. . . .
>
> Make it clear that the staff is not expected to recognize each alter.
> Alters must identify themselves to staff members if they find such
> acknowledgment important.
>
> Explain ward rules personally, having requested all alters to listen, and
> insist on reasonable compliance.

In short, according to the clinical literature on MPD, adopting the
view that more than one subject inhabits a single body is a strategy
that works with these patients when no other strategy does. And we
who are normal can all attest to the strategic wisdom of others'
treating us as if we were each a single subject inhabiting a body, with
only limited capacity to report on what is going on inside us. Thus
other people are certainly users for whom our Joycean user illusions are
valuable.

Notice also that each human brain, posed the multifaceted task of
controlling a highly active and complex body through a complicated
world, needs information about certain of its own states and
activities—but can readily make use of only certain edited sorts of
information. It needs a user illusion of itself. And thanks to the
indoctrination it receives during its apprenticeship, it gets one. We

call it a mind. As Douglas Hofstadter has said, "Mind is a pattern perceived by a mind."[18]

Where does this mind come from? Is it real? What is it made of? It is a virtual machine, running in the brain, a product of three sorts of evolution. And it is *its own* user illusion.

▭

The ideas—memes—presented here have been undergoing population explosion in the academisphere in the last few years, and the task of determining their lines of ancestry—or, alternatively, their convergent evolution—is beyond me. Among the major contemporary phenotypes are those found in the following works, in addition to the works cited in the notes.

Richard Dawkins. *The Selfish Gene.* Oxford: Oxford University Press, 1976.

Gilles Fauconnier. *Mental Spaces.* Paris: Les Editions de Minuit, 1984.

Michael Gazzaniga. *The Social Brain.* New York: Basic Books, 1985.

Geoffrey Hinton (Touretzky and Hinton). "Symbols Among the Neurons: Details of a Connectionist Inference Architecture." In *Proceedings of the Ninth Joint Conference on Artificial Intelligence*, Los Angeles, California, August 1985, pp. 238–243.

Douglas Hofstadter. *Godel Escher Bach.* New York: Basic Books, 1979.

————. *Metamagical Themas.* New York, Basic Books, 1985.

Ray Jackendoff. *Consciousness and the Computational Mind.* Cambridge, Massachusetts: Massachusetts Institute of Technology Press, 1987.

Julian Jaynes. *The Origins of Consciousness in the Breakdown of the Bicameral Mind.* Boston: Houghton Mifflin, 1976.

Stephen Kosslyn. Paper presented to the Society for Philosophy and Psychology, 1984.

————. *Science* 240: 1621–1626, June 17, 1988.

Marvin Minsky. *The Society of Minds.* Cambridge, Massachusetts: Massachusetts Institute of Technology Press, 1986.

Allen Newell. "William James Lectures, 1987." In *Science* 241: 296–298, July 15, 1988; and *Science* 241: 27–29, July 1, 1988.

Gilbert Ryle. *On Thinking.* K. Kolenda, ed. New Jersey: Rowan and Littlefield, 1979.

NOTES

1 Quoted in William H. Calvin, *The River that Flows Uphill* (New York: Macmillan, 1986), p. 159.

2 Ewert, "The neuroethology of prey-capture in toads," *Behavioral and Brain Sciences* 10:3, (November 1987) and commentary. See in particular my commentary, "Eliminate the Middletoad!" *Behavioral and Brain Sciences* 10:3 (September 1987): 372–374.

3 Different versions of this story can be found in D. C. Dennett, *Content and Consciousness* (London: Routledge and Kegan Paul, 1969), Ch. 3, "Evolution in the Brain," and "Why the Law of Effect Will Not Go Away," *Journal of the Theory of Social Behavior*, 1975 (reprinted in *Brainstorms* [Cambridge, Massachusetts: Massachusetts Institute of Technology Press, 1978]); G. Edelman, *Neural Darwinism* (New York: Basic Books, 1987); J. P. Changeux and S. Dehaene, "Neuronal Models of Cognitive Functions" (forthcoming in *Cognition*); William H. Calvin, "The Brain as a Darwin Machine," *Nature* (1987), pp. 33–34.

4 Or it might not be a *virtual* machine at all. It might be a made-to-order hard-wired special-purpose real machine, such as a Lisp machine, which is a descendant of Lisp *virtual* machines, and which is designed right down to its silicon chips to run the programming language Lisp.

5 See, for example, Stephen Jay Gould, *The Panda's Thumb* (New York: Norton, 1980).

6 In *Elbow Room* (Cambridge, Massachusetts: Massachusetts Institute of Technology Press, 1984), pp. 38–43, I tell a "Just So Story" about the birth of this variety of consciousness, involving processes of talking to oneself and drawing diagrams for oneself, for instance. Many other tactics of self-manipulation are also plausible.

7 Sometimes the route of transmission is itself documented: On the American television program *Geraldo* (a morning talk show) the husband of a multiple (as one calls them in the trade) recalled his bafflement about his wife's behavior until he saw a report on MPD on *60 Minutes* (another American television program) and guessed, instantly, what was wrong with his wife. He got in touch with the therapist interviewed on *60 Minutes*, and soon this therapist had diagnosed and begun treating his wife. On need not suppose, skeptically, that the therapist *created* the condition of MPD in this woman; the patient probably already exhibited quite a robust and well-defined multiplicity. But there seems to be very

good reason to suppose that therapeutic encounters are often responsible for the typical explosion that creates the following striking statistic: The mean number of personalities in a well-studied sufferer from MPD is thirteen. See also Nicholas Humphrey and Daniel Dennett, "Speaking for Our Selves," *Raritan*, 1989; and F. W. Putnam, "The Clinical Phenomenology of Multiple Personality Disorder: Review of 100 Recent Cases," *Journal of Clinical Psychiatry* 47 (1986): 253–293.

[8] Just as the wheel is a fine bit of technology that is really quite dependent for its utility on rails or paved roads or other artificially planed surfaces, so the virtual machine that I am talking about can exist only in an environment that has not merely language and social interactions, but probably writing and diagramming as well—since the demands on memory and pattern recognition for its implementation require it to "off-load" some of its memories into buffers in the environment. (See David Rumelhart, *Parallel Distributed Processing* (Cambridge, Massachusetts: Massachusetts Institute of Technology Press, 1986), Ch. 14, for observations on this topic.)

[9] The following discussion owes a great deal to discussions with Nicholas Humphrey.

[10] Nietzsche offered a similar speculation a century ago: "thus it was that man first developed what was later called his 'soul.' The entire inner world, originally as thin as if it were stretched between two membranes, expanded and extended itself, acquired depth, breadth, and height, in the same measure as outward discharge was *inhibited.*" Nietzsche, *Genealogy of Morals*, Essay 2, section 16, trans. Kaufman (Princeton: Princeton University Press, 1950), p. 84.

[11] Quoted in Calvin, p. 147.

[12] Nicholas Humphrey, *Consciousness Regained* (Oxford: Oxford University Press, 1984) and *The Inner I* (London: Oxford University Press, 1986).

[13] It is important to note that this innovation by three processes of natural selection of good software for the incompletely designed brain does not just enhance the individual's chances of coping, but increases the speed and efficiency of the first process of natural selection as well. This is known as the Baldwin effect: Thanks to the plasticity of design, species can be said to pretest the efficacy of particular designs by phenotypic (individual) exploration of the nearby possibilities. If a particularly winning setting is thereby discovered, organisms that are "closer" to it in the adaptive landscape will have a clear advantage over those more distant (and hence less likely to design themselves to the winning position during their lifetimes).

I mention the Baldwin effect because it has a clear counterpart in computer science in the principle that software design is faster and cheaper than hardware design. Thanks to their programmability, general purpose computers have permitted the cheap, swift exploration of varieties of computational architectures that would be extremely costly to build as hardware and then test. Once a design has proven its prowess as a software virtual machine, it sometimes pays to use it as the blueprint for a hard-wired machine. Lisp machines are a good case in point. And DEC computers are perhaps the beneficiaries of a true Baldwin effect—since they were selected for their capacity to turn themselves swiftly and effortlessly into Lisp virtual machines.

14 We might note, for instance, that the value we place on self-consciousness, and on being "reflective," while it might be independently justified, is certainly the result of advertisement by a self-serving or selfish meme. "The unexamined life is not worth living," Socrates proclaimed, thereby suggesting that one should acquire and foster any habits of self-examination that one encounters.

15 It is clearly arguable—but by no means certain—that its rival, MPD, does more harm than good to those who implement it; in any event, the proliferation of MPD through the culture does not in any direct way depend on its being of value, or even on its subjects' (mis)perceiving it as valuable.

16 David Rosenthal, in "Thinking That One Thinks" (paper presented at the Tufts Colloquium, 1988), develops the case for the initially counterintuitive thesis that conscious mental states are all those and only those that are the *objects of* second-order *unconscious* mental states. That is, to be conscious, one must be capable of thinking that one thinks, noticing that one is happy, noticing that one is daydreaming, and so forth, but these second-order mental states do not themselves need be conscious. Only their "perceptual" objects are thereby moved into the class of conscious mental states and events.

17 Directions to ward staff, from R. Kluft: *Directions in Psychiatry* vol. 4, lesson 24, "The Treatment of MPD: Current Concepts": 1986.

18 Douglas Hofstadter, *The Mind's I* (New York: Basic Books, 1981), p. 200.

Simulations of Reality: Deciding What to Do Next

WILLIAM H. CALVIN

It wasn't until I considered the neural setup that would be needed for rapid ballistic movements, such as throwing, that I got to thinking about what secondary uses such a neural mechanism might have—and realized that it was perfect for simulating courses of action or shaping up sentences to speak, as well as for throwing.

Anyone interested in the nature of reality seems to wind up thinking about thought itself. The late physicist Heinz Pagels was very interested in thought—how it came about, how it achieved what we call "reason," and its pitfalls. The title of his last book is only the first half of that famous nineteenth-century cautionary line from Goya: "The dreams of reason bring forth monsters." There are traps for the unwary, snares whose consequences are far more than just making a single mistake—they can entangle you for life in a prison of your own making.

As background, consider Henry David Thoreau's firm-footing metaphor for reality: "Let us settle ourselves, and work and wedge our feet downward through the mud and slush of opinion . . . till we come to a hard bottom and rocks in place, which we can call reality . . . a place where you might found a wall or a state." Pagels, in *The Dreams of Reason*, seems to have had this metaphor in mind when he cautioned about overdoing certainty:

> The characteristic of all fundamentalism is that it has found absolute certainty—the certainty of class warfare, the certainty of science, or the literal certainty of the Bible—a certainty of the person who has finally found a solid rock to stand upon which, unlike other rocks, is "solid all the way down." Fundamentalism, however, is a terminal form of human consciousness in which development is stopped, eliminating the uncertainty and risk that real growth entails. [1]

Notice that Pagels's alternative to those fundamentalist monsters of reason seems to involve uncertainty and risk. That's certainly surprising to many people who treat science as settled certainty, glorified—people who confuse the occasional *products* of science with the scientific *process* of shaping up a truth. But Pagels had recognized, far better than even most of us in biology, that evolutionary thinking—the way that Darwin and his followers tend to look on things—is the key to thought, to reason, to *doing* science—especially to the scientific agenda of the next decade. Pagels's emphasis on uncertainty can be used as a text from which to explore some fundamental aspects of thought and language. In some sense evolutionary thinking is the missing key in the classic search—the search for the seat of the soul. Which is, I suppose, the traditional name for the following story.

◻️

That search is the most obvious example of looking for a *place* or a *product* when you should have been looking for a *process* instead. Asked what goes on inside our heads, we imagine a homunculus—a puppeteer within that pulls our strings, or a voyeur within that evaluates what the senses provide. Some people have even mistaken the uniquely human "language organ" metaphor of Eric Lennenberg[2] and Noam Chomsky[3] (and, I suppose, Emile Durkheim, who started the organ metaphor business in the social sciences[4]) for a place, rather than understanding it as a search for a transformational process. At one time I certainly made that mistake—and I should have known better, since I've spent a lot of time in our neurosurgical operating room watching the language cortex being mapped[5] in awake patients. No one patch of brain seems to be of really central importance; it seems more like a big committee that can work pretty well with half its members missing.

Certainly the most fascinating aspects of the Penfield-like localization data and of Doreen Kimura's studies of hand-movement disorders occurring together with language disorders[6] were the specializations for temporal ordering, for sequence, that were seen by my Seattle colleague George Ojemann in his mapping studies.[7] It all suggested that the stringing-together-words aspect of language might be just one task of a more primitive bit of neural machinery, good not only at stringing together hand-and-arm movements but also throat-tongue-lips movements, and good at analyzing incoming sound sequences as well.

But it wasn't until I got away from cortex and began looking at other serially ordered processes, like the DNA coding in the genome and species evolution, that I was surprised to find that the well-known Darwinian process may suffice to explain a lot of the phenomena we associate with the self, with consciousness in the sense of deciding what to do next, with planning ahead, and with speaking and listening. Thought shapes up guesses.

Xenophanes said, in the sixth century B.C., that there is no certainty in the world, that "all is but a woven web of guesses."[8] And the English geologist William Smith remarked in 1817, a generation before Charles Darwin, "If man was to think beyond what the senses had directly given him, he must first throw some wild guess-work into the air, and then, by comparing it bit by bit with nature, improve and shape it into a truth."[9] In the wake of Darwin's *Origin of Species* in 1859, such thinking about thought accelerated, aided by Darwin's and Wallace's insight about the shaping-up that could be accomplished by repeated rounds of randomness and selection. And, indeed, Darwinian thinking about thought itself dominated the last several decades of the nineteenth century.

No one has been very clear about the shaping-up process, however, probably because they had no notion of the neural machinery that the brain requires to do various jobs. It wasn't until I considered the neural setup that would be needed for rapid ballistic movements, such as throwing, that I got to thinking about what secondary uses such a neural mechanism might have—and realized that it was perfect for simulating courses of action or shaping up sentences to speak, as well as for throwing.

Not long ago, I published an article in *Nature*, entitled "The Brain as a Darwin Machine," that laid out a model for language and thought, suggesting that neural machinery in the left brain was well suited to simulate the Darwinian evolutionary process on a rapid time scale.[10] We have already seen that new antibodies could be evolved in days, rather than taking the millennia required to evolve a new biological species. It's a matter of generation time. So we may just be shortening the time scale another few orders of magnitude, shaping up new mental constructs in milliseconds to seconds. Perhaps sentences—strings of words. Or the string of actions we call a scenario: a plan of action. Or the string of musical notes we call a melody.

<hr>

Rational thought from randomness? That's odd, because purpose seems so different from chance. But Darwinism suggests that you might be able to have your cake and eat it too: Chance plus selection, repeated for many rounds, can achieve much that single-shot randomness cannot. It's like that sampling-without-replacement problem in probability theory: The base from which you're drawing is always changing; furthermore, the unsuccessful are sometimes recycled as food for the successful via the carbon cycle. The next time that someone tells you that the idea of rooms full of monkeys typing the works of Shakespeare is absurdly improbable, tell him to read chapter 3 of Richard Dawkins' recent book, *The Blind Watchmaker*, and learn the difference between one-shot randomness and the dance called the Darwinian Two-Step: randomness and selection, back and forth, over and over, shaping up the improbable.

Can machinery in our heads, using the Darwinian Two-Step, really account for purposeful behavior, especially our planning-for-the-future behavior that has been such a powerful drive toward both civilization and ethics? Is it, indeed, the foundation of our more-than-the-other-animals consciousness?

I think so,[11] and, on my reading of *The Dreams of Reason*, so did Heinz Pagels. He certainly phrased the possibility succinctly, and then went on to offer a moral lesson that arises from it: "Perhaps our thinking exemplifies a selective system. First lots of random scattered ideas compete for survival. Then comes the selection for what works best—one idea dominates, and this is followed by its amplification." I'll return to that word "amplification" later. Pagels continued, "Perhaps the moral of this selective model system is that you never learn anything unless you are willing to take a risk and tolerate a little randomness in your life."[12]

Pagels made selective systems the cornerstone of his analysis of the sciences of complexity that he thought would dominate future science and technology: "A selective system is a pattern producing and recognizing system, be it the pattern of life on earth, the symbolic order of the mind, or the pattern of culture. A selective system manages complexity."[13] Just to show you how important Pagels considered this, recall his preface, where he says: "I am convinced that the nations and peoples who master the new sciences of complexity will become the economic, cultural, and political superpowers of the next century."[14]

━━

And how does Darwinism work inside our heads, compared to the immune system or to biological evolution? Let me begin by examining how the brain circuitry problem has been posed in fields that may be more familiar to some of you than is neurophysiology: namely, the concern with narratives so frequently voiced by those in the humanities. Like the DNA strings of the genome, or the amino acid strings of the antibody, we humans are always stringing things together. Even the cosmologists are belatedly getting into strings! Jean-Paul Sartre said:

> A man is always a teller of tales, he lives surrounded by his stories and the stories of others, he sees everything that happens to him through them; and he tries to live his life as if he were recounting it. [15]

This tendency develops gradually, as the literary critic Peter Brooks recently summarized so nicely:

> About the age of three . . . a child begins to show the ability to put together a narrative in coherent fashion and especially the capacity to recognize narratives, to judge their well-formedness. Children quickly become virtual Aristotelians, insisting upon any storyteller's observation of the "rules," upon proper beginnings, middles, and particularly ends. [16]

Roger Schank has a fine discussion of how children learn "scripts" and chain them together to explain their world. [17]

Well, where did we get this ability to chain things together—an ability in considerable excess of that seen elsewhere in the animal kingdom? A need for planning? Feedback does work pretty well, and if you can do successive approximation, you don't need a detailed plan of action, some sort of serial buffer to chain together movement commands. Goal and feedback, together with inborn action patterns, usually suffice; indeed, most animals don't have such neural machinery. There are, however, some human actions, such as accurate throwing, that require detailed advance planning—strings of modular muscle commands formed up in a serial buffer during ready-set, then shipped out (see the figure on p. 116).

You can't use feedback for ballistic movements like clubbing, kicking, hammering, or throwing, because the movement is over and done with in the tenth of a second that it takes for the feedback loop to

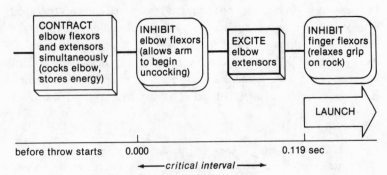

Modular motor commands, strung together to plan throw

operate. So you simply have to make the perfect plan in advance, like silently punching a roll for a player piano and then playing it aloud without feedback corrections.

If it isn't a well-grooved movement like a basketball free throw, you have to generate a family of variations on an approximate plan (the "variations-on-a-theme mode" shown in the figure on p. 117), and then judge each of those candidate strings against memories of what strings succeeded in the past under similar conditions. But you need this array of planning tracks for a second reason: Because throwing doesn't tolerate much jitter in timing the signal to release the grip on the projectile, you have to average a lot of jittery timers that are all trying to do the same job at the same time, something like a whole roomful of player pianos playing copies of one command roll. To halve the jitter, just quadruple the number of planning tracks with identical programming.

So the easy way to get this "choral mode" (on the right side of the figure on page 117) is for the most successful strings (the ones scoring highest in comparison to memories) to replace the lower-ranked candidates. That's the short version of what throwing taught me.[18]

But consider the intermediate steps of shaping up this movement command buffer into the choral mode. Let the highest-ranked of the first round replace the more ridiculous of the proposed candidates (see figure on page 118), but with little variations—copying errors, if you like. This is the "amplification step" that Pagels referred to in that quotation about thought. Some daughter strings may be even better

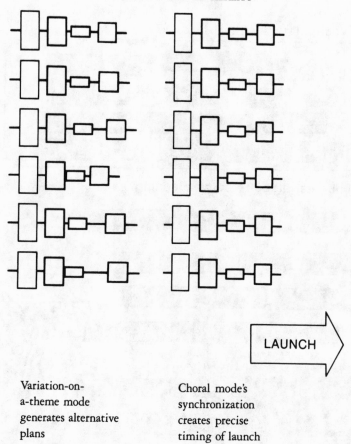

LAUNCH

Variation-on-
a-theme mode
generates alternative
plans

Choral mode's
synchronization
creates precise
timing of launch

than their parent string, have an even better fit to emerging memories
of past successes and failures.

My Darwin Machines metaphor is based on a strong analogy to the
Darwinian Two-Step.[19] This is the biological dance of randomness
then selection, back and forth. Its many injections of randomness are
usually accomplished by the gene shuffling that occurs during crossing over, as sperm and ova are made; we understand the gene shuffling that goes on in the immune response less well, but it's a similar
setup. This achieves a very nonrandom-looking result because of the

Vocabulary in Short-term Memory

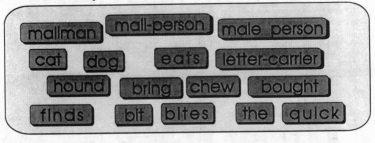

Four serial buffers for planning sentences

ROUND ONE

cat bit hound quick *3*

cat eats teeth finds *2*

hound chew mailman *5*

the dog bit the mailman *8* ✓ NOISY COPY

ROUND TWO

the dog bit the letter-carrier

the mailman bites dog

hound bites mailman

the dog bit the mailman

power of selection effected by an environment full of predators and pathogens, opportunities and obstacles. There are many serially coded individuals (DNA strings in the genome, amino acid strings in antibodies, movement sequences in behavior) existing simultaneously in parallel—but most are nonsense when graded by the "environment."

Hand movements presumably start from serial command buffers, but there are competitions between many such buffers, many rounds of shaping up. Many considerations enter into which command buffer gets switched out onto the main track and carried out as overt behavior: Sometimes instead of opening and closing your hand, you get up and go fetch something from the refrigerator, or merely turn off the commercial, or change channels. Each of which was an alternative command queue that had subconsciously formed up. Nocturnal dreams provide a biological analogue of what is mentally aborted during conscious contemplation, which lets only a few of the best plans loose for the external environment to additionally judge.

To evaluate Darwin Machines as the possible off-line planner, we must briefly consider a topic that philosophers find daunting: the problem of *value*.[20] For throwing plans, memories of closely similar situations might cause a candidate to be rated nine-plus, while other situations (such as throwing while perched on a tree branch) might have few similar elements in memory, and so no proposal receives more than a four. One can imagine quantifying the elements of the problem (distance, height difference, wind, projectile size, target size, etc.) separately and summing up. But for other sequential tasks, such as scenario spinning and language, how does one assign a value to a possible scenario, so that one can rate a scenario as "better" than another? And eventually find the "best"?

━━━

Grading is a procedure presumably analogous to the economist's utility functions, in which essentially dimensionless numbers are assigned to various elements of the problem (not unlike the way a sensation can be graded by guessing where it falls on a scale of zero to ten) and then summed up as if they were "costs" or "revenues" of some factory:

> You're halfway down the stairs of your apartment building when a thought occurs: you've forgotten your umbrella. . . . You glance at your watch and recall the subway schedule. The neural circuits that are dealing with weather award 9 points to the possibility of rain. The likelihood of missing the subway is given an 8. . . . Perhaps there is a dial that controls fear of being late; turn it from 5 to 7. Perhaps this new signal would swing the decision the other way, in favor of forgetting about the umbrella. Or lower the level on another dial that controls one's aversion to rain.
>
> The point is that you can make your imaginary computer as com-

plex as you like, adding dials to control any number of characteristics, making the gradations on the dials as fine as you please, programming the entire system to base its decisions on many times more data. Maybe that's not how the mind works. But it begins to look as though it could be modeled that way, if the simulation were fine enough.[21]

We're actually very good at making relative judgments, comparing two sounds or two lights or two tastes and saying what their relative "strengths" are. S. S. Stevens and coworkers established a series of power-law relationships for such subjective rating scales in the 1950s.

You can use these subjective ratings to compare unlike things, even guns and butter. For some people, an apple is worth 0.73 oranges. The economists in particular are always equating things for planning purposes, even outrageous things such as the "cost" of a worker's life (they are not, of course, proposing exchanges, only trying to establish true costs of building bridges and the like). Consumer organizations rating products are likely to award so many points for this feature, so many for that, so many for relative price, etc. To plan for the future, architects generate alternative scenarios and grade them according to subjective "liking." Environmental impact statements always list alternatives to the favored one, with their advantages and disadvantages; frequently, the public rates the alternatives quite differently than the planners.

Except for lacking the random shuffling and the Darwinian Two-Step, the economists' model of rational planning, as described by computer scientist Herbert A. Simon, sounds rather like my model for the mind:

> [There are] four principal components of the [Subjective Expected Utility] model: a cardinal utility function [which can assign a cardinal number as a measure of one's liking of any scenario of events in the future], an exhaustive set of alternative strategies, a probability distribution of scenarios for the future associated with each strategy, and a policy of maximizing expected utility.[22]

Of course, the "exhaustive set" and the expectation of a unique, optimal solution is where the economists got into trouble with this otherwise fine idea (which Simon calls "one of the most impressive intellectual achievements of the first half of the twentieth century. It is an elegant machine for applying reason to problems of choice"). What economists perhaps have not realized is that successive rounds of shaping up and additional injections of randomness can solve the problem—as evolution demonstrates (just substitute "inclusive fitness" for "utility").

Attention can wander, sometimes being loose (as when daydreaming at the beach), sometimes being fairly well focused (as in trying to decide between known alternatives), and sometimes being tightly focused (as when one gets set to throw). That makes it look as if the process of shaping up a population of sequencers can be held at various levels. To what does this correspond in the original Darwinism?

In the "random-thoughts mode," (Round One in the figure on page 118) exemplified by nocturnal dreams (and also daydreams), the valuation scheme is episodically changing—e.g., from boredom to novelty. One never progresses to near-clones, as might happen if we maintained attention long enough; when we "become interested" in something new, as when the story line in a dream shifts, we also change "grading criteria" and set about trying to make some sense out of the scenario on another track. It is not unlike the child "at the top of the class" changing every day of the week as the teacher's tests switch from emphasizing spelling on Monday to emphasizing American history on Tuesday, to science on Wednesday, and so on. If the teacher gets stuck in a rut, as used to happen when spelling bees stimulated competition, then the leaders of the pack are shaped up by the competition—but to the neglect of other subject matter.

The variations-on-a-theme mode (Round Two in the figure on page 118) would be where attention mechanisms keep the valuation scheme fairly constant but still drift around enough to maintain variation, keeping a pure clone from taking over. Because of the drift in climate (if not continents!), biological evolution seldom progresses to a pure clone, except via the artificial selection practiced by laboratory rat breeders trying to produce a strain with minimal variability. "Making up one's mind" might only require that a majority of the tracks, not nearly all of them, achieve the same string. Pathological processes such as worry might correspond to an inability to break out of such a tightly focused mode: No new string ever has a chance to become good enough to outscore an existing one.

But when does the cerebral choir gang into lockstep to "sing a hallelujah chorus"? To what, in the consciousness version of Darwinism, might the choral mode (Round Three in the figure below) correspond? It, after all, is what would seem to be under the severe selection pressure during evolution, since it should be so helpful in making a regular living as a hunter. What in speech or scenario-spinning

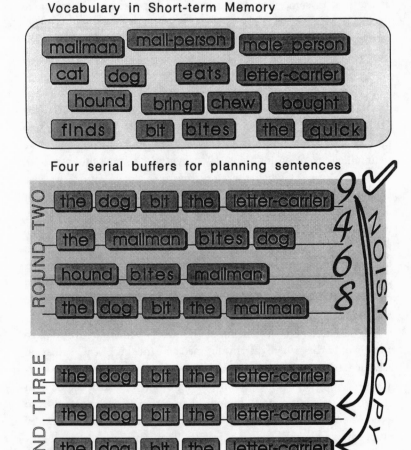

Vocabulary in Short-term Memory

mailman mail-person male person

cat dog eats letter-carrier

hound bring chew bought

finds bit bites the quick

Four serial buffers for planning sentences

ROUND TWO

the dog bit the letter-carrier 9 ✓

the mailman bites dog 4

hound bites mailman 6

the dog bit the mailman 8

NOISY COPY

ROUND THREE

the dog bit the letter-carrier

the dog bit the letter-carrier

the dog bit the letter-carrier

the dog bit the mailman

consciousness corresponds to the ganged-into-lockstep phase? The choral mode would be much closer to a real clone than to a simple majority: Everyone is singing the same "Hallelujah" as close to the "same time" as they can manage. But you probably only achieve such an ultimate state of affairs by "concentrating very hard" and excluding anything that might "distract" you from the task and cause you to value something else more for a while.

Both biological evolution and the immune system seem to value variety, and so a clone takeover isn't often seen. But there are special circumstances, and they are particularly instructive. When rabbits were imported into Australia, there was a big population explosion based on the genes of the "founder population" that arrived by ship from England. The same thing happens naturally when an insect, carried away from the mainland by the wind or a piece of driftwood, comes to rest on an island—and discovers that it has no competitors for the food, and no predators, either. If the insect happens to be a pregnant female, then just one individual's fortuitous arrival can set the stage for a population explosion, and each of her descendants will have gene sequences as similar as in siblings. The Indians of North and South America could be descendants of a relatively closely related tribe that arrived on a virgin continent and expanded over 500 generations.

So shifting attention in our mental life seems analogous to the fluctuating environment that constantly changes what is valued. If selection is also weak, as when a new niche is discovered or a conversion of function has invented a new way of making a living, a lot of different sequences may be pursued at once; in the random-thoughts mode, the "top dog" is constantly switching around, mostly because nothing achieves a very high score. I suspect that the reason our dreams are so changeable is the same reason that they are so absurd: Checking candidate sequences against episodic memory sequences doesn't work very well, and so scores are never very high; nothing gets shaped up very far before something else takes over the lead.

When efficiency is valued because the ecosystem has settled down enough to make competition between individuals more important, then some shaping up occurs—but the environment drifts a little faster than evolution can track it, and so there remain lots of deviant sequences in the variations-on-a-theme mode. Extreme concentration is rare in behavior, probably because it can cause you to be "blind-sided"; flying instructors, for example, are careful to teach student pilots always to be looking around for other planes even after they've spotted one (many a pilot has let another plane approach unnoticed while his attention was riveted on a known threat).

When something extraordinary about the environment (such as the total lack of predators or competitors) *and* something unusual about the circumstances (such as a small founder population) set the stage, then you can wind up with near uniformity. And the same may be true of the choral mode of that Darwin Machine inside our heads when it encounters an unusual set of memories in an unusual setting: The *idée fixe?* The person with the "one-track mind"? The obsessive? The worrier? The person with perfect pitch? The baseball pitcher? It will be interesting to look at some of the correlates of synchrony in the electroencephalogram in such people to explore this new possibility for modeling brain processes.

Shaping up commands is a process that is strikingly like that of the immune response of shaping up antibodies to fit an invader, or the biological evolution that shapes a species' body style and behavior to fit its environment. Thus this throwing circuitry can become a Darwin Machine. And since hand-arm sequencing circuitry in the brain has a strong overlap with where language circuitry is located in the left brain—the words we speak are composed of modular movement command sequences for pharynx, tongue, and lips—maybe the same Darwin Machine can do double duty for language and thinking in the off hours when we're not throwing or hammering or swinging a tennis racket. Instead of sequencing hand and arm commands and grading each candidate train by memories of previous successful throws, suppose that a track planned a throat-tongue-lip movement sequence and graded each such candidate train by the rules of syntax and by the individual's memories of similar verbal situations. The highest-ranked train might tend to replace low-ranked trains—but with occasional substitution of linked elements, such as synonyms. With many millisecond-long rounds, the highest-ranked train will be shaped up to better and better approximations of a plan suitable to the situation. But the best string will also begin having a lot of clones and near-relatives in the population. For a received sequence held in a temporary buffer, we make a model of its actor-action-object relationships; a candidate sequence that achieved many near clones in the Darwin machine would then represent "understanding" the message, in that we could simulate the actor-action-object scenario intended by the sender. Thus, the well-formed sentence and the reliable plan of action have some strong analogies to more familiar Darwinian successes; we may be able to use evolutionary phenomena such as the Baldwin Effect and Gause's Principle to explore language and consciousness.

Language per se has a lot of rules, which surely shape up any string of sensory and movement schemas of the kind we associate with nouns and verbs. Much could be said about language, but I am going to skip over the intermediate stages of generating a sentence to speak and just show you the final stages (see figures on pages 118 and 122). The grading against memory involves not only rules of grammar but suitability to the situation that your attention mechanisms are focusing on: memories of those childhood scripts of Roger Schank's, and variations on familiar phraseology.

Sentences are just a handy example of the more general thought scripts and scenarios. I think that we use this kind of Darwin Machine to analyze the past and to guess the future—attempt, indeed, to simulate reality, to make a model of the world. The concept that the brain comes to contain a *model* of the world was suggested in 1943 by Kenneth Craik and, following Craik's early demise, has been championed by the biologist J. Z. Young. In *The Nature of Explanation*, Craik outlined a "hypothesis on the nature of thought," proposing that

> the nervous system is . . . a calculating machine capable of modelling or paralleling external events. . . . If the organism carries a "small-scale model" of external reality and of its own possible actions within its head, it is able to try out various alternatives, conclude which is the best of them, react to future situations before they arise, utilise the knowledge of past events in dealing with the future, and in every way to react in a much fuller, safer and more competent manner to the emergencies which face it. [23]

These concepts are powerful, but they have lacked a framework with suitable building blocks. A Darwin Machine now provides a framework for thinking about thought, indeed, one that may be a reasonable first approximation to the actual brain machinery underlying thought. An intracerebral Darwin Machine need not try out one candidate sequence at a time against memory; it may be able to try out dozens, if not hundreds, of candidates simultaneously, shape up new generations in milliseconds, and thus initiate insightful actions without *overt* trial and error (just lots of hidden-inside-the-head trial and error).

While not conveying the Darwin Machines concept explicitly, Pagels certainly articulated the consequences of such off-line simulation:

> We are evidently unique among species in our symbolic ability, and we are certainly unique in our modest ability to control the conditions of our existence by using these symbols. Our ability to represent and simulate reality implies that we can approximate the order of existence and bring it to serve human purposes. A good simulation, be it a religious myth or scientific theory, gives us a sense of mastery over our experience. To represent something symbolically, as we do when we speak or write, is somehow to capture it, thus making it one's own. But with this approximation comes the realization that we have denied the immediacy of reality and that in creating a substitute we have but spun another thread in the web of our grand illusion.[24]

> No one can possibly simulate you or me with a system that is less complex than you or me. The products that we produce may be viewed as a simulation, and while products can endure in ways that our bodies cannot, they can never capture the richness, complexity, or depth of purpose of their creator.[25]

▭

Alas, Darwin Machines are not the whole story for the brain's function. But they do seem to handle aspects of imagination, language, subconscious problem solving, and the "self"—that *narrator* who has been so troublesome because of the homunculus confusions. Undoubtedly we will discover, as Darwin did for biological species, that there are circumstances when adapting isn't important, when selection temporarily plays a negligible role—as when a new niche is discovered, or when a conversion of function is possible. And the rules of cultural evolution are considerably more flexible than those of biological evolution, and so there are situations when Darwin Machines can eventually be superseded, can evolve into an efficient algorithm, like that scheme we now use for long division, when guessing the answer isn't sufficient. Culture is good about converting guesses into seeming certainty—just remember Pagels's caution!

Yet the basic phenomena that allow each of us to have a sense of self, to contemplate the world, to forecast the future and make ethical choices, to feel dismay upon seeing a tragedy unfold—these things we may owe to the same kind of Darwinian process that give the earth abundant life. Each of us has under our control a miniature world, evolving away, making constructs that are unique to our own head. There may or may not be life evolving on some planet near one of those other stars in our galaxy, but comparable evolution is taking place inside the head of every reader of this essay.

We have sought links between the laws by which the material world was created and those that created the human mind. And here we seem to glimpse one: the Darwinian principles that shaped life on Earth over the billions of years, that daily reshape the immune systems in our bodies, have again blossomed in human heads on an even more accelerated time scale. In much the manner that life itself unfolded, our mental life is progressively enriched, enabling each of us to create our own world.[26]

AN AFTERWORD: We invented language (and, indeed, thought itself) without any understanding of the neural machinery underlying it. Yet think about what happened to transportation in the wake of understanding Newton's physics of moving bodies: In several centuries, we went from ox carts to moon rockets. Think of what happened to communication in the wake of our nineteenth-century understanding of electricity and magnetism: We went from hand-carried letters to our ability to load up memory telephones with a thirteen-digit sequence that dials a phone on the other side of the world, connecting you at the mere touch of a single button. Or to medicine, once the circulation of the blood and the role of microscopic organisms were appreciated: In several centuries, we went from purging and leeches to physiologically based neurosurgery for epilepsy and Parkinsonism, to persuading lowly bacteria to produce human growth hormone and insulin, merely from snippets of human DNA.

All of which would have seemed like magic to our ancestors, no matter how well educated they were. But most of the people in this world (including the 94 percent in the United States who lack scientific literacy) have no analogies with which to think about a computer or a space shuttle—or even an aspirin tablet. To them, most technology is magic, just as a flashlight might appear to a remote tribesman encountering explorers.

Once we establish a workable explanation for our thinking and language machinery, we will again see a great augmentation in our capabilities. Certainly our educational philosophy should profit from a knowledge of optimal methods of learning new material. Certainly the ergonomic design of our machinery should benefit from knowing how to make a good match between human and helper.

But imagine what knowledge of the mental machinery will do to augment our sense of self, as we feel in better command of our destinies, better able to choose good courses of action. Imagine how it will help us move beyond the present limits in our abilities to appreciate complicated things, whether they be detailed logical arguments, five-dimensional spaces in mathematics, or the complexities of nonlinear systems. Rationality will take on an entirely new meaning, once we understand the underlying neural machinery that we use to reason with. But I think the same thing will happen to music, a whole generation of composers will arise, each with the mental abilities of a Bach or a Mozart. They might even have to redesign golf courses, to make them more difficult. Anything involving versatile serial-order tasks might benefit—even playing poker.

Understanding the mental machinery could make us less susceptible to being manipulated by the powerful. Or perhaps make us more manipulatable: It would be sad if what our understanding of the mental machinery did was simply to make advertising techniques even more persuasive and pervasive, transferring even more power in our society to those who can afford to buy the best in media exposure. Pagels had something pointed to say about that state of affairs, which I will use to close:

Francis Bacon said that knowledge was power [but that] leaves open the question of whether we possess the wisdom to exercise that power, and whether we who possess it are ready to extend it to the billions who are powerless. Sometimes I wonder if it will be the poverty of the poor or the greed of the rich that will be our undoing. Yet I remain an optimist and believe that the distant day will come when the order of human affairs is not entirely established by domination. And even if that day should never come, it seems worthy of our hope.[27]

NOTES

[1] Heinz Pagels, *The Dreams of Reason* (New York: Simon and Schuster, 1988), p. 328.

[2] Eric H. Lennenberg, *Biological Foundations of Language* (New York: John Wiley and Sons, 1967).

[3] Noam Chomsky, *Rules and Representations* (New York: Columbia University Press, 1980).

[4] Emile Durkheim, *The Division of Labor in Society* (Glencoe, Illinois: Open Court, 1947, reprint).

[5] See, for example, William H. Calvin and George A. Ojemann, *Inside the Brain: Mapping the Cortex, Exploring the Neuron* (New York: New American Library, 1980), chs. 3, 4, and 15.

[6] Doreen Kimura, "Neuromotor Mechanisms in the Evolution of Human Communication," in H. D. Stecklis and M. J. Raleigh, eds., *Neurobiology of Social Communication in Primates* (New York: Academic Press, 1979), pp. 197–219.

[7] George A. Ojemann, "Brain Organization for Language from the Perspective of Electrical Stimulation Mapping" *Behavioral and Brain Sciences*, 1983, vol. 6, pp. 189–230. George A. Ojemann and Otto D. Creutzfeldt, "Language in Humans and Animals: Contribution of Brain Stimulation and Recording," in Vernon B. Mountcastle, Fred Plum, and Steven R. Geiger, eds., *Handbook of Physiology. Section 1: The Nervous System, volume 5, part 2, The Higher Functions of the Brain*, (American Physiological Society, 1987).

[8] Karl R. Popper and John C. Eccles, *The Self and Its Brain* (Springer International, 1977), p. 125.

9 William Smith (1817), quoted in Loren Eiseley, *Darwin's Century* (New York: Doubleday, 1958), p. 117.

10 William H. Calvin, "The Brain as a Darwin Machine," *Nature*, November 6, 1987, vol. 330, pp. 33–34.

11 William H. Calvin, *The Cerebral Symphony: Seashore Speculations on the Mechanisms of Consciousness* (New York: Bantam, 1989).

12 Pagels, 1988, pp. 138–139.

13 Ibid., p. 150.

14 Ibid., p. 15.

15 Jean-Paul Sartre, *Nausea* (trans. Robert Baldick), chapter "Saturday Noon."

16 Peter Brooks, *Reading for the Plot: Design and Intention in Narrative* (New York: Random House, 1984), p. 3.

17 Roger Schank, "Johnny Can't Read (and Neither Can His Old Man)," in John Brockman, ed., *The Reality Club*, vol. 1 (New York: Lynx, 1988), pp. 215–260.

18 William H. Calvin, "A Stone's Throw and Its Launch Window: Timing Precision and Its Implications for Language and Hominid Brains." *Journal of Theoretical Biology*, 1983, vol. 104, pp. 121–135.

19 This section is adapted from chapter 13 of *The Cerebral Symphony*.

20 I am grateful to Paul Ryan for noting that Darwin machines do not solve the problem of value and reminding me of Warren McCulloch's model.

21 George Johnson, *The Machinery of the Mind: Inside the New Science of Artificial Intelligence* (New York: Times Books, 1986), pp. 3–4.

22 Herbert A. Simon, *Reason in Human Affairs* (Stanford: Stanford University Press, 1983), pp. 12–13. Simon goes on to note that "in typical real-world situations, decision makers, no matter how badly they want to do so, simply cannot apply the SEU model. [Human beings] have neither the facts nor the consistent structure of values nor the reasoning power at their disposal that would be required . . . to apply SEU principles" (p. 17).

23 Kenneth J. W. Craik, *The Nature of Explanation* (Cambridge University Press, 1943).

24 Pagels, p. 88.

25 Ibid., p. 331.

26 The preceding three paragraphs are adapted from *The Cerebral Symphony*.

27 Pagels, p. 321.

The Two Faces of Creativity

MORRIS BERMAN

. . . modern creative work has a strong addictive or compulsive component; the artist is expected to outdo him- or herself with each succeeding product. It is here that we see the schismogenic character of modern creativity most clearly. The structure is one of "upping the ante," in other words; work is often "unfinished" because it is done in the pursuit of an inaccessible ideal. It must depart from tradition, must create a new genre, and it grows difficult to keep on doing this. As a result, modern creativity tends to have high psychic costs.

There is one aspect of Western creativity that has been commented upon by sociologists and cultural historians alike, and that is its peculiar tendency to burn out or destroy the artist, often at a relatively young age. Why this should be so remains unclear, but the "tortured artist syndrome," represented by figures as diverse as James Dean and John Keats, does seem to be a persistent feature of modern Western life. Thus Elliott Jaques, some years ago, provided ample statistics to show a recurrent pattern of mid-life crisis, frequently leading to death, among creative people, while Katinka Matson, in *Short Lives*, gives the reader a series of extremely interesting vignettes that reveal artistic self-destructive tendencies all too clearly. In a similar vein, A. Alvarez, in his study of suicide, argues that modern creativity is "provisional, dissatisfied, restless." All of this, as the cultural anthropologist Gregory Bateson would have said, comes under the heading of "schismogenesis"—the tendency to move toward climax or breakdown; and in this sense, modern Western creativity is a reflection of the culture in which it is embedded. There are exceptions, of course, but the cliché of the driven (and, frequently, alcoholic) artist is not only common, but actually a kind of cultural ideal—a "good thing," as it were; or at least, something we have come to expect.[1]

That creativity has to be self-destructive or schismogenic is, accordingly, taken as a given. Genius continues to be regarded as akin to madness, and creative individuals are somehow seen as members of a separate species, inhabiting worlds that most of us will never see or even understand. The problem with this way of viewing human creativity is that it is ahistorical. It assumes that the mainsprings of the creative impulse are somehow archetypal, true for all time; that in effect, there is only one way to "do it." As a result, we have thousands of histories of art, music, science, architecture, and so on, but apparently nothing on the history of creativity itself. Of course, if the creative act is fixed for all time, then there is nothing to write. But suppose this were not so? Suppose the creative process itself has evolved over the centuries, or millennia? This would mean that there *is* more than one way to do it, and that future creativity might be a very different animal from the one it is now. My guess is that the creative process can be understood both historically and psychodynamically, in terms of a typology, and that such a typology can lay bare not only the nature(s) of creativity itself, but also of the wider culture(s) of which it is a part. Both in art and in society, schismogenesis leading to breakdown might not be the only option we have. What follows is thus an investigation into the varieties of creative experience as well as an attempt to explore what the alternatives to the schismogenic model are or might be.

One of the best treatments of the subject occurs, surprisingly enough, in an extraordinarily bad piece of historical writing published by Sigmund Freud in 1910, *viz.* his study of the life and work of Leonardo da Vinci.[2] As a historical argument, the essay is a complete failure, a mass of unsubstantiated conjecture and speculation. Yet in a few short pages, Freud generates a typology of the creative process that strikes me as being immensely suggestive, and it is one that stayed in my mind long after I forgot the discussion of Leonardo *per se.* Freud's typology is too stark, and it is also incomplete; yet given the available alternatives, it is not a bad place to start. Freud was specifically interested in intellectual activity, and its relationship to sexuality; but I believe that if we are willing to broaden this and talk in terms of sensual experience of the world in general—an experience that includes curiosity and exploration as major components—his analysis can be extended to all forms of creative work. Let me, therefore, take a bit of poetic license with Freud's exposition, modifying it in certain ways, and see whether it can be helpful to the inquiry at hand.

Freud begins his discussion by noting that there is a certain type of person who pursues creative activity "with the same passionate devotion that another would give to his love. . . ." The crucial event, says Freud, is the fate of what he calls the "period of infantile sexual researches," or, more generally, the pleasure the child takes in the sensual exploration of its surroundings. This may include curiosity about the birth process, but the larger expression is a tactile-erotic one, and this total lack of inhibition tends to make the parents nervous. Unconsciously, they are stirred to remember when they, too, were like this, and how this openness toward the world got quashed. Disturbed by this unconscious awareness, they do the same thing to their own children. The impulse then gets thwarted and repressed, and this, says Freud, has three possible outcomes. In the first and overwhelmingly typical case, the child's curiosity gets shut down. The child learns that such openness, such creative expression, is risky business. The result, says Freud, is that creative expression "may be limited for the whole of the subject's lifetime." In the second case, the child's development is sufficiently strong to resist the repression to some degree. The repressed sensuality then returns from the unconscious "in the form of compulsive brooding, naturally in a distorted and unfree form, but sufficiently powerful to sexualize thinking itself and to color [creative or artistic] operations with the pleasure and anxiety that belong to the sexual processes proper." The brooding never ends; eros is transferred to the creative activity and the latter becomes a substitute for it. In the third case, says Freud, "the libido evades the fate of repression by being sublimated from the very beginning." The transition is smooth, the quality of neurosis absent; the instinct operates freely in the service of creative activity.

In general, Freud's schema (modified) might look something like this:

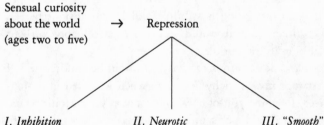

Sensual curiosity
about the world   →   Repression
(ages two to five)

I. Inhibition (most people).	II. Neurotic compulsion.	III. "Smooth" sublimation.
Repression is totally effective; unconscious activity emerges via symptoms such as hysteria and other forms of psychosomatic illness. Posture toward life is one of (usually unconscious) fear and hatred.	Repression is largely but not totally effective; unconscious activity emerges into creative work by a process of breakthrough or eruption. Creative work is the substitute lover.	Individual escapes repression; unconscious activity is freeflowing and not characterized by stress.

There is not much to say about Type I creativity, since it is the counterexample, the decision to give up on creativity (and really on life) altogether. The repression is so effective that all creative expression is blocked forever. Most people mask this early defeat with substitute activity, but it shows up somatically, or psychosomatically, when they are caught off guard. Type II, the neurotic model, was—as far as Freud was concerned—typical of most creative work. As we have said, in this case the person fights back, for the spirit is not completely extinguished. But the result of this partial repression is a situation soaking in ambivalent emotions. The creative work has an obsessive quality to it; one is "married" to one's work, as the saying goes. Tension and passion are the characteristic modes of expression here.

Type III is the least familiar case. The repression is very slight, and the translation of sensual energy or exploring spirit into creative work is carried out with a minimum of trauma. Such work has a relaxed, spontaneous feeling. In the early pages of the da Vinci biography, Freud puts Leonardo into this category; but by the end of the book, he is forced to conclude, based on his own evidence, that the Italian master was a Type II. As a result, Creativity III emerges as an empty category. It is an intriguing possibility, and Freud's insight here is intuitively brilliant; but it would seem to be a category without content, hanging in the middle of nowhere.

One possible candidate for Creativity III might be children's art. I saw such artwork myself many years ago when I worked in a Montessori nursery for three-year-olds, who had not as yet been hit by too much repression. As aides or counselors, we were instructed never to put the children on the spot by asking them what it was they were painting or constructing, and indeed, they exhibited virtually no performance anxiety whatsoever. It was a pleasure to watch their glee as they immersed themselves in their "work." Looking back, I wouldn't call it great art, but it certainly was not compulsive or conflict-ridden. For better or worse, there were no van Goghs in that nursery. The problem is that if that is all that can be put in this category, then it is not very interesting. What I wish to argue is that Creativity III constitutes a mode of expression that includes most medieval art, the art of non-Western cultures, and the art of traditional societies. It approximates what we call craft, as opposed to art as such. As a result, it throws the creativity of the Western, post-Renaissance world into sharp relief, for it involves a psychodynamic entirely different from that of Creativity II. Modern creativity, or Creativity II, should be seen for what it is: a local and, in fact, fairly recent phenomenon that organizes bodily energy in a particular way. In doing so, it produces a mode of expression that is very powerful and focused, but extremely draining, both for the individual and for the culture at large. In its most extreme and perhaps most talented form, it tends to have the effect we have already mentioned—that of taking the lives of its representatives at a fairly early age.

When I first began thinking about this subject, and specifically about how creativity manifested itself in my own life, there was no avoiding the fact that I fell into the second category. I conformed very well to the popular image of the writer who stayed up all night fueling himself with coffee and tobacco, pacing the floor in frustration as ideas refused to come, and sitting down and writing things out in white heat when they finally surfaced. The pattern was clearly addictive-obsessive; neurotic, in short.

Yet as I thought about it more, I began to see that these were the surface manifestations of a deeper drama. The most creative work I had done resulted from a psychic crisis that ran very deep, and which, once triggered, I was powerless to control. The French psychiatrist Jacques Lacan said that we state our problems on the symbolic level before proceeding to solve them, and something like this had happened to me. It began with the speculation that if worldviews were artifacts, the magical worldview that antedated modern science must have real validity. The more I began to follow that train of thought, the more archaic consciousness began to take me over. Finally, I was in deep trouble. How does the line from *Faust* go? "Two souls reside within my breast." I was both a modern and an ancient, a scientist and an alchemist, and neither side would release its grip. It was a rocky ride, but I had no choice except to live out those contradictions. Once the traditional/modern gap opened up within my psyche, my fate was sealed: I had to heal that split or die. And this, I believe, is the number-one characteristic of Creativity II: It is a contemporary form of exorcism. (I am not talking here about *productivity*, which has *no* psychic energy behind it, and which merely involves turning out work in a mechanical fashion.) In Creativity II, you are possessed by an internal conflict, and the work is undertaken to resolve it. You create from pain; or as John Fowles put it in one of his novels, you create from what you lack, not from what you have. It is this that gives modern poetry, for example, what Robert Bly has called a "leaping" structure. Chaucer, by way of contrast, derives his power from the beautifully crafted language of the narrative. *The Canterbury Tales* are not soaking in unconscious power; they do not "leap," as do, say, many of Bly's own poems. [3]

The second characteristic follows from this: You create yourself out of your work; the work is characterized by "self-expression." In the modern period, art and self-expression (something Chaucer was *not* after) have practically become synonymous. Creative work must bear a personal signature or style, whereas in the Middle Ages it tended to be anonymous. Medieval artists typically did not sign their work. Cennino Cennini's essay of 1400, *Il Libro dell' Arte*, announced the artist's intention to break with this tradition, and the book is usually regarded as a turning point, marking the end of the craft tradition and the call for modern artistic creativity. Once again, John Fowles is relevant here. "Romantic and post-Romantic art," he writes, "is all pervaded by . . . the flight of the individual from whatever threatens his individuality." Modern creativity, he essentially argues, is heavily fueled by the desire to prove that one exists. [4]

A third characteristic, which tends to follow from the first two, is that the creative insight is seen to break through, or erupt from, the unconscious. It is this eruption that generates the psychic split that demands to be healed, and that alters the personality structure so that the work of integration becomes self-expression. Traditional creativity would have to be different, since traditional societies tend, in varying degrees, to be swimming in the unconscious already. Hence, there is nothing, or at least much less, to erupt.

Fourth, modern creative work has a strong addictive or compulsive component; the artist is expected to outdo him- or herself with each succeeding product. ("I work as my father drank," George Bernard Shaw once remarked. [5]) It is here that we see the schismogenic character of modern creativity most clearly. The structure is one of "upping the ante," in other words; work is often "unfinished" because it is done in the pursuit of an inaccessible ideal. It must depart from tradition, must create a new genre, and it grows difficult to keep on doing this.

As a result, modern creativity tends to have high psychic costs. The examples of an intense, sustained burst of creative work followed by suicide are legion: Vincent van Gogh, Dylan Thomas (suicide by alcohol), Janis Joplin (suicide by drugs), Jimi Hendrix, Sylvia Plath, Anne Sexton, and on and on. The work ineluctably moves toward breakdown. It is for this reason that so many creative people stop doing what they are doing in their late thirties: They know where it is all leading.[6] This also explains, in part, why the public loses interest in writers such as Norman Mailer. Mailer's first work, *The Naked and the Dead*, remains his best. From the standpoint of modern creativity, the artist is expected to set up and leap over increasingly higher hurdles. This is the structure of an ever-expanding economy; it is not steady-state. Mailer's career was over almost before it began. The modern Western public is trained to expect novelty from its creative sector; it quickly loses interest in artists who have nothing "new" to offer.

Finally, modern creativity often involves, as Freud said, the sexualization, or at least eroticization, of the activity. One's work becomes one's lover—one's central, and obsessive, relationship. All the dramas that are typically played out in such a relationship get played out here: the initial romantic rush, the subsequent tapering off, jealousy and possessiveness, and finally disillusion and the search for a new love. There is a heavy overlap of Oedipal energy here: Male artists are notorious mama's boys, "heroes" winning battles for the mother. And they do this precisely by innovating, by rupturing tradition—*i.e.*, by slaying the father.[7]

We have, in the West, many images that glorify the notion of creativity as being a triumph over adversity. We speak of "the shit that fertilizes roses," or the grain of sand in the oyster that leads to the generation of a pearl. This is the stuff of *Reader's Digest* stories and Ann Landers columns. And these images do capture a truth, though they mask a larger one. The truth they capture is that creative work can and often does emerge out of conflict; the truth they mask is that other psychodynamic patterns of the creative process are possible, and that, historically, the conflict model may actually represent an aberration. My goal in this essay, however, is not to condemn modern Western creativity as "bad" and to enshrine Eastern or premodern creativity as "good." It is, rather, to argue that there are different somatic or

energetic processes involved in each case. There is a way, given my
own upbringing, that no Indian raga will ever move me as much as
Mozart, no Japanese landscape painting resonate for me as deeply as
Cézanne's evocative scenes of the Midi. In fact, modern Western art
has a brilliance that no medieval icon or Eastern painting can ever
approximate, in my view. But my point here is that it takes a
particular energetic configuration to create such an effect, and if
Freud is right about Creativity II, it actually requires early somatic
damage that leads to a distrust of the body, and a corresponding
shunting of that bodily energy upward, toward the head. The center
of gravity is too high, so to speak; there is a way in which the very
brilliance of Western creativity depends on its instability, its extremely high level of tension and stress.

Yet the conflict model of creativity, as Freud realized (though he
wasn't able to prove it), does not exhaust the entire subject. Psychologists from Otto Rank to Rollo May have insisted on the necessity of
stress or tension for the creative act, without realizing that this is a
formula for only one type of creative expression.[8] In *Caliban Reborn*,
Wilfred Mellers addresses himself to the issue of conflict and self-
expression, and emphasizes how specific it is in time and place:

> While this conception of art is our birthright and has gone to make the
> world we live in, we have to realize that in the context of history the
> notion is both newfangled and restricted. It is relevant to only about
> the last five hundred years of Europe's history. . . .

The difference between music as magic (traditional music) and music
as expression, he says, is that the former lacks the element of harmonic
tension. Such music, he adds, has a strong corporeal component:

> In the music of primitive cultures . . . the rhythm is usually corporeal
> and the music is never self-expression but rather a communal act of
> work or play which may have magic[al] as well as social significance.

Mellers goes on to say that "the compositional principles inherent in
European music before the Renaissance are not radically distinct from
those of Oriental music." In both Gregorian chant and the Indian
raga, rhythms such as breath or heartbeat constitute the creative

source. The invention of harmony—something of which traditional and Oriental cultures were aware, but which (says Mellers) they never chose to emphasize—ruptured this pattern. That is, it shifted music from a Creativity III to a Creativity II structure.[9]

Many years ago, living near New York City, I used to play a kind of game, experimenting with the shift between Creativity III and Creativity II energy patterns, without really knowing what I was doing or why. In upper Manhattan, I would go to the Cloisters, which is the medieval section of the Metropolitan Museum of Art, and then, having spent several hours there, would go directly downtown to the Museum of Modern Art. I would recommend this experiment to anybody. If you stay tuned to your physical reactions, the effect is quite remarkable. The immersion in a "craft" environment, complete with tapestries, carved wooden doors, stained glass, and illuminated manuscripts, creates a very soothing sensation. The body lets go, as it were, and time seems to stand still. The sensation of silence and tranquility is particularly striking. To follow this up with an immersion in twentieth-century art is to give yourself a real shock. The sensation here is one of excitement and anxiety; the dreamy and magnetic sense of wholeness, or union, is replaced by a chaos and dramatic brilliance that explodes on the canvas, or from the sculptures. As in the case of van Gogh (see below), it is as if the breakdown of the psyche resulted in the breakthrough of art. Two hours in such a place as this leaves one both exhilarated and emotionally spent. This simple experiment conveys only a fraction (I suspect) of what it means to live in one culture as opposed to the other, and how very different the psychic and emotional pattern that lies at the root of Creativity II is from that which underlies Creativity III.

In December 1986 I unintentionally repeated this experiment, but in reverse. The Metropolitan Museum had mounted an exhibit of van Gogh's last eighteen months—"Van Gogh at Saint-Rémy and Auvers"—and I took the opportunity to see it. I had originally planned to stay several hours; as it turned out, I was totally exhausted in ninety minutes by the intensity of color and emotion that escalated in van Gogh's painting in direct proportion to his increasing madness. Whether it was accidental or deliberately planned by the exhibition's organizers, I do not know, but the show exited onto a very different sort of exhibition, entitled "Individuality and Tradition in

Seventeenth-Century Chinese Art." The impact was enormous; I felt a
sudden "whoosh" as my entire energy returned to ground level. As I
sat and looked at the lovely, relaxed prints of mountains and landscapes, a great feeling of peace came over me. I felt a bodily sense of
centering, coming home. I realized that I loved van Gogh, but that I
couldn't live with him hanging on my living room walls. The intensity was simply too great; and his creative pattern—which is very
typical of Type II creativity—reflected this. In the final seventy days
of his life, living under the care of Dr. Gachet at Auvers-sur-Oise, van
Gogh turned out no fewer than forty paintings. By contrast, Kung
Hsian, one of the seventeenth-century Chinese painters displayed at
the Met, turned out comparatively few; and his comments on this are
all of a piece with the Creativity III style. "Little by little is better
than more and more," wrote Kung Hsian; "this is the advanced stage
of a painter." He wrote: "When you are afraid of producing too much
painting, you will make a good painting." He explained: "Being
clever is not as good as being dull. The uses of cleverness can be
grasped at a glance, while apparent dullness may embody limitless
flavor." These are sentiments that would never have occurred to van
Gogh; nor do they occur to most of us. [10]

My goal here, again, is not to make a judgment, but rather to point
out a very significant cultural contrast. The first four elements I
identified as being characteristic of Creativity II—healing a split,
self-expression, eruption from the unconscious, and an addictive (escalating) pattern—all add up to the schismogenic structure discussed
above. Add to this the fifth factor of sexual and Oedipal or erotic
tension, and you have a situation that cannot help but be as brittle as
it is brilliant, as neurotic as it is rich. It is thus not that Creativity II is
"wrong," but that in the late twentieth century, this mode of expression has been pushed to the breaking point. In an evolutionary sense,
it cannot extend its trajectory any further. As a result, what we are
witnessing in a whole variety of fields is not merely the creation of yet
another style or genre, but the transformation of the creative act itself
into something else. If creativity has a past, it also has a future,
though it is not easy to predict at this stage what it will be. I shall
return to this question later on; for now, it might be valuable to try to
obtain a deeper understanding of the psychological basis of schismogenic creativity.

The schismogenic nature of Western creativity was first (indirectly) recognized by the Jungian writer Erich Neumann in *The Origins and History of Consciousness*.[11] The essential argument of the book is that the consciousness of the individual passes through the same stages as that of the human race at large, and that mythology is the map of that evolution. The first myths, says Neumann, are creation myths: The earth is submerged, or nonexistent, and is precipitated out of a watery chaos. This is certainly the drama described, for example, in the opening chapter of Genesis. The second set of myths are hero myths, and these record the process of differentiation. The symbols of the first category are water, or the egg, or the ourobouros, reflecting a unitary consciousness or the absence of consciousness: no tension, no opposites, no differentiation. The symbols of the second category are the sun—the entry of light into darkness—and also journeys and conquests. The *Odyssey*, for example, can be read as a psychic journey involving the hero's differentiation from the unconscious, and, in general, from the archetype of the Great Mother. It is the drama of ego *vs.* unconscious, light *vs.* dark, male energy *vs.* female energy, that makes the archetypal journey so fascinating, even to the modern reader. Again and again, Odysseus experiences the enormous pull of that great, unconscious, undifferentiated female power, the desire to melt or merge back into it, to go unconscious, as he once was as a very young infant or a fetus. But what makes him a hero is that he refuses that option. He is not interested in the dark energy of the unconscious, and his "victory" over this is symbolized by the blinding of the cyclops, whose eye is the "third eye" of intuitive understanding.[12] With the birth of the hero, which is really the birth of the ego (or, perhaps, of a certain type of ego), the world becomes ambivalent. It is split into masculine and feminine, black and white, left and right, God and the devil, ego and unconscious, and this becomes the great drama that all cultures have to deal with, at root. In the Far East, the solution has been characterized as Taoistic—*i.e.*, "both/and"; yin and yang are seen as transformable, interpenetrating, and as I shall discuss shortly, this has given Eastern creativity a particular style. In the West, and especially since the Renaissance, the solution has been Manichaean—*i.e.*, "either/or"; the two poles are mortal enemies, locked in combat to the death. And in the West or Near East, in particular, this has given rise to a third type of myth that tends to combine the first two: the myth of Set and Osiris, or the twin brothers. In this myth, two brothers emerge from the Void (Primal Unity), or the womb, or the Great Mother, *viz.* the Hero and the Great Mother Representative. The Hero urges separation from the Great Mother; the Representative wants to merge back into her. And so there is a tension that is never resolved.[13]

This is, of course, a mythological struggle, played out in the Western psyche. The twin brothers' conflict is intermediate between hero and creation myths. A defiant ego has emerged, but it is fearful of complete separation. Set and Osiris, or Cain and Abel, are really two parts of the same person. We hear these conflicting voices particularly at those moments when we are about to give in to an addiction: taking a cigarette, smoking a joint, drinking a martini, eating a slab of cheesecake. The body wants merger; the mind says: Resist (or is it the reverse?). This is, in fact, the theme of *Dr. Jekyll and Mr. Hyde*, which is nothing less than a twin brothers' war. Robert Louis Stevenson wrote:

> I thus drew steadily nearer to that truth, by whose partial discovery I have been doomed to such a dreadful shipwreck: that man is not truly one, but truly two. . . . I saw that, of the two natures that contended in the field of my consciousness, even if I could rightly be said to be either, it was only because I was radically both; and from an early date, even before the course of my scientific discoveries had begun to suggest the most naked possibility of such a miracle, I had learned to dwell with pleasure, as a beloved daydream, on the thought of the separation of these elements. If each, I told myself, could be housed in separate identities, life would be relieved of all that was unbearable. . . . It was the curse of mankind that these incongruous faggots were thus bound together—that in the agonized womb of consciousness, these polar twins should be continuously struggling.[14]

What does all this have to do with creativity? The point is that creativity—or at least Creativity II—is the *product* of this internal tension. As Neumann puts it, "[this] tension is what we call culture"; and in this I think he may have been mistaken. Being a Jungian, he saw this dynamic as universal and archetypal, and perhaps to varying degrees, it is; but different cultures express it differently and deal with it differently, and this may be the crucial point. Nevertheless,

Neumann's formulation of twin brothers arguing over the Abyss is an especially important clue as to what goes on in modern creativity. The "game" is to let the whole drama play itself out on the terrain of the psyche, and channel the resulting energy into art, poetry, or whatever. It is precisely here that we find the mechanism that underlies the brilliance of modern Western creativity, giving it its keen edge and also its tragic aspect. For in order for his or her work to be increasingly brilliant, the artist has to generate greater and greater twin-brother splits, or encounters with the Void, from which to recover. Finally, as in the case of Dylan Thomas or Janis Joplin or so many others, the gap becomes too great. The chasm widens beyond their heroic powers, and they cannot manage to get back. Modern creativity is a battlefield of psychic, and often physical, corpses.

A good study of this turbulent or tormented phenomenon in modern art occurs in a work by James Lord called *A Giacometti Portrait*, which is a study of the great sculptor, Alberto Giacometti, at work. It very clearly embodies the first four themes of modern creativity that I have noted. Giacometti is never satisfied with his work; it is never, in his eyes, really finished; he sees his Self totally on the line every time he sits down before an easel or a piece of clay, and so on. Lord writes how he once found Giacometti at a nearby café on a coffee break, his hollow eyes gazing into nowhere, "staring into a void from which no solace could come."[15] Any healing that is engendered tends to be short-lived. You are constantly challenged to create *yourself*, and this process never ends. "I work in a state of passion and compulsion," said the artist Joan Miró in 1959.

> When I begin a canvas, I obey a physical impulse, a need to act. . . . It's a struggle between me and what I am doing, between me and the canvas, between me and my distress.[16]

The problem with this struggle is that it often ends in death or madness.

There are numerous examples of Western creativity one can take as illustrations of Type II, and as I indicated earlier, much of this is well documented. The classic example of the tortured-genius syndrome, and one that has been worked over in great detail is that of Vincent van Gogh, whose art was so clearly "a cry of anguish," an attempt to merge with life, a substitute for intimacy. "The more I am spent, ill, a broken pitcher," he wrote, "by so much more am I an artist—a creative artist. . . ."[17] This is one of the paradoxes of modern creativity—that the search for self-expression actually winds up depleting the Self. The artist of the Type II category is like a broken doll, an *imitatio Christi*, exhausting himself or herself for art's sake, which is "all." In this case, however, you are the agent of your own crucifixion: You make something greater than yourself, seek the unattainable, become a flawed vessel, ultimately emptied or destroyed. For van Gogh and many others, acute depression is somehow welcome, a source of creative drama and energy.

A more complex and interesting example of the Creativity II pattern is Wolfgang Amadeus Mozart, about whom so much has been written in recent years. Exactly what happened in Mozart's infancy we shall never know; but there is evidence to suggest the presence of repressed antagonism toward his father, Leopold, for nearly twenty-five years.[18] Very early on, Leopold Mozart, himself a musician, realized he had a prodigy on his hands, and proceeded to take on the role of impresario, abandoning his own career and dedicating his life to that of his son. He made Wolfgang totally dependent on him, stage-managing virtually every step of Mozart's rise to fame. As a child, Wolfgang was fond of saying, "Next to God comes Papa"; and if antagonism was present, it must have been very deeply buried. Mozart's letters home during this period—about twenty years—were filled with an ostensible love and appreciation of Leopold, and his music during this time was childlike, exuberant, spontaneous. Operas and concerti literally poured from his pen. There is simply no evidence of conflict here, and the style of work reflects this.

All of this gradually began to change in the late 1770s. Wolfgang began to realize that his father had effectively kept him a child all his life, and that Leopold still, after all his (Wolfgang's) achievements, was disappointed with him. He began to realize also that he feared and resented Leopold, and by 1781 the resulting anger began to surface in some of their correspondence. Yet there was only so much Mozart could say, for Leopold was by now an old man, and Mozart did not want to hurt him. But the conflict that had been so deeply buried finally surfaced, with even more needing to come out; and all of this got channeled into his work. Wolfgang Hildesheimer, one of Mozart's more recent biographers, notes that the four years from 1784 to the end of 1787 were Wolfgang's most prolific and creative ones, and that this was also the period of his greatest experimentation and discovery. Mozart's interest in destroying old genres and creating new ones was at its height during this time. As Hildesheimer writes, "The revolutionary Mozart is the Mozart of his last eight years." Repressed Oedipal rebellion surfaces in his two most brilliant operas. In *The Marriage of Figaro* (1786), which was based on a play by Beaumarchais that had long been banned in Vienna, Figaro, the servant of a member of the nobility, Count Almaviva, thwarts the latter in an amorous adventure and emerges the victor. As Hildesheimer tells us, Mozart

> . . . knew [that] Figaro was no fairy tale. His theme yielded a model for his own behavior; an unconscious drive, probably long latent, came to the surface and tempted him to stop living according to the rules imposed on him from outside. He began to "let himself go."

It was this opera, which so antagonized precisely the class that Leopold had toadied to, so as to grease the wheels of his son's career, that marked the beginning of the end of that career: the descent into poverty and, by the end, relative obscurity.

The theme of the upper-class Don Juan character, whose sexual conflicts are so great as to drive him to seduce virtually every woman he meets, and who comes off rather badly for it, is repeated and greatly magnified in Mozart's opera *Don Giovanni*, which appeared the very next year, in 1787, only five months after Leopold's death. It is surely one of the greatest operas of all time; and it is interesting to note that Freud once remarked that it was the only opera that interested him. We need hardly wonder why: One of Mozart's own additions to the libretto was the reappearance of the slain father as an accusing ghost (the statue). Critics said he stole the theme from *Hamlet*, but they hardly had to look that far afield. What we find in Mozart's work, from this point on, with its obvious attack on the aristocracy, its Oedipal themes, and its smashing of traditional genres, is the working out of powerful internal conflicts through the creative act itself. Mozart was not necessarily suffering here; indeed, Hildesheimer claims he was getting high off all this conflict. But my point is that the later Mozart is a classic Type II, and that the energy was coming from a place of anger and frustration. This energy—and it had twenty-five years of repression behind it—was clearly phenomenal. Between *Figaro* and *Don Giovanni* (eighteen months), Mozart wrote thirty-five separate works; between *Don Giovanni* and *Così fan tutte* (thirteen months), sixty-three more compositions. These were followed, in 1791, by a mass of chamber music, cantatas, and court dances, plus two more operas, one of which was *The Magic Flute*. And in *The Magic Flute*, the Oedipal conflict is revealed as finally resolved: Sarastro, the obvious father figure, is the priest of universal love. As Peter Shaffer has Mozart's arch-rival, Antonio Salieri, say in the play *Amadeus*, when Salieri attended the premiere of the opera and saw the silhouette of Sarastro against the sun: "And in this sun—behold—I saw his *father*! No more an accusing figure but forgiving!—the highest priest of the Order—his hand extended to the world in love! Wolfgang feared Leopold no longer: A final legend had been made!"[19]

The catharsis was apparently successful. As Hildesheimer notes, the spontaneous, childlike effect of Mozart's earlier years, absent since 1778, reappears now in the music for the first time in thirteen years; and significantly, *The Magic Flute* would seem to lack the power and brilliance of *Figaro* and *Don Giovanni*. It was, in any event, too late. Believing that someone had poisoned him, Mozart began, in 1791, to write his own requiem, the "Requiem Mass," which was never completed. He died at age thirty-five, for reasons that remain obscure to this day.[20]

I wish to return, finally, to what I have called traditional creativity, or Creativity III. There are endless examples of this, of course, and I could easily furnish at this point texts of Japanese haiku, photographs of ancient Greek or Egyptian vases, or Hopi or Celtic designs, in addition to the seventeenth-century Chinese landscape painting mentioned earlier. Let me, however, refer to only one classic painting, which is, because of its immense popularity, probably familiar to many readers—namely, the famous ink drawing of six persimmons attributed to Mu ch'i, an artist who lived in Szechuan province (central China) in the late thirteenth and early fourteenth centuries. The drawing has been reproduced in many art books and histories of art, and it shows six persimmons, two white, two gray, and two that are black. The simplicity and elegance of the drawing make it one of the most beautiful works of Eastern art ever to have appeared. Here is the commentary of one modern student of Chinese art, Chang Chung-yuan:

> This picture of six persimmons is one of the best works ever produced by Chinese artists. Before Mu ch'i picked up his brush, his mind was in a state of no-thought. Thus, we have in this painting a manifestation of the primary indeterminacy of the uncarved block. What his mind reflected at that moment his brush would put down. First two deep black contours and then to their left two gray contours. To the extreme left and right he placed two plain white contours. The ink wash of the two first contours is pitch black without any shading at all, and the two contours at the left are all gray with only a light touch. The two outside contours are pure white. The shades of the ink wash from dark to gray and from gray to white correspond to the inner process going on in the painter. When he was still in the depth of the preconscious, the density of his creative night found expression in two dark contours. With the awakening of his consciousness, the inner darkness loses its density and manifests in two gray contours. As he awakens fully, his creative innocence is entirely unveiled. So the white contours are its expression. What is expressed in the picture corresponds to what happened in his mind. Through his brush-work, the various states of his mind can be traced from the primary indeterminacy of the uncarved block to transparency.[21]

The first thing that strikes me about this work, and indeed, about the whole Creativity III genre, is the absence of what might be called a "Freudian layer." There is seemingly no pent-up sensual or sexual struggle in this material. Eros and internal conflict do not play much of a role. What Chang describes is a fairly smooth descent *into* the unconscious, not an eruption from it. Hence, it is clear that the dark persimmons would come first, in a state of meditative trance, and the lighter ones after, as the artist comes back to more conscious awareness. The state of "no-mind" familiar to Eastern thought is largely foreign to the modern West (van Gogh was *out* of his mind, not in no-mind). For no-mind is a state of detachment or wholeness, and this indicates that the healing takes place *before* the work begins. This material does not reflect the *search* for unity; it is, rather, an artistic expression of psychic unity *previously attained*. To invert John Fowles, you create from what you have, not from what you lack.

Second, there is no "self-expression" here. It is not a particular person or healing journey being depicted. If there is a twin-brothers' tension here, it is fairly muted. The *unity* is what is being expressed, and that is seen as being universal. As already noted, traditional artists, and Western artists prior to the Renaissance, typically did not sign their work. It is all anonymous because it bears the "mark of God," so to speak; a theme pursued by the great French philosopher and mystic Simone Weil. Weil's idea of creative work was what she called "decreation"—you "decreate" yourself in order to create the world. It would be more accurate to say that you don't create the work, but rather that you step out of the way and let it happen. In this way, it is significant that so much Oriental art and poetry is about nature, about the physical world, not about the Self and its dilemmas.[22]

Third, there is no schismogenic or Manichaean structure here. The work is spontaneous and regarded as finished. It is also part of a craft tradition—*i.e.*, the idea is to stay *within* a genre, not to have to invent a new one constantly. And as with craft, all of this is part of daily life: pouring tea, carving wood, cooking persimmons—all activities are considered worthy of craftsmanship. You don't have a special place called a "gallery" to which beauty is assigned for storage and display, nor do you have a special heroic category in society reserved for creative people (the Balinese are an excellent example of a society permeated by art, rather than having art and artists regarded as exceptional). As Ananda Coomaraswamy once put it, "The artist is not a special kind of person; rather, each person is a special kind of artist."[23] And this necessarily means the absence of an addictive or schismogenic structure. This kind of art is continuous with life; it doesn't attempt to "outdo" life by means of psychic acrobatics.

All of this falls into category III, it seems to me, but it is hardly child art. Creativity III, in fact, can be subdivided into two categories: III(a), child art; and III(b), which is the art of an adult who is training himself or herself to be *childlike*—open, immediate, and spontaneous. The difference here is what the Zen master Shunryu Suzuki labeled as Zen mind *vs.* beginner's mind. The early Mozart was possessed of beginner's mind. He began composing at age five. When he finally became aware of his conflicts, he switched from III(a) to II. This is not surprising; what else would one expect? It is just that the Eastern pattern, or premodern one, is so different. The goal is not to go unconscious, or be a three-year-old at a Montessori school, but to pull back enough "yang" energy so that yin and yang can balance out. It is spontaneity of a different sort.

To complicate things further, it seems to me that Creativity II can also be subdivided into two categories:

II(a). This is what I have described thus far as Creativity II: The healing of the split takes place by playing the struggle out in the work itself. The "exorcism" is, in other words, indirect, or unconscious.

II(b). This represents a slight shift away from II(a), in that the exorcism is direct. One stays fully conscious of the neurotic dramas that have led one to the particular artistic or creative issue at hand, and one goes directly for the liberation from those dramas, through therapy or one's own internal work. In other words, one moves into one's fears. This releases the energy that is tied up in obsessional patterns, which is then available for creative work, and which starts to come out in a more free-flowing way.

The major difference between II(a) and II(b), then, is that II(b) is on the road to Creativity III, so to speak (Creativity III begins when one is finally done with obsessions), whereas II(a) is not. In fact, in II(a) the artist *fears* the loss of obsessions, because he or she believes that this would mean the end of his or her career. "Life" and "obsession" are seen as being pretty much identical; the heroic ego whispers in the ear of this person, "Lose me and you'll never create again." And the voice is sincere, because it honestly cannot conceive of a different form of creativity.

The fact that our categories have now developed subcategories, and that these may even overlap, is possibly an important clue to where our culture is going. Creativity II may be our (Western) path to Creativity III, at least in its II(b) form; it is not all II(a), not all a dead end, and this suggests that within the evolution of Western creativity itself lies a tendency toward genuine cultural liberation. This is no small point: The way in which our private and cultural neurotic configuration is framed, or dealt with, may actually be the key in the lock. Those who choose to work through their fears and repressions in the service of creative work may (if they do it before they die) break through to a liberating kind of creativity, and in so doing recode the culture along nonschismogenic lines. This is an earthshaking possibility.

If we look around at the artistic and literary scene today, especially in the United States, we do find some radical departures from the II(a) model, if only in an attempt to express a unitary type of consciousness. This may be premature; Western culture may have to push through II(b) before it can experiment with III(b) in a truly unselfconscious way. But the alternative attempts are important, nonetheless. Wallace Stevens' work displays obvious "decreative" tendencies in the field of poetry; Henry Moore's work does the same in the area of sculpture. Postmodern minimalist music is clearly in the Creativity III category. This music, as exemplified by composers such as Philip Glass, Steve Reich, and Terry Riley, has so completely eliminated the tension-and-resolution structure typical of Western music since the late Middle Ages that the new form has a curious similarity to Gregorian chant. Reich has stated in public interviews that the study of yoga, Cabala, African and Balinese music, and classical breathing exercises, all of which are aspects of traditional cultures, has had a tremendous impact on his work.[24]

It is not clear what all this means, especially since it can be argued that it represents a retrogression, an attempt to return to an earlier cultural period. For various reasons, I think that unlikely; and we should also keep in mind that a major part of the Renaissance involved a revival of antiquity, or what the English potter Bernard Leach called "revitalization," the going backward in order to go forward. The modern potter, said Leach, takes Sung (twelfth-century Chinese) pottery as a model; not for imitation, as an end in itself, but as a way of revitalizing contemporary techniques.[25] It seems obvious that the limits of Creativity II have been reached, and that beyond the tendencies I have described as Creativity II(b), we are searching for completely different modes of cultural and creative expression, in the arts as well as the sciences. As in the case of Creativity II(b), this is a hopeful sign; it suggests that there are somatic forces at work in our culture that are antischismogenic; that are working, perhaps unconsciously, to reverse what appears to me, in a general way, to be a destructive trajectory. We are engaged in turning a corner as significant as that which was turned in Western Europe roughly four centuries ago. We can still listen to Gregorian chant, of course, but most of us don't do it very often. In two centuries, Mozart may be in the same category, and the tension-and-resolution structure of music may be puzzling to our ears.

Beyond the form that creativity will take during the next historical epoch is the question of the human personality structure, the energetic experience that will underlie it, and the nature of Western culture as a whole. Who can say what these will be? There is obviously no way to know. But the following lines from Mary Caroline Richards's book *The Crossing Point* sounds what to me is the most hopeful, and at the same time most realistic, note possible. She writes:

> Eventually the soul asks to be born again into a world of the same order as itself—a second coming into innocence, not through a glass darkly, but face to face, in consciousness. . . . We pass through cruel ordeals on the way. Estrangement, coldness, despair. Death.
>
> By going through the experience faithfully, we may come through on the other side of the crossing point, and find that our faithfulness has borne a new quality into the world.[26]

A new quality . . . a new history . . . a creativity that can be shared by everyone. Let's hope it is still possible.

NOTES

[1] Elliott Jaques, *Work, Creativity, and Social Justice* (London: Heinemann, 1970), chapter 3, ("Death and Mid-Life Crisis"); Katinka Matson, *Short Lives: Portraits in Creativity and Self-Destruction* (New York: William Morrow, 1980); A. Alvarez, *The Savage God* (New York: Bantam Books, 1973), especially pp. 227–252; Gregory Bateson, *Naven*, 2nd ed. (Stanford: University Press, 1958), and also various essays in *Steps to an Ecology of Mind* (London: Paladin, 1973).

[2] Sigmund Freud, *Leonardo da Vinci and a Memory of His Childhood*, trans. Alan Tyson (New York: W. W. Norton, 1964). See especially pp. 27–30 for the discussion that follows.

[3] On "leaping" see, for example, Bly's essay "Spanish Leaping," in his journal *The Seventies* 1 (spring 1972), pp. 16–21.

4 John Fowles, *The Aristos*, rev. ed. (London: Pan Books, 1969), pp. 52–53.

5 Quoted in Erik H. Erikson, *Young Man Luther* (New York: W. W. Norton, 1962), p. 45.

6 On this especially see the works by Jaques and Alvarez cited in note 1.

7 Matthew Besdine, in "The Jocasta Complex, Mothering and Genius," *The Psychoanalytic Review* 55 (1968), pp. 259–277 and 574–600, identifies a whole number of individuals for whom overmothering seems to have been an important factor in their creativity. The list includes Michelangelo, Poe, Dylan Thomas, Proust, van Gogh, Goethe, Einstein, Shakespeare, Freud, Balzac, and Sartre.

8 Esther Menaker, "The Concept of Will in the Thinking of Otto Rank and Its Consequences for Clinical Practice," *The Psychoanalytic Review* 72 (1985), pp. 254–264; Rollo May, *The Courage to Create* (New York: W. W. Norton, 1975). Similar studies that see creativity only in terms of the conflict model include classics such as Arthur Koestler, *The Act of Creation* (London: Hutchinson, 1964), and Nicolas Berdyaev, *The Meaning of the Creative Act*, translated by Donald A. Lowrie (London: Gollancz, 1955; orig. Russian ed. 1914). See also the more recent work by Albert Rothenberg, *The Emerging Goddess* (Chicago: Chicago University Press, 1979). It seems to me that Freud must be credited, at so early a date, with seeing that an alternative to Creativity II was at least conceivable.

9 Wilfred Mellers, *Caliban Reborn: Renewal in Twentieth Century Music* (New York: Harper & Row, 1967), chapter 1.

10 Quotations from Kung Hsian are taken from translations of texts that were displayed as part of the exhibition at the Metropolitan Museum of Art during 1986–1987.

11 On the following see Erich Neumann, *The Origins and History of Consciousness*, trans. R.F.C. Hull (Princeton: Princeton University Press, 1979; orig. German ed. 1949), introduction, pp. 5–41, and 88–127.

12 I am very grateful to Michael Crisp for this very imaginative, and I think accurate, interpretation.

13 The splitting of the Great Mother is discussed by Neumann (see note 11, above) on pp. 96–97. The terminology "Great Mother Representative" is my own; Neumann's own phrase, which strikes me as being a loaded one, is "destructive male consort."

14 Robert Louis Stevenson, *Dr. Jekyll and Mr. Hyde* (New York: Bantam Books, 1981; orig. publ. 1886), pp. 79–80.

15 James Lord, *A Giacometti Portrait* (New York: Museum of Modern Art,

1965), p. 38. See also Lord's more recent study, *Giacometti, a Biography* (New York: Farrar, Straus and Giroux, 1985).

[16] Miró died in 1984; this quotation appeared in several obituaries that ran in a number of North American newspapers.

[17] Quoted in Albert J. Lubin, *Stranger on the Earth* (New York: Holt, Rinehart and Winston, 1972), pp. 3 and 16. See also Matson, *Short Lives*, pp. 363–374.

[18] The following discussion is based on Charlotte Haldane, *Mozart* (New York: Oxford University Press, 1960), and Wolfgang Hildesheimer, *Mozart*, translated by Marion Faber (London: Dent, 1983), esp. pp. 131, 138, 175, 180–185, 235, 351, and 357.

[19] Peter Shaffer, *Amadeus* (New York: Harper & Row, 1980), p. 83.

[20] According to Hildesheimer (see note 18, above), p. 375, Mozart believed someone had given him aqua tofana, a slowworking arsenic poison common enough in the eighteenth century. Shaffer's play *Amadeus* is built around the possibility that Salieri was the villain, and it is certainly curious that Salieri *denied* poisoning Mozart on his (Salieri's) deathbed (Haldane, *Mozart*, p. 129). An inquest on Mozart's death held in London in May 1983 concluded that he could have been poisoned, not by Salieri, but by a married woman with whom he was having an affair. (This was reported on the BBC.) Dr. Peter J. Davies argued against the possibility of poisoning in a two-part article published in the British journal *Musical Times*, in 1984; see also Donald Henahan, "Rest in Peace, Salieri, No One Killed Mozart," *The New York Times*, November 11, 1984, Section H. The issue will probably never be resolved.

[21] Chang Chung-yuan, *Creativity and Taoism* (New York: Harper & Row, 1970), page facing Plate 4. Mu ch'i's drawing is reproduced on the front cover of this work, as well as on the front cover of Shin'ichi Hisamatsu, *Zen and the Fine Arts*, translated by Gishin Tokiwa (Tokyo: Kodansha International Ltd., 1971).

[22] Weil's essay "Decreation" can be found in *Gravity and Grace*, translated by Emma Craufurd (London: Routledge and Kegan Paul, 1952; orig. French ed. 1947). Matson discusses Weil in *Short Lives*, pp. 375–388. There is of course a large literature on Simone Weil, including studies by Simone Pétrement and John Hellman, among others. T. S. Eliot had already approached the theme of personality *vs.* non-personality in creative work in his essay "Tradition and the Individual Talent," in *Points of View* (London: Faber and Faber, 1941), pp. 23–24.

[23] I have substituted the word "person" for "man," which appears in the

original. See Ananda Coomaraswamy, "Meister Eckhart's View of Art," in *The Transformation of Nature in Art* (New York: Dover Publications, 1956; orig. publ. 1934), 2nd ed., p. 64.

24 On minimal art, see Gregory Battcock (ed.), *Minimal Art: A Critical Anthology* (New York: E. P. Dutton, 1968). Philip Glass is perhaps best known for his opera *Einstein on the Beach*, and for composing the soundtrack for Godfrey Reggio's films *Koyaanisqatsi* (1983) and *Powaqqatsi* (1987). Terry Riley's most famous work (Steve Reich worked on it as well) is probably "In C"; for an interesting interview with Riley see Jon Pareles, "'Terry Riley's Music Moves to Improvisation," *The New York Times*, September 24, 1982. Reich discussed his sources and his own musical development in an interview and performance at the Exploratorium, San Francisco, December 15, 1982; see also the excellent article by Ingram Marshall in *Stagebill* (San Francisco) (December 1982), vol. 2, no. 4, and the interview with Reich in *Parabola* (May 1980), vol. 5, no. 2, pp. 60–72.

25 Bernard Leach, *A Potter's Book*, 2nd ed. (London: Faber and Faber, 1945), p. 42.

26 M.C. Richards, *The Crossing Point* (Middletown, Connecticut: Wesleyan University Press, 1973), pp. 63–64.

Speculation on Speculation

═══════════

LYNN MARGULIS

The crucial ancient beginnings of the human brain lie in the dancing of bacteria: the intricate mechanisms of cell motility. How do cells locomote? The answer to this puzzle is the beginning of enlightenment for the origins of mind-brain.

Whereas in science *theory* is lauded, *speculation* is ridiculed. A biologist accused in print of "speculation" is branded for the tenure of her career. This biologist finds herself like a ballet dancer imitating a pigeon-toed hunchback: All of the intellectual training to keep my toes turned out emotionally backfires with a request to speculate freely. What else, though, does John Brockman ask his Reality Club members when he says: "We charge the speakers to represent an idea of reality by describing their creative work, life, and the questions they're asking themselves. We also want them to share with us the boundaries of their knowledge and experience"?

Only a direct response to Brockman's request permits me the luxury of speculation. Never before would I dare mention out loud the questions I am continually asking myself. Without the Reality Club prod, no speculation on speculation would be possible. In a manuscript lacking data, field and laboratory observations, descriptions of equipment and their correlated methodologies, and deficient in references, I feel a huge restraint as I attempt to comply with John's request to slacken the bonds of professionalism and turn my toes in. My well-seasoned inhibitions are nevertheless titillated by the joys of this Brockman opportunity to really tell you about the hypothesis that I am always testing, that which I am always questioning: my developing worldview of mind. Asking your patience and indulgence to see beyond the inevitable barriers of language, I can at least try to articulate the unmentioned and hitherto unmentionable.

We have an intuitive grasp of the reality to which these terms refer: *perception, awareness, speculation, thought, memory, knowledge,* and *consciousness.* Most of us would claim that these qualities of mind have been listed more or less in evolutionary order. It is obvious that bacteria perceive sugars and algae perceive light. Dogs are aware; whether deciding to chase a ball or not, they seem to be "speculating." Thought and memory are clearly present in nonhuman animals such as *Aplysia,* the huge, shell-less marine snail that can be taught association. *Aplysia,* the sea hare, can be trained to anticipate; it will flee from potential electric shock as soon as a light is flashed. Knowledge, some admit, can be displayed by whales, bears, bats, and other vertebrates, including birds. But conventional wisdom tells us that consciousness is limited to people and our immediate ancestors. Many scientists believe that "mind"—whatever it is—will never be known by any combination of neurophysiology, neuroanatomy, genetics, neuropharmacology, or any other materialistic science. *Brain* may be knowable by the -ologies but *mind* can never be.

I disagree with many versions of this common myth. I believe brain is mind and mind is brain and that science, broadly conceived, is an effective method for learning about both. The results of the -ologies just listed, as well as of many other sciences, can tell us clearly about ourselves and what is inside our heads. Furthermore, humans have no monopoly whatever on any of these mental processes. As long as we indicate consciousness of *what*, I can point to conscious, actively communicating, pond-water microscopic life (and even extremely unconscious bureaucrats). The processes of perception, awareness, speculation, and the like evolved in the microcosm: the subvisible world of our bacterial ancestors. Movement itself is an ancestral bacterial trait, and thought, I am suggesting, is a kind of cell movement.

We admit that computers have precedents: electricity, electronic circuits, silica semiconductors, screws, nuts, and bolts. The miracle of the computer is the way in which its parts are put together. So, too, human minds have precedents; the uniqueness is in the recombination and interaction of the elements that comprise the mind-brain. My contention is that hundreds of biologists, psychologists, philosophers, and others making inquiries of mind-brain have failed to identify even the analogues of electricity, electronic circuits, silica semiconductors, screws, nuts, and bolts. In the absence of knowing what the parts are and how they came together, we can never know the human mind-brain. Only the very recent history of the human brain is illuminated by comparative studies of amphibian and reptilian brains. The crucial ancient beginnings of the human brain lie in the dancing of bacteria: the intricate mechanisms of cell motility. How do cells locomote? The answer to this puzzle is the beginning of enlightenment for the origins of mind-brain.

I cherish a specific, testable, scientific theory. The means for testing it are biochemical, genetic, and molecular-biological. The facilities for the testing are available in New York City. A conclusive proof would require generosity on the part of at least two hugely successful and highly talented scientists and their laboratory assistants, a Columbia University biochemist and a Rockefeller University geneticist. Dr. Charles Cantor, of Columbia University Medical School, has developed new techniques to purify genes (DNA) gently. The purification holds the biological material on agar blocks (a gelatinlike substance) in such a manner that the structures in which the genes reside, the chromosomes, are extracted in their natural long, skinny form. Groups of genes (linkage groups) can be identified. Chromosome counts, difficult to determine microscopically, can be made biochemically.

And Dr. David Luck, an active geneticist at The Rockefeller University for over a quarter of a century, has recently discovered a new type of genetic system. He has found a special set of genes that determines the development of structures, bodies called kinetosomes that are present in thousands of very different kinds of motile cells: those of green algae, sperm, ciliates, oviducts, and trachea, for example. These structures, which I think of as assembly systems for nearly universal cell motors, may be determined by a unique set of genes separate from those of the nuclei and other components of cells. These genes, inferred from genetic studies of Luck and his colleagues, may be exactly the spirochetal remnant genes I predicted still must be inside all motile cells that contain kinetosomes. [1]

Although no exorbitant amount of money would be needed, because testing my theory would be limited by the requirement for time and energy of very busy people, it would be expensive. Furthermore, the results of my testing, even if they are ideal, would cure no disease, stop no war, limit no radioactivity, save no tropical forest, or produce no marketable product. At least in the beginning there would be no immediate profit coming from the work. The very concrete results would simply help us reconstruct the origin of our mind-brains from their bacterial ancestors.

What is the central idea to be tested? I hypothesize that all these phenomena of mind, from perception to consciousness, originated from an unholy microscopic alliance between hungry killer bacteria and their potential archaebacterial victims. The hungry killers were extraordinarily fast-swimming, skinny bacteria called spirochetes. These active bacteria are relatives of the spirochetes of today that are associated with the venereal disease that, in prolonged and serious cases, infects the brain: the treponemes of syphilis. The fatter, slow-moving potential victims, the second kind of bacteria called archaebacteria, were quite different from the spirochetes. By resisting death the archaebacteria incorporated their would-be, fast-moving killers into their bodies. The archaebacteria survived, continuing to be infected by the spirochetes. The odd couple lived together; the archaebacteria were changed, but not killed, by their attackers; the victims did not entirely succumb. (There are precedents for this: Plants are green because their intended victims, the chloroplasts that began as oxygen-producing cyanobacteria, resisted death by ingestion.)

Our cells, including our nerve cells, may be products of such mergers—the thin, transparent bodies of the spirochete enemies sneakily incorporated inextricably and forever. The wily fast movement, the hunger, the sensory ability of the survivor's enemies all were put to good use by the evolving partnership. Cultural analogues of such mergers exist: cases in which two very different warring peoples form new identities after the truce; identities, for example, in which unique domesticated plants of one culture become firmly incorporated in that of the second. The presence of Indian corn, tomatoes, and potatoes in Europe is due to the near annihilation of indigenous Native Americans. I see our cell movement, including the movements leading to thought, as the spoils of ancient microbial battles.

My speculations, two thousand million years later, may be the creative outcome of an ancient uneasy peace. If this reckoning is true, then the spirochetal remnants may be struggling to exist in our brains, attempting to swim, grow, feed, connect with their fellows, and reproduce. The interactions between these subvisible actors, now full member-components of our nerve cells, are sensitive to the experience we bring them. *Perception, thought, speculation, memory*, of course, are all active processes; I speculate that these are the large-scale manifestations of the small-scale community ecology of the former spirochetes and archaebacteria that comprise our brains.

Arcana Naturae Detecta is the name of Anton van Leeuwenhoek's seventeenth-century book revealing the microcosm beneath his single-lens microscope illuminated by a gas lamp. The visible became explicable to him by the machinations of the subvisible. Leeuwenhoek and his followers made clear that "decay," "spoiling," and "rotting food" are all signs of healthy bacterial and fungal growth. In baking, "rising dough" is respiring yeast; in tropical disease, malarial fevers are apicomplexan protists bursting our red blood cells. Fertility is owed in part to semen or "male seed" containing millions of tailed sperm in sugar solution. The disease of Mimi, the heroine of *La Bohème*, is "consumption." From its point of view, "consumption" is the healthy growth of *Mycobacterium* in the warm, moist lungs of the lovely young woman. Speculation, I claim, is legacy of the itching enmities of unsteady truce. Speculation is the mutual stimulation of the restrained microbial inhabitants that, entirely inside their former archaebacterial enemies, have strongly interacted with them for hundreds of millions of years. Our nerve cells are the outcome of an ancient, nearly immortal marriage of two archenemies who have managed to coexist: the former spirochetes and former archaebacteria that now comprise our brains.

Like animated vermicelli married and in perpetual copulatory stance with their would-be archaebacterial victims, these former free-living bacteria are inextricably united. They probably have been united for more than one thousand million years. The fastidiously described speculation is indistinguishable from the theory. I continually play with an idea: The origin of thought and consciousness is cellular, owing its beginnings to the first courtship between unlikely bacterial bedfellows who became ancestors to our mind-brains.

My goal in the rest of this essay is to explain what I mean and why I make such a bizarre assertion.

What needs to be explained? My basic speculation is that mind-brain processes are nutrition, physiology, sexuality, reproduction, and microbial community ecology of the microbes that comprise us. The microbes are not just metaphors; their remnants inhabit our brain, their needs and habits, histories and health status help determine our behavior. If we feel possessed and of several minds, if we feel overwhelmed by complexity, it is because we are inhabited by and comprised of complexities. [2]

The detailed consequences of the theory of spirochete origin of microtubules of brain cells do not belong in an essay about speculation for The Reality Club. Indeed, it is unlikely that such a statement would even be considered for publication in the *Proceedings of the National Academy of Sciences*. Rather, I ask only that the unmentionable become discussable over mulled wine and friendship so that the consequences of the hypothesis may be speculated upon. Could thought, speculation, and awareness really have evolved from fast-moving bacteria and their interactions, their hungers, their activities, their satiations, their associations with their fellows, both like and unlike, and their waste-removal processes? Is it possible that we are as entirely unaware of the microbial inhabitants that comprise us as a huge ship tossing in the waves is unaware that her responses are determined by the hunger, thirst, and eyesight of the captain at the helm and his communications with the crew?

What might be the implications for mind-brains if this bacterial origin of speculation is correct? Let us list a few. They all may be incorrect, but they are all testable within the rigors of the scientific tradition.

1. *Nerve impulses and the firing of nerves.* These become explicable as our motile spirochetes' trying to swim; as Betsey Dyer (assistant professor of biology, Wheaton College, Norton, Massachusetts) says, captive former spirochetes are spinning their wheels unable to move forward. They have become uncoupled motors going around and around. This quasi movement is the nerve impulse. It occurs because small, positively charged ions (*e.g.*, sodium, potassium, calcium) are accumulated and released across what is now our nerve cell membrane. These ions, their protein and membrane interactions, derive from the membranes of the original spirochetes.

2. *Sweet memories.* Two different kinds of memory systems exist: short-term (seconds to minutes) and long-term (indefinite). The storage of memories is markedly enhanced by adrenaline and other substances that lead directly to increased availability of sugar to the brain cells.[3] Sugar, like anything penetrating the blood-brain barrier— that is, entering the brain from the blood—is very carefully monitored and controlled.

Short-term memory arises every time from casual encounters between the sticking-out parts of former spirochetes and their friends. These interactions begin in seconds; it probably takes a few minutes at most while two or more neurons née spirochetes interact. The casual encounters occur by small-ion interactions with proteins on the surfaces of what used to be spirochete membranes (now they are our nerve cell membranes). In brief, short-term memories derive from the physiology of spirochetal remnants in the brain. We know that the pictorial short-term memory, for the recognition of fractal designs, for example, "is coded by temporary activation of an ensemble of neurons in the region of the association cortex that processes visual information."[4] Presumably the short-term memory is stored when visual information is processed and not in special compartments for short-term memory. The "temporary activation," if I am correct, will be directly homologous to spirochete behavioral interaction—not analogous to it or to computer software manipulation.

Long-term memory is stable; it depends on new protein synthesis. Long-term memory works because it stores the short-term. What were repeated casual encounters between former spirochetal remnants become stabilized attachment sites. Synapse, if I am correct, is the neurophysiologist's term for the well-developed spirochetal remnant attachment site. In brief, long-term memories derive from the growth of spirochetal remnants, including their attachment sites, in the brain.

Sugar enhances memory processes because it feeds preferentially the spirochetal remnants so that they can interact healthily and form new attachment sites. Sugar has been the food of spirochetes since they squiggled in the mud.

■□■

As Edelman (1985) has pointed out, no two monkeys, no two identical twins, are identical at the level of fine structure of their neuronal connections. "There must be a generator of diversity during the development of neural circuits, capable of constructing definite patterns of groups but also generating great individual variation. Variation must occur at the level of cell-to-cell recognition by a molecular process. Second, there must be evidence from group selection and competition in brain maps and re-entrant circuits. This must occur not in the circuitry but in the efficacy of preformed connections or synapses."[5] I believe Edelman is discovering the actively growing latter-day populations of microbes that comprise every brain. Edelman's "populations" are nerve cells and their connections. I interpret Edelman's populations literally as remnants of ancestral microbial masses. The spirochetal remnants, either poised or ready to grow, attach and interact depending on how they are treated during a human's crucial stages (fetal development, infancy, and early childhood). Neural Darwinism, differential growth by selection of spirochete associations, determines the way in which the brain develops.

Mental health is, in part, how we feed the normal spirochetal remnants that make up our brain. Learning becomes a function of the number and quality of new connections—attachment sites—that these wily apobeings forge. The spirochetal remnants grow faster, dissolving temporary points of contact while consolidating firm connections that are our nerve cell endings during our infancy and childhood. More potential changes occur early—in infancy and adolescence—relative to those of adulthood. The growth patterns of nerve cells née spirochetes are sensitive to the food, such as essential fatty acids, that the rest of our body provides for them; experience is always active, always participatory and, if registered in long-term memory, unforgotten. Our memories are their physical networks. Our crises and climaxes are their "blooms," their population explosions. Senility is spirochetal-remnant atrophy. It is no coincidence that salt ions and psychoactive drugs, including anesthetics, have strong effects on spirochetal movement of the free-living mud-bound cousin spirochetes.

Clearly these enormous contemplative issues cannot be solved here alone by me. All I ask is that we compare consciousness with spirochete microbial ecology. We may be vessels, large ships, unwitting sanctuaries to the thriving communities comprising us. When they are starved, cramped, or stimulated we have inchoate feelings. Perhaps we should get to know ourselves better. We might then recognize our speculations as the dance networks of ancient, restless, tiny beings that connect our parts.

NOTES

1 J. L. Hall, Z. Ramanis, and D. J. L. Luck, "Basal Body/Centriolar DNA: Molecular Genetic Studies in *Chlamydomonas*," *Cell* (1989), vol. 59, pp. 121–132.

2 L. Margulis and D. Sagan, *Origins of Sex* (New Haven: Yale University Press, 1990).

3 Paul E. Gold, "Sweet Memories," *American Scientist*, (1987), vol. 75, pp. 151–155.

4 Y. Miyashita and H. S. Chang, "Neuronal Correlate of Pictorial Short-Term Memory in the Primate Temporal Cortex," *Nature* (1988), vol. 331, pp. 68–70.

5 Gerald M. Edelman, "Neural Darwinism: Population Thinking and Higher Brain Function," 1985. In *How We Know, Nobel Conference XX*, ed. Michael Shafto, Gustavus Adolphus College, St. Peter, Minnesota, pp. 1–30.

Dreaded States and Cherished Outcomes

DAN OGILVIE

. . . a major difference between the ideal self and the undesired self is this: We know precisely what the undesired self is because we have already been there. By comparison, the ideal self is unknown. It contains ideas about how we would like to be. The undesired self is experiential. The ideal self is conceptual.

During the prime of behaviorism, any academic psychologist who wished to cash his or her paycheck in good conscience kept a safe distance from any concept that bore a relation to "the self." For some, "the self" smacked of "the mind," and the mind was, at best, an epiphenomenon that created usually irrelevant post hoc justifications for behavior that, in fact, scientific psychologists viewed as nothing more than learned habits and responses to various contingencies of reinforcement. Now we are in the midst of a new cycle, where the self is "in" and respectable. Even modern-day behaviorial therapists, called cognitive behaviorists, find concepts containing a hyphenated self (for example, self-esteem, self-regard, self-referential behavior) essential in conducting their research and communicating their ideas.

As academic psychologists took their extended detour into schedules of reinforcement and associative learning, psychoanalytic theorists, other depth psychologists, and several major sociological theorists managed to keep the self alive. While no definitional consensus was reached, references to these writers of the early and middle part of this century are now common.

Given our culture's adherence to the scientific enterprise, nothing is worthy of investigation unless it can be quantified. That gave experimental psychologists an edge over the other members of the field: They counted things like the number of times a rat bit a target or a pigeon pecked a mark. What does someone interested in something as intangible as the self count? Finally, Carl Rogers, humanist and empiricist, developed a method for computing the distance between the real self and the ideal self. His method was this: He presented a subject 100 cards on which were written statements such as "I enjoy being with people" and "I tend to get angry at little things." The subject's task was to sort the cards into a normal distribution whose extremes represented "most like me" and "least like me." The distribution was done according to how the individual felt about his or her self right now, the "real self." Rogers then instructed the subject to create a second distribution, using a duplicate set of cards, according to his or her "ideal self." After these tasks were performed, a distance, or discrepancy, score was calculated by statistically correlating the two distributions. A high and positive correlation was taken to mean that there was a healthy overlap between one's real and ideal selves. On the other hand, a low correlation or, in a dire case, a negative one, would be a sign that a large gap existed between the person's real and ideal selves, indicating that much work would be required to bring the two into closer harmony.

While Rogers's method did nothing to clarify what the self is, it did offer a strategy for hundreds of hungry researchers to count something, and, as an added bonus, what was being computed was considered important. Rogers's theory of real and ideal selves resembled the conceptions of several major psychodynamic theorists who predated him. Notable in this regard was Alfred Adler.

Adler was one of the original members of Freud's inner circle in Vienna. Over his nine-year association with Freud, his notions regarding how personality operates became increasingly incompatible with Freud's basic postulates. Finally, the two broke relations and Adler created his own school, called individual psychology. Adler's view was that we are incapable of appreciating or having true compassion for another person if we do not know his or her conscious goals, what the person is working on or working toward. Adler did not deny that the child was, in some respects, the father to the man or the mother to the woman he or she would become—that early experiences did affect later relationships and one's perceptions of those relationships—but he believed that adult behavior is misrepresented when construed solely on the basis of the clashing forces of infantile ids and superegos. Inspired by the ideas of the philosopher Hans Vaihinger, Adler embraced the notion of fictional finalism. According to this view, we all create fictions or stories about how we will be in the future. These fictions take shape as mental images of ourselves at some future time, and once they are established in our minds, they act as powerful incentives for behavior. Our fictions are our guides. They organize our lives and shape our behaviors, giving us hope that, with hard work, craftiness, luck, faith, or a few good breaks, we will step into the pictures that have preoccupied us. Fictions, Adler claimed, are essential to healthy lives.

Fictions are also the stuff of neuroses when they become rigid and inflexible. For example, it would be self-defeating for a student who has failed every biology, physics, and chemistry course in high school and college to hold fast to the fiction of becoming a surgeon. Adherence to that fiction could become the breeding ground for serious trouble.

Unrealistic and unbending fictions can be harsh masters. They can lead to all sorts of miseries. An undeniably good college football player who is not drafted by a professional ball club may consider his life to be over. A hardworking teacher who is denied tenure cannot face her friends. An actor who cannot find a part, an author unable to find a publisher, or an ambitious pianist whose hand is crushed in an accident may turn in desperation to alcohol.

More flexible fictions allow individuals who have not succeeded in achieving something important to them to experience their discouragement, pick up the pieces, and begin again. If necessary, fictions can be revised, to be made more compatible with native skills and demonstrated talents. For our sense of well-being, it is important to hold fictions in a manner that makes their modification possible when experiences dictate that they be changed. It is equally important to update and nourish our fictions, because they are what make our lives meaningful. According to Adler, in no case should an individual operate without a fiction. No fiction, no purpose. No purpose, no motivation. For Adler, the tension between what an individual is now (the real self) and what that person could be (the fictional, or ideal, self) is the point of life. No tension, no meaning. Life would be pointless without personal fictions beckoning us to move from where we are to where we could be. Lacking a fix on some clear image of one's self in the future, an individual might suffer the condition that I assume Lily Tomlin refers to in her bag-woman character's line, "I always wanted to be somebody. Now I realize I should have been more specific."

Adler found receptive audiences in the United States. It's not what I am now that counts, it's what I'm gonna be. The combination of a Protestant ethic of hard work, a pioneering spirit, and our cultural emphasis on individualism and achievement created a kind of homecoming setting for Adler and others who pointed out that life is lived between now and the future. So, when Rogers discovered a way to "measure" the discrepancy between the real and ideal selves, he made an already important issue scientifically respectable. Since then, numerous social scientists have become obsessed with calculating the real/ideal self discrepancy score, which has become one of the leading variables in personality research. And why not? Social scientists are as much involved in the fabric of mainstream beliefs as merchants, politicians, filling station attendants, prospective brides and grooms, and tired factory workers looking forward to life-renewing, invigorating retirements.

Given the pressure we feel to "be all we can be," what are the consequences of failure? What happens to a person who simply cannot get into medical school, a budding executive who is repeatedly passed over at promotion time, the woman who wishes to bear the perfect child and cannot get pregnant? Under these conditions, we stand face to face with what I call the undesired self.

The concept of an undesired self occurred to me on a miserable day when I was delivering a lecture about the ideal self as contained in various theories of behavior. My experiences with the topic had led me to expect students to engage in lively public descriptions of their grand images of themselves in the future. On that day, however, class members were apathetic, and no one spoke. Sometimes I can make up for students' lack of enthusiasm by generating some of my own. But I was in no shape to perform, because of my obsession with the broken transmission in my car, my dismay that some materials I had promised to pass out to the class had not been collated as promised, my unhappiness about a recent letter from a distressed family member, and various administrative matters that were taking too long to resolve. I was in no shape to lead a class discussion on the self made perfect. After a moment of reflection, I set my prepared notes aside and stated, "Ladies and gentlemen, I could care less about the ideal self. At this moment, the concept is meaningless to me. The very idea of it makes me ill. None of the authors we are considering had anything to say about our worst selves, our undesired selves, those self-conceptions that arise when nothing, I stress *nothing*, works. The ideal self is too nice. It leaves out the nitty gritty of life. It's too clean, and life is sometimes dirty." Encouraged by a chorus of "Right on!" and "Go for it, brother!" responses, I proceeded to question psychology's obsession with the disparity between real and ideal selves. This cathartic episode not only woke up a dreary class; it also opened up a new area of psychological research.

As mentioned earlier, in my field of academic inquiry, colleagues don't pay much attention to new ideas unless numbers can be attached to them. So I designed and conducted a study that showed rather forcefully that life satisfaction is more a function of the *distance* between the real and undesired selves than it is a function of *discrepancies* between the two. People applauded the study, and as some applauded, they also said they had known it all along. The undesired self concept and the results of my research rang true to their experiences. It seems to me quite likely that we commonly operate in the field between how we are and how we don't want to be—our dreaded states—but we usually keep our dreaded states encapsulated and private. Publicly, it is much more common to speak of our fictions, of what we are doing and where our work and lives are heading, of our cherished outcomes.

Why is the undesired self a better peg for assessing our well-being than how close or far we are from our ideal selves? Here are some of the words people have used in describing their worst states to me: afraid, unloved, bad-tempered, fat, impatient, tired all the time, jealous, stupid, raw, awkward, dumped on, despairing, anxious, out of sorts, worthless, lonely, rejected, unsure, confused, out of control, helpless, wimpy, nervous, depressed, shy, a loser, hated, disgusting, dependent, despicable. Compare these descriptors with words commonly used to characterize ideal selves: powerful, rich, respected by all, serene, peaceful, in great shape, open-minded, successful, admired, creative, well-rounded, warm, knowledgeable, humble about my accomplishments, open, accepting of others, productive, and—my favorite—pretty wonderful in all respects.

There is a qualitative difference between these word groupings. In general, words used to describe dreaded states, often referring to specific affects and bodily states, are more concrete than those used to characterize hoped-for conditions. Witness the respondent who tried to explain to me what well-rounded (an ideal state for her) would feel like. "Well-rounded? That's easy. I will feel well-rounded when I am not only this, but I am also that and that and that. I'm sure you know what I mean. It will be something like being surrounded by a glow."

Compare the abstractness of her attempt to describe this ideal state to the tangibility of her associations with feeling stupid (an undesired condition for her): "When I am stupid, I get disgusted with myself. I tell myself that I should know better. That if I keep it up, nobody, absolutely nobody, will like me. I feel as though my head is crashing in on itself, like I had been hit with a sledgehammer. There is a pulsating sensation in my temples. I get a weak feeling in my knees and ankles. I wonder if my legs will continue to hold me. I get sweaty and embarrassed. One time I felt so stupid that I wished I could disappear. I wanted to turn into a snake or insect and crawl into a corner where no one could see me." I can form specific and personal associations to this person's description of feeling stupid. In fact, I can easily re-create some of the physiological manifestations of tension she put into words. On the other hand, her definition of well-rounded sounded very nice to me, but I didn't know what in the world she was talking about.

In short, a major difference between the ideal self and the undesired self is this: We know precisely what the undesired self is because we have already been there. By comparison, the ideal self is unknown. It contains *ideas* about how we would like to be. The undesired self is experiential. The ideal self is conceptual.

It would be foolhardy and unscholarly for me not to mention that the concept of the undesired self is, in some respects, old wine in a new bottle. For example, a primary concept in Carl Jung's arsenal of terms was the shadow. This archetype is the underside of the persona, the masks we show to the public, costumes we wear as we attempt to influence how others perceive us. The shadow is the unconscious counterpart of the ego, but as Jung construed it, the shadow is more similar to Freud's id than to the undesired self. Jung described it as "the one who wants to do all the things we do not allow ourselves to do." I don't think we *want* to feel stupid, embarrassed, afraid, or alone.

A more direct and compelling comparison can be made between the undesired self and Harry Stack Sullivan's concepts of the bad-me and the not-me. According to Sullivan, as individuals go through childhood, they form various "personifications" of others and of themselves. One of the earliest "other" personifications is the good mother and the bad mother. The good mother is the tender, caring, loving mother often portrayed in children's stories as the good fairy. The bad mother is the forbidding, angry, upset, or anxious mother. The infant's interaction with the good mother leads to a self-personification of the good-me. The good-me receives praise, warmth, and all the nice feelings that accompany tenderness. The bad-me personification emerges in response to the punishing mother, the upset mother, the evil stepmother. The not-me comes into being when mother–child interpersonal relations are infused and surrounded by anxiety. The not-me is filled with such dread, such awe, that it is dissociated from the self. Thus compartmentalized, it is a primary candidate for projection onto hated and hateful others, people or nations, in adult life.

It does not seem to be stretching the point to state that the good-me forms the base upon which the ideal self later develops. A suitable elaboration of the good-me would be the wonderful-me in a position of respect and admiration, or the grand-me surrounded by worldly treasures. Similarly, the undesired self can be considered an amalgam of the child's experiences of the bad-me and the not-me.

Rather than continuing on a parallel path with Sullivan, it is useful to delve directly into the substance of his theory, for his notion of the self opens new avenues for our consideration. In fact, Sullivan rarely uses the word *self*. Instead, he speaks of the "self-system." For him, the self-system is the "equilibrating factor in living . . . the extensive organization of experience within the personality." It consists of "security operations" intended to reduce the experience of anxiety. For me, Sullivan's next observation is a mind-stopper. Here I paraphrase him. *Without the experience of anxiety, there would be no emergence of a self-system.* If I had the power of the Queen of Hearts in *Alice in Wonderland*, I would say to you, the jury, "That's important. Write that down." A person who never experienced anxiety would go through life much as Chauncey Gardner (played by Peter Sellers) did in the film version of Jerzy Kasinski's novel *Being There*. Life would be lived by imitation of others. One thing would be just as important or unimportant as anything else. Certainly, nothing would be self-referenced, because there would be no self-system to refer to.

Whether we pity Chauncey Gardner or envy him, there is no chance of emulating him because it is nearly impossible to imagine even a child, let alone an adolescent or adult, moving through life without at least a taste of anxiety. Anxiety, in raw form, is what Karen

Horney described as feeling alone and isolated in a potentially hostile world. Perhaps at an even deeper level, it is the distinctively human experience that comes about when we recognize that at one time we did not exist and at a later time we will cease to exist. The insecurity that accompanies this recognition of mortality is countermanded by a sometimes desperate search for security.

So the discomfort that emerges with the appearance of the undesired self is the discomfort of insecurity. Insecurity is like a warning signal indicating that if things continue to go badly, the self-system will no longer be able to do its job of guarding against the flood of anxiety and despair that have, at their roots, the dread of nonexistence. It seems that one of the major ways we defend ourselves from this chasm of chaos is to create systems of order. If we can organize a disorderly world and manage to keep the thing in place, then security will be won. Security, ease of mind, freedom from fear, from danger, from risk of loss. Security, safety, certainty, protection, shelter. That is what we seek.

A major function of society is to provide avenues of security to as many of its members as possible. Our society, like all others, does that by providing roles. One thing that has vanished in the process of creating modern civilizations are highly ritualized and sometimes painful ceremonies that ushered groups of initiates into new and clearly delineated positions within their tribe. With the demise of these rites of passage has come the freedom to choose among various havens that, once occupied, promise that life will flow in an orderly, familiar, and expected fashion. These havens, as I mentioned, are roles that we seek to occupy because we believe that they will bring with them greater security than we now experience.

The power of anticipated roles in how we construe internal representations of our ideal selves has been underlined by the research of students who have worked with me for several years. We have asked hundreds of people, "Can you describe to me what it was, is, or will be like to be at your best, your ideal you?" The vast majority of our respondents first mention roles.

Young adults (over 85 percent of them) state that the best is to come. Some examples: A twenty-one-year-old female replied, "I will be at my best in about ten years. By then, I should be established in my career. I expect I'll be married and have at least one child. My husband and I will be financially secure, he in business and I as a therapist. We will own our home, and we will be active in various organizations."

One twenty-two-year-old male said this: "My ideal for myself will be reached when I get an advanced degree in engineering. Then, I am confident that things will start falling into place. I've worked hard up to now and I don't plan to quit. I even think about opening up my own electronics firm someday. Whether or not marriage is in the cards for me remains to be seen."

And a twenty-four-year-old construction worker gave this answer: "I hope the best comes soon. I have two children, and things are tough right now. I think I am good enough to become a job supervisor in a couple of years, and then my wife and I can think about moving out of that crummy apartment we're living in. I would do anything to own a house. I even thought of selling drugs like some of my former high school buddies. But I'd probably get caught, and all hell would break loose."

These young adults are maintaining tension between their now-me's and their future fictions. Notice how they describe their fictions in terms of roles: homeowner, wife, mother, engineer, supervisor, therapist.

Even some elderly respondents use role terminology to define their best. A seventy-three-year-old woman who devotes her days to tending to her invalid husband said, "I was at my best when I was between forty and fifty. My children were grown. My husband and I had a small farm that we operated as a hobby. We were active in the Grange, in our church, and in several other community organizations."

So roles are crucial to the way we envision and talk about cherished outcomes. We see roles as fastening us into the social system, linking us up with the (imagined or real) stable fabric of society. When roles mentioned by respondents are probed (by such questions as, "What will it be like when you are established in your career?"), positive features are called forth ("I will be happy, secure, confident." "Finally, my life will be organized." "Things will be certain." "I will be free from stress and worry.").

On the other side of the coin, what do people say when they are asked to describe themselves at their worst, their undesired selves? "I was at my worst when I was lonely and confused." "I am at my worst now. I am lost, anxious about the future, and feeling helpless." "I will be at my worst when I am old, dependent, and despairing. I will have lost my mental capacities, and everything will have gone haywire." "I was at my worst during adolescence. Adolescence was dreadful. I had zero self-confidence. I didn't fit in anywhere. I was fat and felt terrible about getting good grades when it wasn't fashionable to do that."

Individuals asked to describe a time when they were lonely, confused, anxious, or feeling helpless almost invariably describe a time when they were roleless ("I didn't fit in anywhere") or committed to a role that was unavailable (the student who could not get into medical school), disrupted (the worker who got fired), rendered inoperative (the man or woman who has lost a spouse), or no longer interesting (the woman who said, "I just woke up to the fact that I simply didn't want to be a housewife anymore"). It is during times like these that the self-system undergoes a severe challenge and must work hard to restore a sense of order. Otherwise, disorder will reign and the organism stands ripe to be invaded by feelings of confusion, insecurity, fear, panic, or hopelessness.

One buffer between a sense of order and the experience of personal chaos is religion. If things on this planet are not right, or if things are right but I can't figure them out, God has reserved a place for me in His home where I can finally find the peace and security that I so desperately seek. Every formalized religion issues directives to its followers. Religions throughout the world assist believers in organizing and structuring their lives around sets of rules and requirements that, if followed faithfully, assure a better existence after death. Thereby our confusion is eased and life on earth is given new purpose. Our belief that God's household is in order and offers us final refuge from feeling alone and helpless means that He and His order must be defended. Most urgently, it must be defended against the intrusion of other religions that have misconstrued God's grand design. Therefore, various armies of God emerge, defending not only His kingdom in heaven, but His kingdom on earth as well. If either of these interwoven kingdoms were to fall, beliefs would be shaken, faith would be meaningless, and masses of followers would stand face-to-face with the dread of nonexistence. In the meantime, Beirut burns, skirmishes continue in Ireland, Indian immigrants are terrorized in Jersey City, and ideological leaders around the world brace their followers for an invasion.

All this, of course, is based on misreading the myths that have inspired religions. For many years, I have been an admirer of the writings of Joseph Campbell, a specialist in myths, whose book *The Hero with a Thousand Faces* contains the structure of ideas elaborated upon in all of his other works. Mythic heroes throughout the ages and across all cultural lines have been portrayed as leaving the world as it is known and understood by its occupants and entering another world, a world of chaos and disorder, where they face many dangers and potential annihilation. These voyagers, who either survive their agony and return or are destroyed and resurrected from death, are renewed by the vision of the coincidence of opposites, by a new kind of order, a cosmic order. Although nearly every heroic voyage is depicted as an external venture through clashing rocks, fire-breathing dragons, or barren deserts, Campbell claims that a proper reading of myths opens the door to an *inward* voyage and ultimately to a reconciliation among opposites.

When a voyage is completed, the hero's next task, perhaps the most formidable of all, is to communicate a message—a message assured from the outset to be misunderstood by masses of people looking for rules that will guarantee security and peace of mind. The transformed hero, now coming from a completely different place from his audience, states something like "This is it" or "Christ is within you" or "What is the sound of one hand clapping?" Thus the hero attempts to point the way to individual transformation. Lacking courage to endure personal journeys or simply being unable to fathom the message, we seek out the person with the pointing finger and worship him.

What the hero has done is to have explored the contents of his own temple, his inner sanctuary, and, in the vocabulary of this essay, disassembled his self-system in the process. As a snake that has shed its skin rests defenseless to certain dangers, a dismantled self-system can no longer provide its accustomed service. Since the purpose of the self-system is to guard against the emergence of fear and anxiety, the hero, defenseless during much of his journey, boldly faces and experiences the intersection between being and nonbeing. His "rebirth" is nothing more or nothing less than the construction of a revised self-system that has freed him from former attachments, including life-assuring cherished outcomes. As the snake grows a new encasement to surround and contain a larger mass of tissues, a properly revised self-system can take in more of the world as it actually is: a world filled with uncertainty. The hero takes that uncertainty for granted and incorporates it into his life. It is no longer a matter of personal concern. But the recognition that it *is* a matter of personal concern to others adds to his compassion for, and frustration with, people engaged in the hopeless struggle to maintain attachments with their eyes riveted on that day when the world will say, "You were right all along."

So we construe cherished selves in terms of roles. Roles attach us to the social structure. Once we are able to occupy one or more of these roles, we believe we will be secure, life will be more certain. A twenty-two-year-old female college graduate said, "I will be my best after I finish law school and am employed in a law firm." But a thirty-one-year-old female lawyer stated, "I really won't be comfortable until I get to be a partner in this or some other law firm." And the struggle continues.

Although as a culture, our lenses are focused on cherished outcomes and what we must do to accumulate them, we are only dimly aware of dreaded states, because our self-systems will not hear of them. This was brought to my attention time and again a few years ago when my work on the undesired self was highlighted in *The New York Times* science section. Numerous individuals wrote to thank me for unveiling the key to happiness. Happiness is avoiding the undesired self. Some heroes we are! No reconciliation of opposites here—just a further extension of their polarities.

If we are going to solve the problems confronting the preservation of life on our planet—for many of these problems clearly result from human activity—we must confront earth-destroying, shortsighted self-systems and experience what lies behind them (insecurity, fear, anxiety, chaos). That done, the way will be cleared for visionaries to create new solutions to matters of pressing importance.

On a less grand scale, it is certain that life cannot be *experienced* when it is lived somewhere between now and the planned-for future, especially when, without recognizing it, our lenses are being focused by dreaded states we seek to avoid. In our drivenness, we fail to see that what we seek to avoid has little to do with actual survival but a lot to do with human divisiveness. It requires hard mental work to seek and attempt to maintain order in the world of conscious existence, given the context of the background noise of a biological system that has stored information that contradicts everything we "know"; a mostly unconscious system that threatens to rip us apart with uncertainty, ambivalence, and anxiety; a nonrational system based, in part, on infantile memories that "know no time." To prevent this disruption, we put our children, our parents, our neighbors—indeed, entire nations—in their places and try to keep them there. We categorize, label, and look for rules that always work in the hopes of guarding against any signs of external entropy that might match our inner condition of uncertainty. In sum, failure to come to terms with our personal confusions, our own dreaded states, serves to preserve the struggle, limit our fictions to visions of personal security, maintain human divisiveness, and bar us from a here-and-now engagement in life.

Nowadays, when I become aware that I am attempting to resist a sense of confusion by envisioning myself in the center of some fabled future, I think of the words of an eighty-three-year-old man who participated in one of our surveys. He said to me, "My best and worst? My best and worst are over. And you know something? The best was never all that great, and the worst was never as awful as I thought it would be. I wish I had known that before. I wouldn't have struggled so much. I could have done what I do now. I get up, experience the day, and then go back to bed. Had I discovered the joke when I was a young man, I would have gotten more accomplished, had more fun doing it, and I would have had a lot more time for others along the way."

Behind Closed Doors: Unlocking the Mysteries of Human Intelligence

---

ROBERT J. STERNBERG

We do not yet have a fully integrative model of human intelligence. . . . Such a model would have to specify, at minimum, the mental processes and strategies underlying intelligent behavior, the patterns of differences among people generated by these processes and strategies, the various brain sites at which the processes and strategies operate, and how the processes and strategies are brought to bear upon everyday life in one's social-cultural setting.

Some years ago, the Akira Kurosawa film *Rashomon* presented a single sequence of events from multiple points of view. Often, it was hard to tell that the events were the same ones. Similarly, an automobile is a source of transportation to a commuter, a livelihood to a car salesman, and a set of potentially malfunctioning parts to a mechanic. Human intelligence in some ways resembles the film and the automobile. From different points of view and, especially, various levels of analysis, human intelligence sometimes seems to be a different entity or set of entities. Yet if one looks deeply enough into the phenomenon of intelligence to penetrate the multiple points of view, a certain unity emerges that transcends any one perspective. In this essay, I describe some of the points of view from which intelligence has been perceived and then discuss the fundamental unities underlying them. I will argue that the multiple points of view are basically complementary, and that each responds to a different set of scientific and societal needs. In responding to various scientific and societal needs, these points of view taken together have brought us a long way toward understanding a complex and often elusive psychological construct, namely, human intelligence.

What does it mean for someone to be intelligent, or for one person to be more intelligent than another? To some extent, this question is definitional, and the answer will depend in part on how one defines intelligence. Indeed, definitional questions are perhaps more central in the social sciences than in some of the natural sciences. Although experts have reached no consensus on the definitional issue, many would agree that intelligence involves mental activity purposively directed toward adaptation to, shaping of, and selection of environments. Acceptance of a definition such as this one involves a conception of intelligence that is quite a bit broader than the definition that would emerge if intelligence were equated with IQ, which is generally inferred from performance on a range of fairly academic tasks. But what are the nature and origins of intelligent mental activities? The answer to this question depends upon the level at which the question is addressed. Consider three levels of analysis: biological, cognitive, and social-cultural.

THE BIOLOGICAL LEVEL

Many theorists of human intelligence, as of other psychological phenomena, have believed that good scientific explanation is ultimately reductionist: True understanding of intelligence will emerge when we understand intelligence as an essentially biological phenomenon. Indeed, biological work on intelligence goes back at least to the work of phrenologist Franz Gall, who sought to understand the mind in terms of patterns of bumps on the head. To many biological theorists, other levels of explanation are only temporary expedients on the way to understanding of biological bases. For example, Hans Eysenck, a British psychologist, seems to believe that the deepest understanding of intelligence is through understanding brain function.

Psychobiological studies of human intelligence have been nothing if not intriguing. Consider just a couple of the ways in which psychologists have sought to relate intelligence to brain functioning.

Evoked Potentials

Some of the earliest modern biological work on human intelligence involved evoked potentials from the brain, and this work continues. Imagine what for some would seem to be the ultimate intelligence test. The examinee sits in a booth listening to tones presented at irregular intervals. The individual is doing next to nothing—just sitting and listening to tones. But a computer monitoring the subject is doing quite a bit. Attached to the subject's head are electrodes measuring various aspects of brain function, which are combined to yield averaged evoked potentials (AEPs). These evoked potentials represent the amount and kinds of brain activity occurring within the examinee. The figure on page 189 shows auditory AEPs for six bright and six dull subjects, from the work of A. E. and D. E. Hendrickson, as measured by a conventional standardized intelligence test. Visual inspection immediately suggests a difference between the two sets of

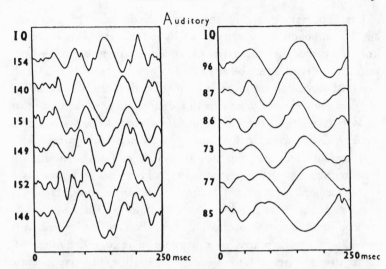

Averaged evoked potentials of six high- and six low-IQ subjects. Sources(:)
H. J. Eyenck, "Intelligence and Cognition," in *Advances in the Psychology of
Human Intelligence* (vol. 3). R. J. Sternberg, ed., (Hillsdale, New Jersey:
Erlbaum, 1986). Reprinted by permission.

AEPs: The bright individuals seem to have more complex wave forms.
The Hendricksons have derived a measure that essentially simulates a
string being lain atop the wave form. The greater the string length—
representing a more complex wave form—the greater the presumed
intelligence of the individual. The surprising finding in this work is
that the string-length measure correlates very highly with IQ (as high
as 0.8 on a scale of 0 to 1). Thus, there appears to be a substantial
relationship between what goes on in the brain and the response
produced on a conventional IQ test.

The Hendricksons' work stimulated a great deal of interest both in
the scientific community and in the popular media. The findings
responded to the longings of some scientists for the ultimate reductionist measure of intelligence and to a perceived societal need for a
"culturally fair" intelligence test. After all, what could be more
culturally fair than to have someone just sit there doing essentially
nothing? The stimulus material is not culturally bound, because there
is no stimulus material. But as is usually true in science, things are
not as simple as they seem.

First, not everyone obtains the same high correlation between AEP and IQ, although some relation usually exists. Second, it is not yet known whether the same relations, or any relations, are indeed obtained for all cultures; the research has not yet been done. Third, averaged evoked potentials are a fairly gross measure of functioning, and it is not clear just what it is in the functioning of the brain that leads to the relation between AEP and IQ. Fourth, some psychologists would question whether IQ ought to be the standard against which new measures are assessed. IQ, like AEP, is a gross measure of functioning, and many psychologists believe that it represents a highly incomplete measure of intelligence, broadly defined. Finally, it is not clear just what the direction of causality is. The AEP may be responding to cognitive functioning rather than causing it; hence, the physiological measure may be a proxy for more cognitive measures, rather than vice versa. Or both the AEP and the cognitive measure may be dependent on some other aspect of psychological functioning that is not yet understood. Thus, exciting as the relation between AEP and IQ may be, it is as yet poorly understood.

BLOOD FLOW

In an attempt to further pin down the specific parts of the brain involved in intellectual functioning, John Horn, formerly at the University of Denver and now at the University of Southern California, and his colleagues have attempted to measure loci of blood flow during intellectual functioning. The underlying idea is that flow of blood through bodily tissues is a direct indicator of functional activity in those tissues. If we could observe blood flow while people are thinking, then we might be able to pinpoint where in the brain intellectual functioning is taking place.

This work goes beyond the evoked potential work, in a sense, in its greater possibilities for locating sites of specific brain activity during thinking. Horn and his colleagues have had their subjects breathe a radioisotope, 133-Xenon, and measured the rate at which the isotope arrives and disappears at each of thirty-two sites, or scintillation detectors, within the brain while the subject is thinking. The investigators found that blood flow decreases with age, and that some areas of the brain are more affected by this decrease than others. Their results go beyond the Hendricksons' in suggesting at least some differentiation in brain functioning during intellectual activity, but these results still do not pinpoint the exact regions of the brain involved (for example, the hippocampus or amygdala). Moreover, some of the questions arising from the Hendricksons' work arise in Horn's as well. In particular, one could argue that blood flow is a proxy for cognitive processing, rather than vice versa.

THE COGNITIVE LEVEL

We saw above that the biological level of analysis seems to go hand in hand with the cognitive level. We need as much to understand the mental processes of intelligence as the sites within the brain at which these processes operate. Ideally, we would be able to map individual cognitive processes into the sites in the brain where they appear to be operative. In particular, we have to decide what the mental processes are that underlie intelligence and how they work together.

FACTORS OF INTELLIGENCE

Early cognitive research did not deal with cognitive processes at all, but with structures, or what were called the factors of intelligence. In the technical use of the term, a factor is usually viewed as a source of individual differences in observed performance. Early theorists of intelligence would give people a series of mental tests—involving such tasks as solving analogies, visualizing objects rotating in space, or solving arithmetic problems—and then apply the statistical technique of factor analysis to identify what they believed were latent sources of individual differences in intelligence. Although different factor theorists have had different lists of latent factors, all have agreed that intelligence is decomposable into such factors.

A particularly influential model of intelligence, Louis Thurstone's, posited seven basic factors of intelligence—verbal comprehension (as measured, for example, by a vocabulary test), verbal fluency (producing large numbers of words quickly), number (arithmetic computation and problem solving), spatial visualization (mentally rotating objects), perceptual speed (quickly perceiving features of stimuli), memory (remembering lists of words or numbers), and inductive reasoning (as measured by analogy and similar tests).

The work of the factor theorists responded well both to certain scientific needs and to certain societal needs of the first half of the twentieth century. The theories and the tests based on them seemed to be the right things in the right time and at the right place.

The scientific issues were straightforward. First, some behavioral scientists were envious of the ability of physical scientists to obtain fairly precise measurements of physical phenomena. Factor theory seemed to offer much the same opportunity to the behavioral sciences: perhaps attributes of people could be measured precisely. Second, factor theory seemed to offer the possibility of creating a map of the mind, much as the periodic table constitutes a map of the structure of the elements. Through factor theory, it seemed possible to decompose intelligence into its basic elements. Third, factor theory seemed to offer a scientific rationale for a sometimes controversial technological innovation, the intelligence test.

The societal issues seemed just as important. By World War II, there was a pressing need to measure some of the mental attributes of inductees in order to know just what could be expected of them both in training and in the mental rigors of combat. The IQ tests offered by psychometrists (those who measure psychological attributes) seemed to be tailor-made to the task. Additionally, and perhaps unfortunately, as Leon Kamin of Princeton and others have pointed out, certain parties were concerned about the effects of immigration on the intelligence of the U.S. population. IQ tests seemed to provide a potential measure of quality control for the influx of immigrants. Unfortunately, the tests were often inappropriate for those who were tested and were interpreted in ways that probably did more to camouflage than to reveal the truth about the mental abilities of the immigrants. Finally, it became clear that the tests had much more use for screening and diagnosis than for the purpose for which they had been developed during the war. The first major intelligence test was devised by Alfred Binet and Theophile Simon at the turn of the century to screen for mental retardation, and the test proved to be somewhat useful not only in distinguishing retarded performers but, more generally, in predicting performance in various kinds of academic and nonacademic tasks.

As usual, however, things were not as simple as they seemed. First, theorists of intelligence did not agree as to just what the right factor model was. A peculiar property of factor analysis is that it can support multiple (in fact, infinite) interpretations of a given analysis. The reason for this can be seen in the figure below. The result of a

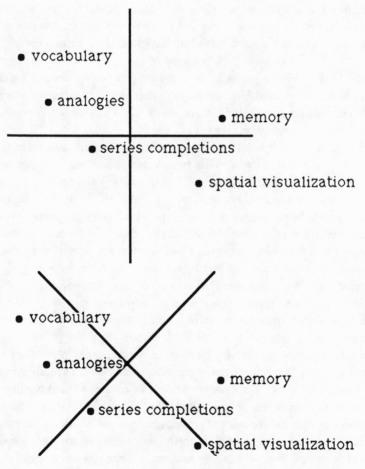

Results of a factor analysis showing fixed locations of points (tests) but variable orientations of axes (factors)

factor analysis is a set of points (the tests), which are fixed in a theoretical space of mental abilities. But in most kinds of factor analysis, whereas the locations of the points in the space are fixed, the orientation of the axes in the space, representing hypothesized abilities, is arbitrary. It is up to the factor analyst to decide on the proper orientation.

Factor theorists differed widely in their preferred orientations of axes and in the numbers of factors they chose to extract. Thus, the turn-of-the-century British theorist Charles Spearman believed that there was really only one important factor in intelligence: He labeled it the general factor and believed it corresponded to "mental energy." At the other extreme, J. P. Guilford of the University of Southern California, writing primarily in the 1950s to 1980s, argued for as many as one hundred fifty factors. Most theorists came out somewhere in the middle. But, clearly, there was no one consensually accepted number of factors or orientation of axes.

Second, the output of a factor analysis is completely dependent on the input. One can extract only factors that reflect the tests that are factor-analyzed. Investigators differed in terms of their views of just what tests should be used, and, indeed, there was really not much a priori basis for the selection of any of the tests. Hence, at least some of the disagreements among theorists derived from differences in beliefs as to what tests should be used. Third, users of the tests often overinterpreted scores, believing that IQ is a fixed and stable property of the individual. We now know that this is not true. Moreover, the tests were often used inappropriately, as in the case of the immigrants. Finally—and, from a scientific point of view, perhaps most important—most of the factor models gave little insight into the mental processes underlying intelligent performance. What does it tell us to say that scores on a reasoning test reflect an underlying "reasoning" factor? The same score could be obtained in many different ways, depending on the items solved correctly and the mental processes used in the tests. Psychologists needed a way to identify these mental processes. The cognitive revolution of the 1960s and 1970s seemed to provide a way to identify these processes.

PROCESSES OF INTELLIGENCE

Research on the mental processes underlying intelligence was motivated by the work of Herbert Simon and Allen Newell at Carnegie-Mellon University in the 1960s, as well as others, suggesting that the workings of the computer might provide a model of the mind. People, like computers, might be viewed as sequential information processors. In 1973 Earl Hunt and his colleagues Nancy Frost and Clifford Lunneborg, at the University of Washington, published a seminal paper in which they argued that intelligence should be understood in terms of mental processes. Others, such as Lee Cronbach of Stanford University and William Estes, then at Rockefeller University and now at Harvard, had made similar arguments, but Hunt and his colleagues were perhaps the first to start a detailed analysis of these processes using experimental techniques. By 1975 Hunt, Lunneborg, and Lewis (also of the University of Washington) adopted a very simple task from the literature of cognitive psychology in order to study verbal intelligence. The task requires the subject simply to decide whether successive sets of two letters are, in one condition, a physical match (for example, AA or bb) or not, or, in another, a match in name (for example, Aa or bB) or not. The task had been used previously by Michael Posner of the University of Oregon to study perceptual processing. But Hunt and his coinvestigators showed that when physical match time is subtracted from name match time (in order to control for sheer speed of responding), the difference score is correlated with scores on tests of verbal intelligence. Although the correlation is relatively modest (about 0.3 on a scale of 0 to 1), it is reputable and appears to reflect some underlying component of verbal intelligence. The investigators argued that the difference score measures speed of access to lexical information stored in long-term memory, and that the reason for the correlation is that higher-verbal people tend to process lexical information faster than lower-verbal ones and thus are able to take in more verbal information.

I argue that although speed of lexical access may well underlie aspects of verbal ability, the approach taken by Hunt and his colleagues was an oversimplification: The tasks were just too easy, and they told us more about perception and simple memory processes than about intelligence. I contend that instead, we should use more complex tasks, of the kinds found on standard intelligence tests. For example, Janet Powell and I argued in a 1981 article that verbal ability would be better understood in terms of the mental processes involved in people's learning the meaning of words from context. We analyzed these processes by presenting examinees with a passage in which are embedded words encountered only very infrequently in the English language and asking them to define those words. An example of a passage used appears below. Three key processes appear to be (a) selective encoding—picking out relevant clues for figuring out word meanings; (b) selective combination—putting the clues together in an internally consistent way; and (c) selective comparison—using old information to help in understanding new information.

In my 1977 book, *Intelligence, Information Processing, and Analogical Reasoning: The Componential Analysis of Human Abilities*, I proposed a general method and theory for the analysis of mental tasks, which I called componential analysis. The idea was that through the method, mental-task performance could be decomposed into its constituent underlying mental processes. I showed how the method could be

---

According to legend, on the night of Francesco Louis-Philippe's birth, there streaked across the midnight sky a *bolide* more blindingly magnificent than any seen before. Indeed, under his rule, the kingdom of Montaldo flared to sudden, brilliant prominence, only to be extinguished when it was overrun by the barbarous Guntherians. The constant state of warfare was a fact of life in the reign of King Louis-Philippe, and although the *spaneria* was a high price to pay, the nation overflowed with riches and national pride. Religious and political leaders took measures to ease the effects of the *spaneria* by relaxing the strict marriage laws requiring monogamy. All in all, the period was marked by a meteoric rise and decline: the many deaths, the many victories, and ensuing collapse. The Montaldans ruled the region until the armies of Guntheria destroyed them.

Passage containing extremely low-frequency words (in italics), which subject has to define on the basis of context.

applied to one of the tasks most frequently encountered in mental tests, namely analogies. The figure below presents an outline of the mental processes alleged to underlie analogical reasoning performance.

Consider, for example, the following analogy:

Rung: Ladder :: Link : (a) Net (b) Gap (c) Ring *(d) Chain.

In encoding, one perceives each of the analogy terms and retrieves from long-term memory attributes of each that may be relevant for solution of the analogy. In inference, one figures out the relation between the first two terms, here, Rung and Ladder. Thus, rungs are put together to form a ladder. In mapping, one perceives the higher-order relation that connects the first part of the analogy to the second, in this case, that both parts are about how components connect to form a whole. In application, one applies the relation inferred in the first part of the analogy to the third term to arrive at an answer. And in response, one actually chooses the correct answer, here, (d) Chain.

The diagram in the figure on page 198 shows the decomposition of a typical test item in terms of the amounts of time spent on each mental process. The decomposition shows that only a relatively small amount of time is actually spent in reasoning, as opposed to encoding and response processes.

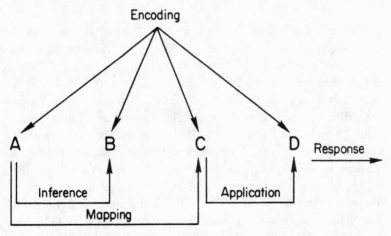

Schematic representation of theory of analogical reasoning

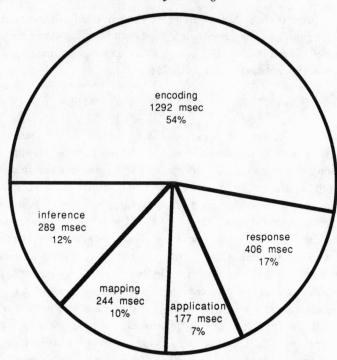

encoding
1292 msec
54%

inference
289 msec
12%

response
406 msec
17%

mapping
244 msec
10%

application
177 msec
7%

Distribution of component time on a typical verbal analogy

Whereas I and colleagues such as Robert Glaser of the University of Pittsburgh and James Pellegrino, formerly of the University of Pittsburgh and now of the University of California at Santa Barbara, argued that the tasks Earl Hunt was using were too simple, other psychologists felt that they were perhaps too complex. Arthur Jensen of the University of California at Berkeley contended that intelligence could be understood in terms of speed of mental processing on even simpler mental tasks, such as reaction. The illustration in the figure on page 199 shows the apparatus Jensen used in his studies of the relationship between mental speed and psychometric intelligence. The subject's task is to move her finger from the central button to a button in the semicircle as soon as the light above it goes on. Only one light goes on for each trial. Jensen found that performance even on this very basic task could be viewed as an indicator of intelligence, again under the view that faster mental speed enables one to extract

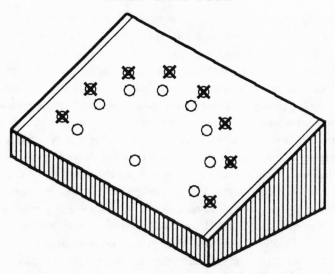

Subject's console of the reaction time-movement time apparatus note: "Push" buttons are indicated by circles, green jeweled lights by circled crosses. The "home" button is in the lower center, six inches from each response button.

more information from the environment and to retrieve it more quickly as the need arises. Jensen also found, however, that the greater the number of choices to be made, the greater the correlation with IQ. Thus, increasing the mental-processing load seems to increase the association. This finding is consistent with the notion that I and others have advanced that at least some complexity seems to enhance the extent to which a cognitive task taps intelligence.

The cognitive-based research programs of Hunt, Jensen, and others, as well as my own, responded to a societal need to understand just what it is that underlies IQ and, possibly, to generate alternatives to the standard intelligence test. At the same time, they responded to a scientific need to understand intelligence in a way that reflects the mental processes involved in intelligent performance. By the 1970s some scientists had come to view much psychometric theorizing as having reached a dead end, and the new cognitive work seemed to offer a promise of a new start toward understanding intelligence. In particular, individual differences in intelligence could be understood in terms of differences not only in speed of mental functioning, but also in the mental processes, strategies, and representations brought to bear on problems requiring intelligent thought. In these years, the computer metaphor was king.

By the 1980s some researchers were becoming somewhat disenchanted with the new cognitive enterprise for at least three reasons. First, although cognitive analysis helped understand intelligence at a micro level of analysis, some scholars believed that the big picture was being lost. It was not always clear how all the elementary processes of cognition worked together in an intelligent way. Second, some scholars had come, at least partially, to reject the computer as a model of the mind. There seemed to be enough disanalogies between the workings of computers and of minds so that some less mechanistic model seemed to be called for: For example, people, unlike computers, are influenced by their motivations and emotions. Third, the cognitive researchers never really went beyond the IQ in their understanding of intelligence. Their criteria for assessing their analyses were the very psychometric IQ scores that they were criticizing. But to some psychologists, IQ seemed both narrow in the understanding of intelligence it provided and culturally bound in the types of things it measured. By the 1980s psychologists sought to understand intelligence in a broader way that did justice both to the mental processes underlying intelligence and to the cultural limitations of the psychometric and cognitive models underlying the study of the IQ. Such investigations proceeded by attempting to understand the social-cultural as well as the cognitive underpinnings of human intelligence.

THE SOCIAL-CULTURAL LEVEL

The findings of cross-cultural psychologists working in the 1970s and 1980s, such as Mallory Wober, Michael Cole, and Sylvia Scribner, were demonstrating that Western theories of intelligence simply do not do justice to notions of intelligence as they exist around the world. Although the cognitive factors and processes elicited in cross-cultural work did not seem to differ from one culture to another, the ways in which they were applied both to simple cognitive tasks and to everyday life did. For example, Wober, working at Maykerere University in Uganda, found that what was considered to be intelligent in the Baganda tribe of Uganda was considered to be unintelligent in the Batoro tribe, and vice versa. The Baganda associate intelligence with mental order, whereas the Batoro associate it with mental turmoil. Now of the University of California at San Diego, Cole, and Scribner, now at City University of New York, found that people in some cultures simply would not accept the task of solving abstract syllogisms because the problems posited information that they would not accept as true. Joe Glick of the City University of New York found that the kind of taxonomic categorizations that forms the basis for Western thinking just did not apply in the same way among the Kpelle tribe in Africa.

Findings such as these have yielded a variety of positions among cross-cultural and other psychologists regarding the relativity of the nature of intelligence as a function of culture. John Berry of Queens University in Canada, considering results such as those described above as well as his own, has gone so far as to suggest that intelligence is a completely different phenomenon from one culture to another. Michael Cole and the members of his Laboratory of Comparative Human Cognition have suggested that limited comparisons among cultures can be made. According to their view, it is possible to draw a kind of conditional comparison across cultures, in which the scientist sees how different cultures have organized experience to deal with a single domain of activity. Least extreme, perhaps, are the views of psychologists such as Paul Baltes of the Max Planck Institute in Berlin and Daniel Keating of the Ontario Institutes for the Study of Education, who combine contextual views with more or less standard kinds of experimentations.

INTEGRATIONS OF LEVELS

Two theorists, Howard Gardner and I, have sought to integrate at least some of the levels of understanding intelligence by testing theories that address the role of intelligence in society.

MULTIPLE INTELLIGENCES

In 1983, Howard Gardner of Harvard University proposed what he called a theory of multiple intelligences, according to which mental abilities are understood as contributing not to a single entity, intelligence, but rather to multiple independent entities, or intelligences. On the basis of a review of diverse research literatures, Gardner proposed a tentative list of such intelligences: linguistic, logical-mathematical, spatial, bodily-kinesthetic, musical, interpersonal, and intrapersonal. Below is a list of examples of tasks that would be included within each of these intelligences.

Gardner's view of intelligence differs from conventional ones in several respects. First, he proposes that each intelligence is independent of the others, having its own perceptual, memory, reasoning, and other processes. Second, he includes within the domain of intelligence talents that usually have been considered outside its purview. For example, musical ability has not conventionally been viewed as an "intelligence," and bodily-kinesthetic ability would correspond roughly to what in the past has been called athletic ability rather than intelligence. This extension of the concept of intelligence has generated a great deal of controversy. Some would question, for example, whether a spastic, or an individual with cerebral palsy, should be viewed as "unintelligent" in any sense, even though that person's bodily-kinesthetic ability may be low.

---

1. Linguistic—writing poetry or novels
2. Logical-mathematical—solving mathematical and scientific problems
3. Spatial—forming mental images
4. Bodily-kinesthetic—dancing, throwing or catching a football
5. Musical—composing, playing an instrument
6. Interpersonal—noticing and understanding other people's moods, temperaments, intentions
7. Intrapersonal—accessing one's own feelings, understanding oneself

---

Gardner's list of intelligences, and tasks involving these intelligences.

A TRIARCHIC VIEW

In 1984 I suggested an alternative formulation that incorporates more conventional notions of intelligence into a broader framework. In my triarchic theory, I propose that intelligence needs to be understood in terms of three aspects—its relation to the individual's internal world, its relation to the individual's external world, and its relation to experience.

The relation to the internal world is understood in terms of the mental-processing components and strategies that formed the basis of my earlier componential theory. These processes and strategies are proposed to be universal with respect to the cultures of the world. The relation to the external world is understood in terms of how these mental processes and strategies are applied to adapt to, shape, and select environments. In my view, intelligence in context represents a balance between knowing when and how to adapt to a given environment and when and how either to mold the environment so as to make it more suitable for one's pattern of abilities, interests, values, and so on, or to leave it in favor of another (selection). In one's work, for example, it is important to know when to accept a given system for getting things done and when to create a new one. I have found in my research that people with high IQs are not necessarily very high in terms of their contextual intelligence, and vice versa. For example, knowledge of tricks of the trade in business is only minimally predicted by IQ. Contextual instantiations of intelligence can differ from one culture to another, as with the Baganda and Batoro. Finally, I propose that the components of intelligence as applied to the environment most critically involve intelligence when they are applied either to relatively novel tasks and situations or to the automatization of information processing. The degree of novelty of a task or situation can also differ across cultures. Navigating by the stars, for example, is routine in the Puluwat society, but not in our own. Automatization involves the transition from mental processes' being conscious, deliberate, and serial to their being subconscious, automatic, and parallel in their execution. For example, when one first learns to read, one's reading is quite controlled; eventually reading becomes fairly automatic for most of us. The figure on page 204 shows how the various aspects of the theory fit together, and on page 205 are examples of tasks used to measure each aspect.

The broader views of intelligence Howard Gardner and I proposed are new enough so that all the evidence is not yet in with regard to both their scientific validity and their utility. But it is clear that the theories respond to what had become a need both within science and within the society at large—the need to view intelligence in a way that is broad enough to reflect its full richness, rather than merely through the tasks that happen to appear on conventional intelligence tests. Some psychologists find these conceptions of intelligence too

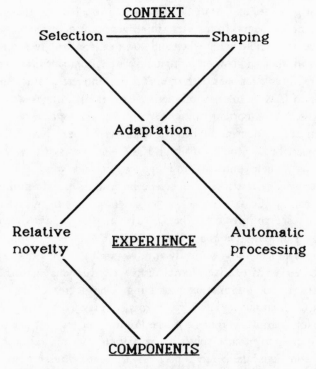

Structure of the Triarchic Theory of Intelligence. Note: Mental-processing components are applied to experience to serve three functions in everyday contexts: adaptation to, selection of, and shaping of the environment.

1. In our society, where families are often spread across the states and neighbors are strangers, *mid* is a constant complaint. Mental health professionals treat the condition primarily through extended counseling sessions, but when anxiety and nervousness are pronounced, tranquilizers may be necessary.

Mid most likely means:
  (a) fear of travel
  *(b) fear of loneliness
  (c) fear of instability
  (d) fear of dependency

2. These numbers are *bir*: 9, 27, 6, 42, 33
   These numbers are *taz*: 10, 12, 14, 2, 24
   Which one of the following numbers is both *bir* and *taz*?
   (a) 8   (b) 52   *(c) 36   (d) 21

3. Suppose that all villains are lovable. Which completion would now be correct?
   Hero is to admiration as villain is to _____
   (a) contempt   *(b) affection   (c) cruel   (d) kind

4. A gum machine contains 20 white gum balls, 30 blue gum balls, and 40 red gum balls. Each piece of gum costs a penny. How many pennies must you put in to make sure you get two pieces of gum the same color?
   (a) 2   (b) 3   *(c) 4   (d) 5

5. The advertisement for the Sweet Life Savings Bank reads, "We guarantee the highest possible interest rate on all savings accounts." Professor Economos looked at the ad and immediately switched his money from the Drysdale Savings Bank to Sweet Life.

Assuming the Sweet Life Savings Bank advertisement was honest, Professor Economos could be guaranteed to:
   (a) earn higher interest at Sweet Life than at Drysdale
   (b) earn the same interest at Sweet Life as at Drysdale
   *(c) earn at least as much at Sweet Life as at Drysdale
   (d) earn the same interest at Sweet Life as at any other bank making the same claim as Sweet Life

Typical items from the Sternberg Multidimensional Abilities Test (SMAT), based on the triarchic theory of intelligence.

broad. The greatest problem with such broad theories is perhaps that they are difficult to disconfirm: It is not clear just what sorts of evidence would, in fact, wholly disconfirm them. At the same time, each theory has enough testable stipulations so that at least parts of each can be disconfirmed—for example, Gardner's claim regarding the independence of the intelligence or my claim that intelligence can vary drastically, depending on the kinds of contexts to which it is applied.

CONCLUSION

Scientists studying intelligence have a problem that scientists studying phenomena such as electricity or star formations do not have: The former do not quite agree as to what their subject is. As Ulric Neisser of Emory University has pointed out, intelligence is an ill-defined construct. But most psychologists studying intelligence agree on a number of essential points, such as the need to understand the cognitive processes underlying intelligence and, ultimately, the biological functions underlying these processes.

We do not yet have a fully integrative model of human intelligence. But I suggest that such a model would have to specify, at minimum, the mental processes and strategies underlying intelligent behavior, the patterns of differences among people generated by these processes and strategies, the various brain sites at which the processes and strategies operate, and how the processes and strategies are brought to bear upon everyday life in one's social-cultural setting. Although the mental processes required for intelligent problem solving can differ somewhat from one problem to another, one set of processes, sometimes called executive mental processes, seem to be critical in the solution of virtually every kind of problem, regardless of the way in which problem solving is analyzed. These processes include recognizing the existence of a problem, defining the nature of the problem, selecting processes and strategies for solving the problem, mentally representing the problem, allocating one's mental and material resources in solving the problem, and monitoring and evaluating one's progress in solving the problem.

Consider, for example, the solution of an algebraic problem. The factor analyst might attribute successful solution of the problem to a high level of a "quantitative reasoning" factor, whereas the psycho-biologist might attribute it to patterns of evoked potentials. The cognitive psychologist would define the quantitative reasoning factor in terms of executive mental processes, such as problem definition and representation, and of nonexecutive ones, such as computing arith-metically. All of these accounts would be complementary in under-standing algebraic problem solving at various levels of analysis.

By studying intelligence at different levels, psychologists are piec-ing together what they hope will be a comprehensive view of the whole multifaceted phenomenon. Research is proceeding rapidly on a number of fronts, dictated by the needs of both science and society. This rapidity of progress is a relatively new development. In the first sixty or so years of the century, progress on the research front was slower, perhaps in part because of curious interaction between science and technology. The enormous success of conventional intelligence tests, and the financial profits to be made from them, probably resulted in a slowing of research that might lead to new types of instruments. Paradoxically, then, technological success can slow down basic research if the success of the technology leads to the belief that a basic problem is solved, or solved well enough. Technological innovations sometimes have too long a shelf life, as we have seen in typing with the QWERTY keyboard or in computer science with the Fortran language. Both innovations have stayed around longer than they probably should have, largely because of the tremendous invest-ment individuals and collectivities have had in them and their spin-offs. New ideas for keyboards and computer language have not been lacking, but gaining acceptance for them has been a slow process, as it undoubtedly will be for new kinds of intelligence tests that are proposed. But as new theories of intelligence emerge, new tests of intelligence based on them seem likely to gain acceptance, even if their acceptance is still some way off.

Memes vs. Genes: Notes from the Culture Wars

MIHALY CSIKSZENTMIHALYI

> . . . *cultural forms can evolve and grow without necessarily enhancing the biological fitness of the individuals who produced them. The monks who developed European culture in the Middle Ages transmitted art and learning instead of genes. That these two ways of transmitting information across time are often in conflict was recognized long ago by the Latin saying* libri aut liberi—*books or children. It is indeed difficult to spawn biological and cultural progeny at the same time.*

Humanity discovered evolution just a little more than a century ago. For the span of a few generations we thought this meant that the future belonged to humankind. During the Victorian era and up to World War I, it seemed that we were slated to be benevolent rulers of the entire planet. This brief period of optimism had barely time to blossom before it already seemed part of a nostalgic past. As we approach the end of the century it is getting more and more difficult to believe that we are making progress toward the rational control of evolutionary processes. Indeed, the very concept of evolution is coming under attack.

Despite these setbacks, evolution still seems the best way to explain what has happened in the past, what is happening now, and, to a certain extent, what will happen in the future. But in order to understand events in human history from the evolutionary perspective, which so far has taken into account changes in the biological structure and function of living organisms, evolution must be expanded to include events of a different kind, following different laws from those that hold for the transmission of genes—changes that take place in the realm of society and culture.

Scholars have debated the relative contributions of biology and culture to human evolution, especially after Edward O. Wilson formulated the theses of sociobiological determinism. The question is whether changes in art, science, religion, economics, politics, and other cultural systems obey their own rules, or whether they are shaped by the same forces that account for the selection and transmission of genes.

It makes sense to assume that evolution consists of the interaction of two parallel but related processes, one biological and the other cultural. They have separate mechanisms for producing new information, for selecting certain variants, and for transmitting them over time.

For example, art historians trace the evolution of domelike structures in Western Europe from the Roman Pantheon rebuilt by Hadrian in the second century, through the baptistery of Florence in the twelfth century, through Brunelleschi's dome of the Cathedral of Florence in the fifteenth century, and ending with Michelangelo's dome over St. Peter's in Rome about a hundred years later. The changing shapes of the dome were not due to genetic mutations in the architects' chromosomes, but to attempts to improve on culturally mediated instructions—plans, theories, calculations, and information passed on from masters to apprentices. Each dome may not have been "better" than the previous one, but it is clear that one "evolved" from the other in the sense that the latter included the technical and esthetic knowledge of earlier forms, plus changes that had not been possible before.

This means that cultural forms can evolve and grow without necessarily enhancing the biological fitness of the individuals who produced them. The monks who developed European culture in the Middle Ages transmitted art and learning instead of genes. That these two ways of transmitting information across time are often in conflict was recognized long ago by the Latin saying *libri aut liberi*—books or children. It is indeed difficult to spawn biological and cultural progeny at the same time.

Occasionally people try to eliminate information they fear. The Romans systematically destroyed everything written in Etruscan so that they could impose their cultural hegemony over Italy. When the great library of Alexandria was put to the torch, much of our Greek heritage perished with it. During the Great Cultural Revolution the Chinese lost so much of their culture that very few people are left now who know how to read the ancient texts that were saved from the flames. But the opposite also happens: Ideas, beliefs, and wrong information kill people perhaps more often than the other way around. Sometimes a small difference in religious interpretation leads to the death of tens of thousands of people, as during the Albigensian wars of the thirteenth century.

Cultural forms depend on the environment of human consciousness. Ideas and artifacts reproduce and grow in the mind, responding to selective pressures that are in principle independent of those that constrain genetic evolution. Because of this independence, it is perfectly possible to start up trains of thought that in the long run will be injurious to our survival. We tend to select new cultural forms that promise to give more power, comfort, or pleasure. But like selective mechanisms that operate in biological evolution, this one, too, has potential dangers as well as obvious advantages.

Cultural evolution can be defined as the differential transmission of information contained in artifacts—in objects, concepts, beliefs, symbols, and behavior patterns that exist only because people took the trouble to make them. While artifacts are human products, they in turn shape human consciousness. A person with a gun, for instance, is different from an unarmed man. It makes no sense to say, as the National Rifle Association does, that "guns don't kill people, people do." People in the abstract don't exist. They are made by the culture in which they live, by the objects they use, the words they hear, the ideas they come across. We have biologically programmed propensities for aggression as well as for compassion and for cooperation. Which of these potentials we realize depends on the cultural environment. When everyone carries a gun, it becomes "natural" to act out the aggressive script instead of the cooperative one.

Artifacts contain implicit instructions for how to behave because they define the reality within which we operate. Children born in a fishing village automatically adapt to a technology of boats and nets, just as spontaneously as they adopt the local language. Some artifacts also contain *explicit* directions for action; they are the norms, regulations, and laws. They parallel even more clearly the function of genetic instructions that direct behavior. But while genetic instructions are coded chemically in the chromosomes, the information contained in artifacts is coded and stored outside the body—in the action potential inherent in objects, drawings, texts, and the behavior patterns of other individuals with whom one interacts. We might use the term "meme," coined by Richard Dawkins for the replicating unit of cultural information.

⊏===⊐

We like to believe that cultural evolution serves the goal of human adaptation. According to this view, memes survive only if they enhance the inclusive fitness of the individuals who use them. Artifacts evolve because they help to make our lives better. Cultural forms become destructive and dangerous only when they are misused. For instance, the reason armaments have evolved from stone axes to space lasers is that we have not been able to resolve competition for resources without resorting to aggressiveness. If people only learned to curb their belligerence, weapons would cease to multiply. This perspective on the evolution of culture is basically reassuring because it holds that the growth of artifacts is held in check by human control.

But thinking this way might blind us to the real state of affairs. It is possible that weapons and other artifacts evolve regardless of our intentions. In effect, the multiplication and diffusion of artifacts follows its own logic to a large extent independently of the welfare of its carriers. The relationship of memes to humans is sometimes symbiotic, sometimes parasitic. Although they need consciousness as their growth environment, this dependence is not different, in principle, from our dependence on plants or on a breathable atmosphere. And just as we might kill the environment that made and supported us, the artifacts we created could well destroy us in the end.

Memes often spread in human cultures despite people's initial opposition. Some of the most important steps of civilization, such as the transition from the free life of the hunters to the more regimented life of the nomadic shepherds, and then to the even more restricted life of the farmers, were at first bitterly resisted. The diffusion of coins and currency across the globe initially caused an enormous amount of unhappiness. People just didn't take easily to a money economy, which seemed so much more impersonal and arbitrary, and so much less fun, than bartering had been.

Whenever there is a change in the culture, we assume that it was something we meant to happen, even though on reflection it seems that we are rather helpless in the matter. For instance, most people believe that new car models are introduced because manufacturers are greedy. But in reality they can't help doing what they do. As long as customers automatically prefer novelty, each new advance in technology makes it mandatory to add the latest gimmicks to existing models. In a free market this means that even if all the manufacturers declined to change, new capital would be attracted to produce a car that included the up-to-date features. We are in the habit of thinking that businesspeople use technology to achieve competitive advantages. From a less anthropocentric viewpoint, the same scenario could be described as technology using producers and consumers as a medium in which to prosper. Unless actively restrained, memes continue to grow and multiply on their own.

Cultural evolution has its own propaganda apparatus, complete with ideology and slogans that people repeat over and over mechanically. One of my favorites is the phrase "It's here to stay," applied to new products and processes. It serves as a handy Trojan horse to lull our sense of judgment. This innocuous-sounding phrase heralds the territorial ambitions of the meme: Ready or not, here I come.

Weapons provide a clear example of how memes change and propagate. The information in a weapon, when decoded by our mind, says that the amount of threat must be countered with a weapon that contains at least as much threat as the first, and possibly more. Thus, the threat of the knife begets the sword, the sword begets the spear, the spear begets the arrow, the arrow begets the bolt, the bolt begets the bullet . . . and so on to Star Wars. This progress may or may not benefit the biological survival of the human host. There is no evidence, for example, that the people of the Tuscan city of Pistoia, who first manufactured the pistol more than five centuries ago, have received any particular benefits in terms of inclusive fitness over their neighbors. On the other hand, the relative decline of Native Americans is due in large part to the fact that the Caucasian invaders had more and better firearms.

Like other patterns of organization, whether physical, chemical, biological, or informational in their composition, memes will propagate as long as the environment is conducive to growth. There is no reason to expect, for instance, that weapons will stop taking over more and more resources unless their growth environment in human consciousness is made less hospitable. The problem is, of course, that many people find the information contained in weaponry congenial. For some, paradoxically, weapons provide a relief from existential anxiety. Others find in the manufacture of weapons a source of profit. A few are intellectually challenged by the technology—Robert Oppenheimer used to refer to his work on the nuclear bomb as "that sweet problem."

Weapons are an obviously problematic species of memes, but the same argument holds for cultural forms that on the surface appear to be more benign. The control over the transformations of matter that modern physics and chemistry have brought about, when translated into uncontrolled technology, has reached a point of diminishing returns. Physical energy gets compressed in ever more explosive concentrations, without a clear idea of whether we shall be able to control its release. New substances are being created regardless of how useful they are, simply because it is possible to produce them. As a result the planetary environment, polluted by noxious substances, is growing to be increasingly unfit for human existence. And when genetic engineering becomes a going concern, it is doubtful that the new forms of life that gene splicing makes possible will be designed with the ultimate welfare of human life in mind—partly because it is impossible to know at this point what that is. Rather, the proliferation of new life forms will be dictated by whatever the technology can accomplish, regardless of consequences. Unless, of course, humankind realizes that its physical survival might be threatened by the evolution of culture, and it is willing to take this threat seriously.

Because artifacts are born and develop in the medium of the human mind, in order to understand the dynamics of cultural evolution it is necessary to consider how consciousness selects and transmits information.

While the *content* of socio-cultural evolution exists outside the body, the *process* that makes it possible takes place within consciousness. The three phases common to all evolutionary processes—variation, selection, and transmission—are mediated by the mind. Cultural variation begins when new memes arise as ideas, actions, or perceptions of outside events. Selection among variant memes, and retention of the selected ones, also involves a more or less conscious evaluation and investment of attention. And so does the transmission of the retained meme. Unless people invested time and attention—psychic energy—in the new variant, it would not survive long enough for the next generation to be aware of its existence. New products, political ideas, and path-breaking works of art will disappear without a trace unless they find a receptive medium in the minds of a large enough audience.

This difference between biological and cultural evolution has some important consequences. Perhaps the most important is that in genetic evolution, selection, to a very large degree, is accomplished by impersonal environmental conditions. Whether a given mutation will be retained or not generally depends on the climate, the nature of the food supply, the mix of predators and parasites, plus a myriad of other factors that interact with the mutation and determine its contribution to the fitness of the organism. In socio-cultural evolution, selection is mediated by consciousness. Whether a new idea or practice is viable does not depend directly on external conditions, but on our choices.

This does not mean, of course, that such things as climate or predators have no effect on cultural evolution. To the contrary, external conditions often dictate which innovations are selected. Two of the most fundamentally early cultural inventions, fire and stone weapons, are obvious examples: They were selected because they helped us cope with the climate and compete for the food supply. Our current fascination with nuclear physics is basically not that different: The energy of the atom is sought both to warm our homes and to destroy our enemies. But in cultural evolution the constraints of temperature and competitive pressure do not affect the survival of information through the differential reproductive rates of the organisms that carry it. The constraints are represented in human consciousness, and it is there that the decision is made whether to replicate the meme. It is clearly not the case that atomic reactors have multiplied because those who developed them have had more children—if anything, the contrary is probably true.

Because the variation, selection, and retention of memes occur in consciousness, we must consider their dynamics in order to understand socio-cultural evolution. Perhaps the most fundamental issue is the limitation of the mind as an information-processing apparatus. There is so much we will never know, simply because our brain is not equipped to handle the information. The limitation is both qualitative, referring to the kind of things we are able to recognize, and quantitative, referring to how many things we can be aware of at a given time. Although the qualitative limitations of consciousness are probably the most interesting in the long run, in this context only the consequences of quantitative limitations will be explored.

Information matters only if we attend to it. It is impossible to learn a language or a skill unless we invest a sizable amount of attention in the task. This means that each person is an informational bottleneck; there are only so many memes that he or she can process at any given time. According to the best estimates, the human organism is limited to discriminating a maximum of about seven bits—or chunks—of information per unit of time. It is estimated that the duration of each "attentional unit" is of the order of one-eighteenth per second; in other words, we can become aware of about 18 times 7 bits of information, or 126 bits, in the space of a second. Thus a person can process at most in the neighborhood of 7,560 bits of information each minute. In a lifetime of 70 years, and assuming a waking day of 16 hours, it amounts to about 185 billion bits of information. This number defines the upper limit of individual experience. Out of it must come every perception, thought, feeling, memory, or action that a person will ever have. It seems like a large number, but in actuality none of us finds it nearly large enough.

To get a sense for how little can be accomplished with the amount of attention at our disposal, consider how much it takes just to follow an ordinary conversation. It is claimed that extracting meaning from speech signals would take forty thousand bits of information per second if each bit had to be attended to separately, or 317 times as much as we can actually handle. Fortunately, our species-specific genetic programming allows us to chunk speech into phonemes automatically, thereby reducing the load to forty bits per second—or approximately one-third of the total processing capacity of attention. This is why we cannot follow a conversation and at the same time do any other demanding mental task. Just to decode what other people are saying, even though it is to a large extent an effortless and automated process, preempts any other task that requires a full commitment of attention.

As the above example suggests, "chunking" information greatly extends the limits for processing it. Some people conclude from this fact that consciousness is a boundless "open" system, and that the information we can attend to can be indefinitely multiplied. This optimistic reading of the situation, however, flies in the face of the facts. Despite our spectacular success in chunking phonemes, it is still impossible to listen to more than three conversations at the same time. It is unlikely that we will ever be able to pull up two socks simultaneously, and it is difficult to imagine a person being able to talk to a child and write a sonnet at the same time.

Because attention is the medium that makes events occur in consciousness, it is useful to think of it as "psychic energy." Any nonreflex action takes up a certain fraction of this energy. Just listening to an ordinary conversation closely enough to understand what is being said takes up one-third of it at any given time. Stirring a cup of coffee, reaching for a newspaper, and trying to remember a telephone number all require information-processing space out of that limited total. Of course, individuals vary widely in terms of how much of their psychic energy they use (how many bits they process), and in terms of what they invest their energy in.

The limitations on the information-processing capacities of consciousness have clear implications for the evolution of culture. Only a few new memes out of the variations constantly being produced are noticed, few are retained, and even fewer are transmitted to a new generation.

The rate at which new variations are produced depends to a large extent on how much attention free from survival demands is available. In addition, it depends on what cultural instructions there are regarding new memes. Some cultures, like the ancient Egyptian civilization, actively discouraged variants. Others, like current Western societies, are ideologically primed to encourage their overproduction. Thus, how frequently new memes appear is a function both of the basic scarcity of attention and of the social organization of attention that may either facilitate or inhibit the emergence of new artifacts.

After a new meme is produced, its retention is also constrained by the amount of attention available in the given human environment. According to the census there are at present about two hundred thousand Americans who classify themselves as artists. It is probably safe to assume that no more than one in ten thousand from among their works will be preserved even one generation from now as part of the information that constitutes the symbolic system of the visual arts. Every year about fifty thousand new books are published in the United States. This number already constitutes a selection from probably one million manuscripts submitted, most of which do not get published. But how many of these volumes will be remembered in ten years, how many in a hundred? The same argument holds for scholarly articles, inventions, popular songs, or new products. The environment of consciousness that allows artifacts to exist is restricted and provides a severe selective pressure on their survival.

The rate of selection and retention of new memes is again a function of both the scarcity of attention and the social organization thereof. Each person must have a theoretical upper limit on how many paintings he or she can admire, how many scientific formulas he can remember, or how many products of each kind he can consume. Thus, societies must also have limits on how many works of art, scientific facts, or commercial products they can recognize and assimilate. It is naïve to assume that progress can be enhanced by encouraging more people to be creative: If there is not enough psychic energy available to recognize creative changes, they will simply be wasted. At certain historical periods, some communities have disposed of unusual amounts of free attention. Greece twenty-five centuries ago, Florence five hundred years ago, and Paris in the nineteenth century were able to stimulate and to retain cultural variations at unusually high rates. Occasionally communities become specialized niches for certain kinds of memes; music flowered in eighteenth- and nineteenth-century Vienna; Göttingen in the late nineteenth century and Budapest in the early twentieth century provided fertile soil for mathematics; Goethe's Weimar was receptive to poetry, and so forth. But eventually no human community has enough attention to keep more than a few of the many new artifacts that are constantly produced. At the point of saturation, a selective process begins to operate.

Of the few innovations that eventually end up in the symbolic system of society, even fewer will be transmitted to the next generation. It is not enough for a meme to be preserved in a book or an object. To survive, it has to affect the consciousness of at least some people. A language that is no longer spoken or at least read becomes a "dead" language. When people forget the key to its meaning, as has happened with Etruscan, the language loses its informational structure and stops growing and reproducing. The transmission of cultural information through time requires expensive investments of attention. Several institutions exist primarily to carry out this function. For instance, schools specialize in the transmission of memes, although anyone familiar with them knows what a small fraction of the cultural heritage is actually passed on within their walls. Another example are the public behavioral instructions codified in political constitutions. All of the nations of the world have constitutions that specify appropriate behaviors concerning the same dozen or so units of information (such as work, property, income, education, decision-making, and so on), although the hierarchical relations between these units vary. The continuity of constitutional texts can be traced back to Roman law and the British Magna Carta. But they don't survive naturally. Great social resources must be invested for their preservation. Without courts, judges, lawyers, police, schools, and a host of other institutions, the instructions contained in constitutions would be disregarded and eventually forgotten.

Human environments favorable to cultural evolution are characterized by surplus attention, by a social organization that encourages novelty, by social arrangements that facilitate the retention and transmission of new variants, and by informational skills that are far enough developed to recognize and integrate the variation within their symbol systems. When a society has these characteristics, it becomes a favorable medium for the spread of artifacts. But whether this will benefit the people who become hosts to cultural evolution is another issue entirely.

▭

The survival of new memes does not depend only on environmental factors, such as the amount and the social organization of attention in the human milieu. It also depends on how the information itself is patterned. In other words, some memes are fitter than others in the sense that the information contained in them is going to spread to more minds and be remembered longer. It is impossible to give a general description of what makes a new artifact successful, any more than it is possible to describe a successful genetic mutation, and for identical reasons. Just as the fitness of a new mutation depends on the environment to which the phenotype is adapted, so is the viability of a new cultural form dependent on the prior state of the culture and the human environment in which it appears.

Nevertheless, it is possible to point out some characteristics of memes that help their diffusion in a wide range of contexts. The first requirement of a new cultural form is that it be identifiable as such. Every symbolic domain has formal or informal criteria for establishing whether a meme is a genuine new variant. The Patent Office and the copyright laws use formal definitions, while in other fields like science and art a consensus of experts decides whether an artifact is really new. To be so identified a variant must depart from previous artifacts to a substantial extent, yet not so much as to be unrecognizable. The range of optimal variation is one characteristic that defines the viability of new memes.

In social contexts where new memes are seen to be dangerous, elaborate institutions might be established to test new ideas and other artifacts to determine whether they constitute variations from the accepted orthodoxy. In some historical periods the Christian Church spent great efforts to identify "heresy," which referred to cultural variants that had to be eliminated from the consciousness of the population. Even now the function of the Vatican's Sacred Congregation for the Doctrine of the Faith, a successor to the Inquisition and to the Holy Office, is to eliminate books and teachings that introduce unacceptable variations into the religious meme pool. Similar institutions exist in the Soviet Union, and in all societies built on the assumption that the structure of information they already have is superior to any possible new form. Such mechanisms of social control try to separate new artifacts that are beneficial to the commonwealth from those that are not. In principle this could be a useful function once it is admitted that cultural evolution need not coincide with human welfare. Historically, though, the censorship of new ideas has been informed more often by the desire to maintain a particular power structure than by the desire to maximize the well-being of the population.

Once it is established that an artifact is genuinely new, the next question becomes: Should it be preserved? A great variety of reasons determines why one meme will be selected for retention while thousands of others are eliminated and forgotten. Economy is one general criterion. Any artifact that saves scarce human resources has a better chance of surviving. And, attention being one of the most precious resources, artifacts that save time and concentration generally have an edge in fitness. Thus, the evolution of symbol systems representing language, quantities, and other forms of representation always tends toward memes that will accomplish equal or better effects with a saving of attention. The ascendancy of the metric system over competing systems of measurement or the general adoption of the North Semitic alphabet are good examples of how savings in attention will positively select a more efficient set of symbols. The same is true of the evolution of tools, appliances, and social customs. A cheaper price is just a corollary of the same principle, since the advantage of saving money is simply a special case of saving attention—money being what is exchanged for psychic energy invested into productive tasks. If a book or a car is less expensive than an equivalent brand, buying the cheaper one saves psychic energy that would have gone into earning the difference in price; the attention saved can then be invested either into making more money or into pleasurable experiences.

While economy of attention is a very important criterion for the selection of artifacts, it is certainly not the only one. Perhaps the most universal qualification of positively selected artifacts is that they improve the quality of experience. Whenever a new cultural form promises pleasure or enjoyment, it will find a receptive niche in consciousness. This reason for the adoption of a new artifact is well expressed by the Greek poet who welcomed the invention of the water mill two thousand years ago, as quoted by the historian Marc Bloch: "Spare your hands, which have been long familiar with the millstone, you maidens who used to crush the grain. Henceforth you shall sleep long, oblivious to the crowing cocks who greet the dawn." Compared to the millstone, the water mill offered women smoother hands, less physical effort, and more disposable time—presumably adding up to an overall improvement in the quality of life.

Clearly enjoyment is the main reason why we select and retain most works of art. Painting, music, drama, architecture, and writing are symbolic skills adopted because they produce positive states of consciousness. So do mystery novels and television programs, which appear to "waste" psychic energy but do so while providing pleasurable information in return for the investment of attention.

But some of the most utilitarian artifacts also survive because they provide enjoyment to those who use them. In discussing the introduction of the first metal objects at the end of the Stone ages, Colin Renfrew writes:

> In several areas of the world it has been noted, in the case of metallurgical innovations in particular, that the development of bronze and other metals as *useful* commodities was a much later phenomenon than their first utilization as new and attractive materials, employed in contexts of display. . . . In most cases early metallurgy appears to have been practiced primarily because the products had novel properties that made them attractive to use as symbols and as personal adornments and ornaments, in a manner that, by focusing attention, could attract or enhance prestige.

Products with novel properties continue to attract attention regardless of utilitarian considerations. Interest in automobiles started not because of their usefulness, but because stunts and races captured people's imagination. A recent promotional brochure from Alfa Romeo states: "In 1910, a car company was created that was destined to distinguish itself from all others. A company built on the simple philosophy that a car shouldn't be merely a means of transportation, but *a source of exhilaration* . . ." This is wrong only in claiming that such a "philosophy" was unique to this particular manufacturer; in fact, most early cars were built with that goal in mind (a point recognized six pages later in the same brochure: "The Triumph TR3. The Austin Healey 3000. The Jaguar XKE . . . They were sleek, sensual, agile . . . Designed and built for the sheer joy of driving, *they made no pretense whatsoever of practicality*"). The same trend can be recognized at the inception of many cultural innovations, from the airplane to the personal computer.

According to the great Dutch cultural historian Johan Huizinga, human institutions originally arise as games that provide enjoyment to the players and the spectators; only later do they become serious elements of social structure. At first, the thoughts and actions these institutions require are freely accepted; later they become the taken-for-granted elements of social reality. Thus, science starts as riddling contests, religion as joyful collective celebrations, military institutions start as ceremonial combat, the legal system has its origins in ritualized debates, and economic systems often begin as festive reciprocal exchanges. Those forms that provide the most enjoyment are selected and transmitted down the generations.

But once a set of memes, for whatever reason, finds a niche in consciousness, it can go on reproducing without reference to the enjoyment of its hosts. Coins were first minted to enhance the prestige and the economic power of kings and to facilitate trade. When the exchange of necessary products becomes dependent on a monetary system, however, people become helpless to resist its spread and will have to adapt to it whether they like it or not. As Max Weber noted, capitalism began as an adventurous game of entrepreneurs but eventually became an "iron cage," an economic system with peculiar shortcomings from which it is very difficult to escape.

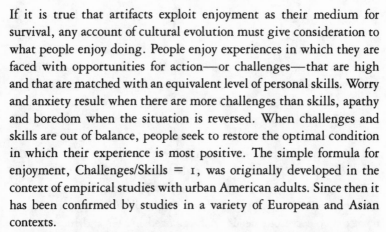

If it is true that artifacts exploit enjoyment as their medium for survival, any account of cultural evolution must give consideration to what people enjoy doing. People enjoy experiences in which they are faced with opportunities for action—or challenges—that are high and that are matched with an equivalent level of personal skills. Worry and anxiety result when there are more challenges than skills, apathy and boredom when the situation is reversed. When challenges and skills are out of balance, people seek to restore the optimal condition in which their experience is most positive. The simple formula for enjoyment, Challenges/Skills $= 1$, was originally developed in the context of empirical studies with urban American adults. Since then it has been confirmed by studies in a variety of European and Asian contexts.

Because of this relationship, people tend to overreproduce memes that raise the level of existing challenges, provided that at the same time they can raise the level of their own skills. Anything we do for a long time eventually becomes boring. At that point we look for new opportunities for action, which in turn forces us to develop greater skills; this dialectic leads to a process of *complexification*. This principle accounts for both the generation of new artifacts and, to a lesser extent, for their subsequent acceptance and transmission.

The relationship between complexification and enjoyment does not mean that people are constantly motivated to seek higher challenges. In fact, the opposite is true. When free to use time at their discretion, most people most of the time prefer to relax. They engage in low-intensity activities such as sitting with a bottle of beer in front of a television set. "Pleasure" is a homeostatic principle that drives people to save energy whenever possible, and to derive rewards from genetically programmed actions that are necessary for the survival of the species, such as eating and sexuality.

Enjoyment that requires developing new skills to meet increasing levels of challenge is relatively rare. Yet this is the experience that people all around the world mention as the high point of their lives. Thus, while pleasure is generally conservative, selecting and transmitting already existing artifacts, enjoyment that leads to complexification is more often responsible for generating and selecting new cultural forms.

At the most general level, then, it can be said that the process of complexification, which is experienced as enjoyable, defines the symbiotic relationship between the evolution of human beings and the evolution of culture. Cultural forms that offer the possibility of increasing enjoyment will survive by attracting attention. Similarly, people who invest attention in such forms acquire a more complex consciousness. In each generation, individuals who develop and learn to use new artifacts form a new breed.

Up to a point, this coevolution is beneficial both to us and to the world of things. However, there is always the possibility that memes will move from a symbiotic to a parasitic relationship. To prevent this from happening, we must entertain the possibility that culture does not exist to serve our needs. As organized matter and information, artifacts compete for energy with other forms of organization, including ourselves. When this possibility is faced, it becomes easier to evaluate cultural forms more objectively, and to make decisions on a sounder basis concerning which ones to encourage and which ones to restrain.

The joint complexification of consciousness and culture, brought about by the evolved trait of finding joy in complexity, has given the human race a great advantage in its competition with other forms of organized matter. Because the mind enjoys a challenge, people have lustily explored the hidden potential in all forms of information, thereby acting as midwives to artifacts of every kind. In so doing they have learned how to survive at the expense of other animals and plants they found useless. But just because enjoying the challenge of complexity has served us in the past does not guarantee that it will do so in the future. There is increasing evidence that this Faustian restlessness is making us vulnerable to the mindless replication of artifacts. If we are to take charge of the direction of evolution, a first step might be to recognize the fact that unless we find ways of controlling the evolution of culture, our own survival might be in serious jeopardy.

Media-Neutral

WIM COLEMAN
AND PAT PERRIN
FEATURING
DANIEL C. DENNETT
AS HIMSELF

So it really was true! I was just a helpless fictional character, trapped in some clumsily written novel or short story—or maybe even some preposterous movie script no producer in his right mind would ever put on film. But if I was just ink trails on a page, how could I be conscious? Was I conscious? And how was I supposed to live with it? I had to talk to somebody, and there was only one man I could think of. That was philosopher Daniel Dennett at Tufts University in Medford, Massachusetts.

FADE IN:

On HECTOR GLASCO, wearing a hat and an overcoat, climbing a long flight of stairs. Mournful, bluesy saxophone music plays in the background.

> GLASCO (Voice-over)
> It was Monday in L.A. The kind of Monday where you don't dare draw a breath. If they took all the ozone out of the air I was breathing and put it back where it belonged, the world would be a safer place for sunbathers.

GLASCO reaches a stairwell door and enters a long hallway.

> GLASCO (Voice-over)
> Yeah, Monday. The worst day of my work week. In my business, there ought to be a law. No Mondays. Period.

GLASCO comes up to his office door, on which is written:

> HECTOR GLASCO, M.D.
> CLINICAL PSYCHOTHERAPIST

> GLASCO (Voice-over)
> My name's Glasco. Hector Glasco. I'm a psychiatrist. Psychiatrists hate Mondays.

Glasco fumbles wearily with his keys and saunters into his front office. He opens up his appointment book and scans the names of his patients.

> GLASCO (Voice-over)
> So who was it going to be today? Father Larry, the flasher priest? Rudy, the Peeping Tom talk show host? Or Cindy, the shy house-wife with a private compulsion for whipping cream and leather? Whoever it was, I could be sure of one thing: Monday would bring out the worst in them. It always did.

There is a THUMP. Glasco looks toward the door, where a folded copy of the *L.A. Times* has just fallen through the mail slot.

GLASCO (Voice-over)
But this Monday would be different. I was going to get a little vacation from all that. It was going to be the kind of vacation I didn't want.

Glasco picks up the newspaper and opens it. The following headline is sprawled across the front page:

Deconstructionist Critic Goes Insane
Tenth Scholar Struck Down This Month

Glasco sees the picture of the critic in question—a gentle, scholarly-looking man in a bow tie. Glasco shudders.

GLASCO (Voice-over)
Yeah, there's nothing a psychiatrist hates more on a Monday than to find out that one of his star patients has wound up in the psych ward. It puts a damper on his whole day.

CUT TO:

EXT.—THE VISITORS' PARKING LOT OUTSIDE THE PSY-CHIATRIC HOSPITAL.

Glasco parks his car and walks into the unattractive, clinical-looking main building.

CUT TO:

INT.—A HALLWAY INSIDE THE HOSPITAL.

Glasco is walking down the hallway with another THERAPIST, who is wearing the proverbial white coat.

THERAPIST IN WHITE COAT
I'm sorry you had to find it out from the *Times*, Glasco. I guess our staff didn't know who to call when he flipped out last night. When these literary critics go, it's just like that.

GLASCO

It's okay. It's just that kind of Monday.

They reach a heavy, iron door.

GLASCO

He's been violent, I take it.

THERAPIST IN WHITE COAT

Well, he's under heavy sedation just at the moment. It'll wear off pretty soon. Think you can handle him? These deconstructionists can really go berserk on you.

GLASCO

I'll just have to risk it.

The great door opens, creaking noisily. Glasco steps into the padded cell.

THERAPIST IN WHITE COAT

If you need any help, just scream like crazy and pound on the walls.

GLASCO

Thanks. I'll take it from here.

The door closes behind him. Glasco is alone with his PATIENT, the utterly innocuous gentleman whose picture we saw earlier. At the moment, he happens to be wearing a straitjacket and is strapped to the wall.

PATIENT
(trying to be amiable)
So! At least I made my appointment this morning, eh, Doc?

GLASCO

Boris, Boris, Boris.

We gather from this that the patient's name is Boris.

BORIS

Don't get mad at me, Doc. I can't handle that. I really can't.

GLASCO

So you were messing around with deconstructionist theory again, huh? I thought we decided not to do that anymore.

BORIS

It's not what you think, Doc. This time it was different. This time I found out something really important.

GLASCO

Yeah?

BORIS

A foray into experimental criticism! I found out I was a fictional character. I found out *everybody's* a fictional character. Let me tell you how it happened. You know how we use nonreferential methods in deconstructionist criticism? Not even the author matters! Well, I decided to apply those same methods to my life—to deconstruct my own life, you see, without referring to anything outside it! This is what happened . . .

Boris's ravings fade away. We watch him speak animatedly—or at least as animatedly as one can when one's arms and legs are immobile. Glasco listens with increasing alarm and surprise.

GLASCO (Voice-over the preceding)

So that's when the horrible truth came through. The guy wasn't crazy at all! He'd just made a solid, academic argument for a simple fact that I'd been trying to ignore all my life. He'd figured out that I was purely fictional—that my whole world was purely fictional.

A MONTAGE OF SHOTS:

Glasco runs desperately down the hallway, out of the building, jumps into his car, and drives frantically to the airport. He buys a ticket and gets on the first flight to Massachusetts. We see him restlessly sipping Scotch and munching on macadamia nuts on the plane. A little tipsily, he squeezes the arm of the man sitting next to him, to see if he's real. His neighbor is not pleased. Then we see Glasco scurrying across the Tufts University campus. He charges into an office and excitedly shouts at a secretary, who seems to give him directions. Glasco rushes out.

GLASCO (Voice-over the preceding)

So it really was true! I was just a helpless fictional character, trapped in some clumsily written novel or short story—or maybe even some preposterous movie script no producer in his right mind would ever put on film. But if I was just ink trails on a page, how could I be conscious? *Was* I conscious? And how was I supposed to live with it? I had to talk to somebody, and there was only one man I could think of. That was philosopher Daniel Dennett at Tufts University in Medford, Massachusetts. I'd read Dennett's book *Brainstorms*, an extraordinary collection of essays on the nature of the brain. Clearly, this man knew a lot of the ins and outs of human consciousness. Maybe he could help me with my quandary. During my trip to Massachusetts, I kept pinching myself to see if I was awake—or even there. I started pinching other people, too. I was afraid my whole world would vanish. When I got to Dennett's office, his secretary told me he was in a seminar. I couldn't wait around till he got out. I had to see him right away.

INT.—A HALLWAY AT TUFTS UNIVERSITY

Glasco walks down the hall, looking for Daniel Dennett's seminar room. His FOOTSTEPS ECHO weirdly down the hall.

GLASCO'S POINT OF VIEW

He wanders on down the hallway, looking into one classroom after another. In one, he sees a rotund instructor writing elaborate mathematical formulas on the blackboard.

INSTRUCTOR #1

. . . so as we can see, Heisenberg's uncertainty principle shows that our ignorance about reality can actually arise out of our attempts to *measure* reality—

(seeing Glasco)
—or perhaps *you'd* care to enlighten us, Mr.—?

GLASCO

No, no. I was looking for somebody else.

Embarrassed, Glasco moves on.

GLASCO (Voice-over)

I left in a hurry. Uncertainty wasn't a subject I needed a lecture on. I was already an expert.

He looks into another classroom and sees a pompous literature professor, spectacles perched on a beak of a nose, hair tousled in the passion of his own eloquence, reading to his students from a huge volume of Shakespeare.

INSTRUCTOR #2

. . . These our actors,
As I foretold you, were all spirits and
Are melted into air, into thin air:
And, like the baseless fabric of this vision,
The cloud-capp'd tow'rs, the gorgeous palaces,
The solemn temples, the great globe itself,
Yea, all which it inherit, shall dissolve
And, like this insubstantial pageant faded—
                (seeing Glasco)
I do hope I'm not disturbing you.

GLASCO
(embarrassed again)

No, no. Not at all.

The professor continues as Glasco walks away.

INSTRUCTOR #2

And, like this insubstantial pageant faded . . .

GLASCO (Voice-over)
I didn't hang around there, either. He was just getting to the "We are such stuff as dreams are made on" bit. I knew it was more truth than poetry.

Glasco moves on to another classroom, in which another, more amiable professor addresses his class. This, in fact, is DANIEL DEN-NETT.

DENNETT
(to his students)
. . . so now that I've won my suit under the Freedom of Information Act, I am at liberty to reveal for the first time a curious episode in my life—

GLASCO
Excuse me, uh—

The entire seminar turns to look at him.

GLASCO
(horribly intimidated)
—are you Professor Dennett?

DENNETT
(politely)
Yes.

GLASCO
Could I, uh, speak with you for a moment?

DENNETT
Certainly. My seminar will be over in forty-five minutes.

GLASCO
No, it's really very urgent. You see, I—
(summoning up his courage)
I've discovered that I'm a fictional character.

In unison, the students do an enormous double-take at Glasco.

                                                    CUT TO:

EXT.—TUFTS CAMPUS

Glasco and Dennett sit on a bench in the cool spring air, discussing
Glasco's latest dilemma.

GLASCO

. . . so how can I possibly be conscious if I exist only on paper?

DENNETT

First of all, I don't think you exist only on paper. You may be a
fictional character, but it seems to me that you also exist in other
media as well.

GLASCO

For example?

DENNETT

Well, certainly, Hamlet isn't made out of ink. In fact, Hamlet's
existence is quite media-neutral at this point.

GLASCO
(puzzling over this)

Yeah?

DENNETT

Not originally.

GLASCO

But now he's in the media of millions of people's imaginations, isn't
he? The media of all sorts of different theater and film productions,
classrooms, and—

DENNETT

And that's important.

Inexplicably, a chess board appears between them. As Glasco and Dennett move about, the pieces seem to change in shape and material.

DENNETT

In that regard, Hamlet is rather like a chess piece. Some chess pieces are made out of ivory or wood, some out of metal, but of course people can play chess just in their heads. And when they do, then the white bishop that's on the white square isn't made out of anything. Still, there always has to be a medium. It might be patterns of excitation in the brain or it might be ink trails on a page.

Glasco looks a little relieved.

GLASCO

Well, if I started out as ink trails on a page, the likelihood is that I've resonated out from that through a number of different readers who may have communicated about me in a lot of different ways, expanding on that fiction!

DENNETT

Indeed.

GLASCO

That's very reassuring. The idea of being ink on paper is a rather terrifying thought—a rather deterministic thought.

DENNETT

It's rather demeaning, yes. And, of course, it is true that most characters have a primary relation to one body, which no other character can share with them, and to which they sort of have squatter's rights. And, I gather from what you say, that's not true of you. You have to share your primary body medium with at least one other character.

Glasco's discouragement returns.

GLASCO

I'm afraid so.

DENNETT

Indeed, perhaps with a character who, if asked, would say yes, he was your "author."

GLASCO

That's exactly what concerns me.

DENNETT

Well, let's put it this way. You have a biography, don't you?

GLASCO

Yes. I'm certainly convinced I do.

DENNETT

There are lots of biographies around. In fact, there are rather more biographies than there are people—that is to say, more than there are human bodies—because each human body generates at least one biography, and then some human bodies generate a whole lot of others. Novelists, for instance, generate quite a few.

GLASCO

Certainly.

DENNETT

But sometimes people who are not novelists—that is, human bodies that are not novelists—will generate more than one biography. For instance, multiple personality disorder sufferers often generate half a dozen, twenty, or thirty different biographies. And those have an existence that is, oh, sometimes partly on paper, partly in other media. But what makes you think that some of those biographies are truer, or realer, or less fictional than others?

GLASCO

Well, my concern is, if I am *authored* by someone else, doesn't that make me less free? I've always wandered through life thinking I could make my own choices. But if, in fact, somebody else is calling the shots by writing me or creating me in some other way, I find that rather disturbing.

DENNETT

Yes, I agree with you about that. If you're authored by somebody else, then that is a particular sign of diminished status. Most selves are not authored by any other *self.* They are *created*, but not authored by any particular other author.

GLASCO

Is this true even, say, in the case of a multiple personality? If I were a facet of a multiple personality, then might I still consider myself autonomous and separate?

DENNETT

Oh, yes. That's almost the rule.

GLASCO

One of the surprising things about this kind of consciousness— this state of being a facet of somebody else's consciousness—is the illusion of continuity. Perhaps I become someone else during intervening moments. But I feel that my consciousness continues from one moment to the next.

DENNETT

No doubt it does, more or less. It's discontinuous every twenty-four hours, for a number of hours. And there may be brief absences that go without much notice during the course of the day. But aside from that, it seems that your consciousness is more or less continuous. Well, so it is.

(He stops to consider.)

But actually, I wonder if that's true in the case of Hector Glasco, as opposed to the author of Hector Glasco. It all depends on how assiduous an author you have. Let's consider a person I've always been interested in, someone a little older than I am—Rabbit Angstrom, from the books *Rabbit Run, Rabbit Redux*, and *Rabbit Is Rich*. It seems that his life is not exactly continuous. At least, we've only been given some samples of his life over the years. There are many questions I would have about what his life was like in between the parts that Updike has told us about.

Glasco squirms a little at this comment.

CUT TO:

INT.—TUFTS LIBRARY. Glasco seems aware of the sudden shift in location, wondering what became of the time "between scenes." Dennett is pulling books off the shelves, stacking them in Glasco's arms.

GLASCO

But is there any way on earth I can find out who this author is? It seems grossly unfair that I am denied that information, whereas the author seems to be rather jocularly aware of everything in my life.

DENNETT

This raises several issues. One is that a great many authors complain about the way their characters take them over and won't leave them alone. Sometimes these authors have to wait and see how they'll come out.

GLASCO

Well, I've heard authors make just that complaint, but I've never taken them at all seriously. I always thought they were just spouting some sort of writerly nonsense.

Dennett pulls down several volumes of Dickens and adds them to Glasco's stack. Glasco is very nearly buried under books.

DENNETT

Yes, I've had that feeling on occasion. But Dickens, here, claims to have wept—*wept*—over the fate of Little Nell in *The Old Curiosity Shop.* It made him just as sad as it made his readers.

Dennett finds a copy of *The French Lieutenant's Woman* and passes it along to Glasco.

DENNETT

And John Fowles has discussed his own emotional reactions to things he has written, finding that they were just too heartbreaking, so he had to go back and tone down the drafts he'd written. They were too upsetting to him. I think these things happen. I don't doubt, either, that many authors exaggerate and put on airs, and tell a much more robust and flamboyant story about the way their characters push them around. But I don't think there's any impossibility in a fictional character's becoming somewhat unmanageable and imperious and obstreperous in the hands of its creator.

GLASCO

That gives me some reassurance that, even without my knowing it, life may not be quite so easy for my creator on my account as I might guess it to be.

DENNETT

Let's think about the importance of what a philosopher would call intentional objects, and I'm just going to mention two—one of them animate, one of them not.

Dennett, with an utter lack of amazement, produces an enormous gold bar from a bookshelf. Glasco is, understandably, astonished.

DENNETT

The one that isn't animate is the gold in Fort Knox. Now, the only reason the gold in Fort Knox is important is that people believe in it. And if somebody could spirit the gold out without anybody's being the wiser, it would have no effect at all, of course, on the world's economy. The intentional object—the gold in Fort Knox—is what's important; it's what plays the role it does. The actual, physical gold is there only because its absence would make the intentional object somewhat perilous.

Now Dennett produces an enormous picture book of British royalty from off the shelf.

ENORMOUS CLOSE-UPS—of photographs of Queen Elizabeth II and family.

DENNETT

Let's compare the gold in Fort Knox to another interesting intentional object: Queen Elizabeth II. I remember some years ago seeing on the BBC in England a series of interviews with young schoolchildren—they were probably five years old—about Queen Elizabeth II. They were asked, "Well, what does she do? Tell us about her day." And it was fascinating. These children were very sure they knew exactly what the queen did. For instance, she vacuumed Buckingham Palace while wearing her crown. And she sat on her throne while she watched television, things like that. It was wonderful. And it struck me then that Queen Elizabeth II, the intentional object constituted by the beliefs of these children, had a much more important role to play in British social history than the actual living woman, who, no doubt, finds that the intentional object Queen Elizabeth II is much more important than she is, and also has a certain power over her. Well, that's just a sort of laboratory case. We're all that way: the intentional objects that we become, or that we conspire to create along with those who know us.

GLASCO

So in a sense, we're fictions of everyone we know, and they're fictions of us as well.

DENNETT

Absolutely. In my current work, I'm developing a notion of human consciousness as a "virtual machine"—a computer scientist's term—imposed on the parallel architecture of the brain. Well, virtual machines are defined by computer scientists in terms of the so-called user illusion that they generate. So the question arises, Who's the user? Well, all the friends and associates we have are our users. And we present a certain user illusion to them—that is to say, our body presents a certain user illusion to them. If our body happens to be the body of a multiple personality sufferer, then it may present a strikingly different user illusion, in which there is more than one person inhabiting the body. But that still seems to suggest that there are these ultimate users who are the victims of these user illusions.

GLASCO

One of the things I gather from all this is that I shouldn't be looking for *a particular author*, but should pay more attention to *authors*—plural, including myself.

DENNETT

Sure! And just remember, the fact that you're a fictional character doesn't necessarily mean you have an author. One of the things we have to come to grips with is the fact that there can be narratives without authors—in the sense of conscious, deliberate, planning authors. Some fictions get created without any author at all.

GLASCO
(a bit startled by this)
Can you give me an example?

A FAST CUT:

Suddenly Dennett and Glasco are outdoors, late at night, at the door of somebody's home. LOUD PARTY MUSIC AND CONVERSATION emerge from inside. Dennett knocks on the door.

DENNETT

Oh, yes. There's a lovely party game, called Psychoanalysis. I don't know if you've ever played it.

GLASCO

I don't believe so.

DENNETT

Well, the next time you have a party with some of your fictional
friends, you can try this out on them.

The host comes to the door and lets them in. Dennett and Glasco
wander through the party, observing the activities almost invisibly.
Then the partygoers begin to act out the very scenario Dennett
proceeds to describe:

DENNETT

You announce that we're going to play Psychoanalysis. One person
is designated the psychoanalyst and has to leave the room. He is
told, before he leaves, that another member of the group is going to
relate a dream that he or she has recently had to the rest of the party.
Then the psychoanalyst comes back into the room and begins to ask
yes-or-no questions in order to dope out the narrative of the dream.
Once he's got the story line down, he's supposed to guess which of
the assembled party dreamed that dream and to psychoanalyze that
person.

Well, after the psychoanalyst leaves the room, you announce that
nobody is to recount a dream. Rather, when the psychoanalyst comes
back into the room, his questions are going to be answered according to the following entirely arbitrary rule: Questions where the
last letter of the last word are in the first half of the alphabet get
answered yes, all others get answered no. But to avoid confusion,
later answers are not allowed to contradict earlier ones. As you
might imagine, what happens when the psychoanalyst comes back
and begins asking questions is that a bizarre and, typically, obscene
narrative begins to evolve, much to everybody's intense amuse-
ment. It helps if people have been drinking. Eventually, usually
the psychoanalyst will say, "Well, I'm sure nobody ever dreamed
that dream. It's too bizarre and obscene. But whoever made it up is
extremely ill, very sick indeed." And then, of course, the joke can
be told, and it's on him: that he, in fact, was the author of that

dream. Well, in one sense he was the author. That is, nobody else suggested putting those three nuns in a rowboat with a gorilla. But at the same time, in a sense it's a narrative that has no author, because it's just a random process.

I think that ALL of our dreams and hallucinations are created by a process that is strongly analogous to that. So Freud is wrong. There is no "dream playwright." There doesn't have to be.

ANOTHER VERY SUDDEN CUT:

Dennett and Glasco are in the hallway of the very building where they started. It is late at night. As they walk past all the empty classrooms, a janitor is mopping the floor.

GLASCO

That reassures me that I'm not necessarily limited by somebody else's "script," and even if I am in somebody else's script, I have a great deal more freedom than I might assume.

DENNETT

I think you should be reassured. The only fictional characters that are completely lacking in free will are a fait accompli. Just don't let any of your authors think that they are the *sole* author of your biography.

GLASCO
(with a strange sense of realization)
I have a very strong hunch that they wouldn't.

DENNETT

Well, that's good.

They arrive at Dennett's classroom. Dennett opens the door. The seminar students are still sitting there, exactly as they were when Glasco and Dennett left them at least twelve hours ago, waiting faithfully for the return of their professor. Dennett resumes his lecture exactly where he left off.

DENNETT

As I was saying, I can reveal for the first time an episode in my life that may be of interest not only to those engaged in research in the philosophy of mind, artificial intelligence, and neuroscience, but also . . .

He closes the door behind him, leaving Glasco in the semidarkened hallway. The saxophone music starts up again.

GLASCO (Voice-over)

So that was the answer! Just try to keep my author busy. Well, as Monday came to a close, I had much more hope for the Tuesday to come. And whoever was writing my story was going to have a lot of work ahead, that much was for sure.

Glasco wanders off into the semidarkness, passing a lonely saxophone player huddled in a doorway, playing soulfully as he goes.

FADE TO BLACK

What Narcissus Saw: The Oceanic "I"/"Eye"

DORION SAGAN

As a virus reproduces itself by infiltrating the cell, so some notions would appear to latch on to the human imagination by being suggestive, self-contradictory, or symbolic. The great ideas leave an "empty space" in which believers recognize themselves. Fascinated with their own reflection, intrigued with the way a notion speaks directly to their own experience, the converted then proselytize to others on behalf of the idea and its amazing truth. Yet in reality they may be just passing a mirror and saying, "Look."

Sense-knowledge is the way the palm knows the elephant in the total pitch-dark. A palm can't know the whole animal at once. The Ocean has an eye. The foam-bubbles of phenomena see differently. We bump against each other, asleep in the bottom of our bodies' boats. We should try to wake up and look with the clear Eye of the water we float upon. [1]

—*Rumi (1207–1273)*

Certain ideas take root in the psyches of their believers, coloring all their perceptions. Kierkegaard noticed that the less support an idea has, the more fervently it must be believed in, so that a totally preposterous idea requires absolute unflinching faith. This perverse balance helps account for the wide variety of beliefs—some "self-evident," others dogmatic—to which people attribute certainty. Abstract and profound ideas, like drawings with an unfinished quality, may contain a certain open-endedness that makes them appeal to many different people. As a virus reproduces itself by infiltrating the cell, so some notions would appear to latch on to the human imagination by being suggestive, self-contradictory, or symbolic. The great ideas leave an "empty space" in which believers recognize themselves. Fascinated with their own reflection, intrigued by the way a notion speaks directly to their own experience, the converted then proselytize to others on behalf of the idea and its amazing truth. Yet in reality they may be just passing a mirror and saying, "Look."

Whether true or not, subscription to certain philosophical notions puts hinges in the mind with which we can swing open the doors of perception. You may believe (with the Buddhist) that time, space, and individuality are illusions (perpetrated by samsara, the merry-go-round of regeneration). You may believe, as Nietzsche did, that everything you do will recur in the future an infinite number of times—or, conversely, like novelist Milan Kundera, that each act in the play of reality comes only once (floating away into "the unbearable lightness of being"). For the Nietzschean, each thought can have an immense significance: It will be repeated throughout eternity. For Nietzsche the thought of the eternal recurrence of the same raises the stakes of being, since any crisis or pain must be dealt with not just here and now, but forever. For the Kunderan, however, events and thoughts may have no special significance, and may appear meaningless, arbitrary, and random, slipping into the future never to return. Since Nietzsche's idea of the eternal recurrence and Kundera's notion of the lightness of being are diametrically opposed, they cannot both be continuously entertained. Yet each dramatically colors the perception of the true believer.

Again, if you hold that your life has been preordained by God, or that interacting waves and particles whose antecedents were present at the origin of the universe determine your every thought and action, you may be inclined to act less responsibly—and more nihilistically —than if you believe you have perfect freedom of choice. Nietzsche sought to prove his doctrine of cosmic rerun with reference to thermodynamics. Using the example of a Christian belief in eternal damnation, he indicated that an idea need not be true to exert a tremendous effect. The truth or falsity is not a prerequisite for ideational power, the ability of an idea to transform a consciousness. Whether there is heaven and hell or starry void, free will or predestination, reality recurring forever or never, there will be believers. The human mind abhors uncertainty; in the absence of tutelage, whatever philosophy is current will rush in to fill its vacuum. (The disturbances generated by French philosopher Jacques Derrida's tortuous prose result precisely from his "deconstructive" ploy of making scintillating suggestions but anticipating and defusing all would-be conclusions.[2])

People ascribe certainty to their beliefs, reality to their perceptions. From an evolutionary epistemological approach, existence is hindered, discourse impeded by the playful suspension of disbelief. So belief returns. Sheer survival requires that we arrive at and act upon conclusions, no matter how shoddily they are based. Doubt is a stranger to the human heart: To love or live we must believe—in *something*.

Let us explore now the perceptual implications of one powerfully riveting idea—that the Earth is alive. This is one of those doors which, swung open, reveals a changed world. Many in the past have believed that the whole universe is alive. A corollary of this is that the

Earth's surface—our planet with its atmosphere, oceans, and lands—forms a giant global organism. We can say that the Earth is alive. But what does that *mean*?

Imagine a child of a present or future culture inculcated from childhood to believe that the planetary surface formed a real extension of his or her person, a child whose language implicitly reinforced this connection to such a point that to him or her it would not even seem to be a connection but rather an *equation*. Such a person would make sense differently. Were nature not a dead mechanism but an immense "exoskeleton" (as the more limited exoskeleton or protective shell of a lobster is not only its house but part of its body), he would be less concerned by what we could not explain. And his perception of the organic would be altered. The arrangement of objects in his home, offhand comments by strangers, walks in the woods, cinema, and vivid dreams would all be linked to the organization of a living organism whose fullness of activity would be beyond his powers of comprehension. His ego no longer encapsulated by skin, he would experience the seas, sands, wind, and soil as numb parts of a body—just as feet and fingers, which, while open to tactile sensation, were yet incapable of speech and sight. The mountains between earth and air would seem to him anatomically placed, as "our" skeleton is between "our" bone marrow and flesh. Putting ourselves in his shoes, landscapes from jungles and glaciers to deserts and glens become body parts in a new anatomy, even if, from the limited perspective of that body's minute and only partially sentient parts, the global or geoanatomy remains largely unintelligible. The incomplete sensations of the planetary surface as a live body is no more a metaphor for ignorance than the idea of a skin encapsulated anatomy. Take an ant crossing a bare human foot. Does it perceive it is touching a life form? With this scale of differences, would it be able to distinguish a toenail from a rock or shell? Or, what can a bacterium living in the human gut conclude about the life form that feeds it? Likewise, if we in our daily activities were meandering about upon the surfaces of a giant being, it need not be immediately apparent. Indeed, if one (not a positivist) believes in the necessity of metaphor as a system of explanation to "make known" our ignorance, then the image of a live planetary surface may itself—like Democritus's theory of atoms—be enough to launch an entire new epoch of scientific research and individual action. Though inevitably we would reach the borders upon which such a program would be based, it is possible to imagine language itself embedding the structure of such an altered state of affairs and "making it real." The blue Earth itself would color all our perceptions.

Imagine someone from this culture picnicking. She believes her environment—and not just individual plants, animals, fungi, and microbes—to be part of her self. The grass on which she sits is a patch of tissue lining the inside of the superorganism of which she forms a part. The bark at her back, the dragonflies, birds, clouds, the moist air and ants tickling her foot—all these sensations represent from her point of view not "her," but that which from our point of view we pedantically term "the self-perception at one site of a modulated environment." Like the ants, "she" senses what is beyond "her." When "she" pulls her T-shirt over "her" knees, this is no longer human, but one locus of sensation within the kaleidoscopic entrails of a planet-sized photosynthesizing being.

The physiology is vast. The prostaglandins in people's bodies have many functions, ranging from ensuring the secretion of a protective stomach coating that prevents digestive acids from acting on the walls of the stomach to causing uterine contractions when ejaculated along with sperm in the male semen. So, too—looking at it now from an artificial position outside the physiology—the whole woman, by what she says, makes, and does, performs multiple functions within the global anatomy. A hormone is a biochemical produced in one part of the body that is transported through the circulatory system and causes biological reactions. The pituitary gland, at the base of the human brain, for example, stimulates sex hormones in the ovary and testes, causing pubic hair to grow. As an animal in the Earth breathes, it affects the entire system. Water and atmosphere act as veins conveying matter and information within the geoanatomy. Indeed, the environment is so "metabolic" that minor actions may be amplified until they have major effects, while seemingly major effects may be diminished or negated. The ground is a live repository for metabolisms like the rings of tissue left in the wake of a growing tree. Treelike, the Earth grows, leaving behind it archaeological and paleobiological rings. The "woman" herself is part of a currently active geological stratum; and, far from dead, the air around the body that we, from habit, distinguish as human is fluid and thriving, part of an external circulatory system exploited by life as a whole. To one raised to believe in the textbook notion of a static geology to which biology adapts, the young woman seems to be eating alone, surrounded only by plant life. Yet from "her" perspective the environment around "her" pulses with communicative life; "she" is at a busy intersection in the heart of nature. A part of nature, "she" is not simply "human" but an action within the self-sensing system of a transhuman being. (Indeed, language's personal pronouns falsify; they do not do justice to "her" but make "us" see "her" as a "thing" in a way that is in fact alien to "her." The self-extension to the environment has altered everything.)

Bearing in mind the idiosyncrasies of "her" perception, let us return to more ordinary language on the condition that without quotations "she" and "her" are still recollected as being imprisoned in such jail bar–like quotes by our more fractured word-biased views. With that said, there are things that to her would seem bona fide but remain quite mysterious from our worldview. Being called by a long-lost friend during the very moment she was thinking of him would not necessarily strike her as being what Carl Jung termed "synchronicity"—coincidences with such deep significance that one concludes they are more than mere coincidences. For her, strange coincidences come from her ignorance of the huge physiological system of which she forms a small part. Rain forests and seaside sludge she *sees* as vital organs, as inextricable to the biosphere as a brain or heart is to an animal; humans, however, she may construe as lucky beneficiaries of the establishment of superorganism, fluff like fur or skin that can be sloughed off without incurring major harm to the planetary entity as a whole. Her uncle, a "geophysician," tells her that humanity has caused in the biosphere a physiological disturbance. "The Earth," he says (in so many words), "is oscillating between ice ages and interglacials; it has the global equivalent of malarial chills and fevers . . . Oil in the ground has become a gas in the atmosphere . . . tall tropical forests are being flattened into cattle . . . our vital organs are plugged with asphalt." Deserts, he tells her, are appearing like blotches on the fair face of nature. "But," he tells his niece, "we don't even know if these 'symptoms' are indicative of transformative growth—in which case we are experiencing normal 'growing pains'—or debilitating disease. Perhaps it is both, as in pregnancy, which, if encountered by a being as minute in relation to a pregnant woman as we are in relation to the Earth, might be misdiagnosed as the most bloated and dangerous of tumors."

Let us adopt the mask of metaphysical realism for a moment, and peer through the empty spaces, the (w)holes, which are all it has in the way of eyes. The example of the physical appearance of the Earth's altering due to the popularity of an idea—whether true or not—is an indication of what can happen when philosophy meets technology. But all this speaking of the Earth as if it had a "face" and a "fever"—as if it were some sort of comprehensible living entity—begs the question: Is the Earth really alive? And, if it is an "organism," what kind of organism is it? Can it think? Certainly the biosphere cannot be an animal, but only animal-like. And if the Earth does not resemble any other organism we know, have we *reason* to call it an organism at all?[3]

Scientific evidence for the idea that the Earth is alive abounds. The scientific formulation of the ancient idea goes by the name of the Gaia hypothesis. The brainchild of British atmospheric scientist James Lovelock, the Gaia hypothesis proposes that the properties of the atmosphere, sediments, and oceans are controlled "by and for" the biota, the sum of living beings. In its most elegant and attackable form, the hypothesis lends credence to the idea that the Earth—the global biota in its terrestrial environment—is a giant organism. Lovelock's Wiltshire neighbor, the novelist William Golding, suggested the name Gaia after the ancient Greek goddess of the Earth. In part because Gaia resonates with a prescientific animism and can bring about a radically different way of perceiving reality, it has been the object of academic dismissal, suspicion, and, now, close scientific scrutiny. The British evolutionary biologist Richard Dawkins (a metaphysical realist if ever there was one) rejects Gaia, arguing that since there is no evidence for other planets with which the Earth has competed, natural selection could never have produced a superorganism. Without planetary competition, how could homeostatic or self-regulating properties on a global scale arise? Nevertheless, evidence for organismlike monitoring of the planetary environment does exist. Reactive gases coexist in the atmosphere at levels totally unpredictable from physics and chemistry alone. Marine salinity and alkalinity levels seem actively maintained. Fossil evidence of liquid water and astronomic theory combine to reveal a picture in which the global mean temperature has remained at about 22 degrees Centigrade (room temperature) for the last three billion years; and this constancy has occurred despite an increase in solar luminosity estimated to be about 40 percent. Under the Gaia hypothesis such anomalies are explained because the planetary environment has long ago been brought under control, modulated automatically or autonomically by the global aggregate of life forms chemically altering one another and their habitats. All these anomalies suggest that life keeps planetary house, that the "inanimate" parts of the biosphere are in fact detachable parts of the biota's wide and protean body.

It was during the NASA Viking mission to Mars with its quest to find life there that Lovelock first thought to use his telescope "like a microscope," pointing it toward the laboratory of the skies. As a thought experiment he examined the red planet from Earth for signs of life. His discovery of an unremarkable absence of reactive gases produced under the control of life led him to conclude before the spacecraft landed that Mars was uninhabited (which, however, it became as soon as the outer human or Earthly limb of the sensing spacecraft landed).

To answer Dawkins and others who required a mechanism of how a self-regulating biosphere could arise in the absence of other competing biospheres, Lovelock and his associate, Andrew Watson, developed computer models that simulated the ecology of a planet containing only light and dark daisies. These models show that neither populations of planets nor foreknowledge on the part of organisms is necessary to stabilize environmental factors on a global scale. Individual organisms grow selfishly when they can bring their environment under control merely by their activities, their continuous metabolic existence. In the model, Daisy World cools itself off despite the increasing brightness of a nearby sun. The cooling comes naturally as clumps of black and white daisies absorb and reflect heat as they grow within certain temperature levels that would be normal for them in any field.

On Earth, temperature modulation may be accomplished, at least in part, by coccolithophores, a form of marine plankton invisible to the naked eye but shockingly apparent in satellite images of the northeastern Atlantic Ocean. These tiny beings produce carbonate skeletons as well as a gas called dimethyl sulfide. The gas, pungently redolent of the sea itself, reacts with the air to produce sulfate particles that serve as nuclei for the formation of raindrops within marine stratus clouds. The plankton, then, by growing more vigorously in warmer weather, may enhance cloud cover over major sections of the Atlantic Ocean. But the enhanced density of the clouds leads to more reflection of solar radiation back into space so that the same plankton growing in warm weather cool the planet. In these sorts of ways the subvisible but remotely sensible beings may be part of a global system of temperature control similar to the thermoregulation of a mammalian body. Without attributing consciousness or personifying them as minute members of some global board of climate control, the organisms may be seen to act together as part of a system of thermoregulation like the one that in us stabilizes our body temperature at approximately 98.6 degrees Fahrenheit. Locally acting organisms apparently can affect the entire planetary environment in a way that builds up organismlike organization.

In a way it is not so surprising that individual action leads to the appearance or, indeed, the actuality of global controls. Academically, the disinclination to accept the possibility that the Earth regulates itself in the manner of a giant living being seems to have less to do with physical and chemical evidence—which lends itself to such interpretation—than it does with the status of modern evolutionary theory. Darwin considered the individual animal to be the unit of selection, but in the modern synthesis of neo-Darwinian theory, natural selection is seen as operating on genes as much as individuals, and evolution is mathematicized as the change in frequency of genes in populations consisting of individual animals. So, too, altruism in sociobiology is often seen as the tendency of genes to preserve themselves in their own and other gene-made organisms; biologists tend to dismiss the idea that groups above the level of the individual can be selected for, since they are not cohesive enough as units to die out or differentially reproduce. Evolutionary biologists lump arguments for selection of populations of organisms with the archaic oversimplification "for the good of the species"; they then perfunctorily dismiss such arguments as misguided, if not altogether disproved. Yet, as elegant as the mathematics combining Mendelian genetics and Darwinian theory sometimes may be, sociobiologists have a deep conceptual problem on their hands with their insistence that natural selection never works at a level above genes and the individual.

First of all, it is not clear what sociobiologists think an "individual" is; they fail to analyze or define this term, assuming that it is self-evident because of a parochial focus on the animal kingdom. The problem is that certain microscopic entities, cells called protists, which in the form of colonies must have given rise to the ancestors of all modern plants, animals, fungi (as well as "protoctists"—algae, slime molds, protozoans, and the like), did, and still do, assume the form of individuals. How, then, can evolution not work at a level above that of the individual, if the very first animals were themselves multicellular collections—populations—of once-independent heterogeneous cells?

The animal body itself has evolved as a unit from a morass of individuals working simultaneously at different levels of integration. Sociobiologists and neo-Darwinian theorists disdain "group selection" because they don't have strong enough cases for its existence in populations of *animals*. But it may well be that, due to their large size and late appearance on the evolutionary stage, animals have not yet achieved the high level of group consolidation found in microbes. No matter how elegant the mathematics, dismissing "group selection" as an evolutionary mechanism requires dismissal of individual animals also, for the body of the academic itself provides a counterexample to the thesis that natural selection (if it "works" at all) never works on "groups." A person is a composite of cells. Part of the problem here is the restrictive focus on *animal* evolution when animals themselves are the result of multigenome colonial evolution and represent only a special intermediary level of individuality midway between microbes and multianimal communities. But cells, animal species, and the biosphere all evolve concurrently. The first plants and animals began as amorphous groups of cells, later evolving into discretely organized and individuated communities of interacting cells. The evolution of individual cells led to the group of cells we recognize as the animal body. Groups of animals such as insect societies and planetary human culture begin to reach superorganismlike levels of identity and organization. The human body is itself a group that has differentially reproduced compared to other, more loosely connected collections of cells. That cells of human lung tissue can be grown in the laboratory long after the victim from which they were taken has died of cancer shows that the cells in our body are tightly regimented into tissue groups but still retain the tendency for independent propagation.

To be consistent, mainstream biology should explain how something called "natural selection" cannot be "acting" on groups of organisms if the animal "individual" is in a very deep sense also a "group" of organisms, namely cells with their proposed histories and origins. Here we can accept for the sake of argument that several hundred million years ago multicellular assemblages began to evolve into the animal lineage. These groups left more offspring than their free-living unicellular relatives. Their very bodies contained the principle of social altruism, in which some cells specialized and curtailed their "selfish" tendency toward indefinite propagation for the "benefit" of the group to which they belong. Working within the framework of evolutionary theory, we must accept the argument that "group selection" exists in the *origin of animals*—therefore, we must (again, within this framework) concede that evolution favors populations of individuals *that act together to re-create individuality at ever higher levels*. This somewhat freaky assertion calls into question the very usefulness of trying to isolate the units of natural selection: *Because of the articulation or community relations of living things, the differential reproduction of units at one level translates into the differential reproduction of units at a higher, more inclusive level.* I anticipate that the mathematical theory of fractals, in which the same features are present in interlocking geometrical figures at various scales of analysis, may be useful in illustrating the principle of emergent identity in the series cell, multicellular organism, superorganismic society. In principle, the "animal-like" nature of the Earth can be considered fractally as resulting from the Malthusian dynamics of cells reproducing within a limited space.

If this essay's evolutionary understanding (qualified by placement under the rubric "metaphysical realism") is "right," it may be that the Earth itself represents the most dramatic example of emergent identity. As in Lovelock's Daisy World, the properties of global regulation on Earth result from the metabolic activities of the organisms that comprise our biosphere; on a less inclusive scale, "global" human consciousness and unconscious physiological control mechanisms can be traced to the synergistic effects of billions of former microbes acting locally to comprise the human body and its central nervous system. As an individual, the human body has evolved in isolation from other organisms, whereas the biosphere as a whole does not even have as clear a physical boundary separating it from the abiological cosmic environment, let alone from other organisms. In this sense the biosphere is much less an individual than an animal. But the lack of biospheric individuality may be as artifactual as it is temporary. A superorganism as large as the Earth has not had the chance to evolve distinctive characters in isolation. Moreover, even if it were far more complex (anatomically, physiologically, and "psychologically") than a mammal, we may have difficulty understanding it precisely because of that complexity. In short, because the Earth is so huge, the Gaian organism may not be as apparent—or as consolidated—as a single animal. Over time, however, the Gaian superorganism can be expected to consolidate and become increasingly apparent; it may in the next centuries even become "obvious" to the majority of human beings.

Russel L. Schweickart, a NASA astronaut from 1963 to 1979, is an adviser on Biosphere II—a private-capital project to build a multimillion-cubic-foot biosphere near Tucson, Arizona, for about the price of a modern skyscraper. "The grand concept," he said recently at a meeting of those working on the project, "of birth from planet Earth into the cosmos—when, 1993, 1994, 2010, 2050, whenever—is a calling of the highest order. I want to pay a lot of respect to everyone associated with that grand vision for their courage to move ahead with this in the face of the unknowns which make the lunar landing look like a child's play toy. There were a lot of complexities there, but we were dealing with resistors, transistors, and optical systems which were very well understood. Now we're wrestling with the real question: that natural process of reproduction of this grand organism called Gaia. And that's what all the practice has been about." Many astronauts space-walking or gazing at the Earth report on the tremendous transformative power of the experience. That looking at the Earth from space could so totally change a person's consciousness suggests that the experience has not yet fully registered upon the body politic. People such as Schweickart who have seen the Earth from "outside" in space may be more prepared to accept the unorthodox idea that the biosphere is not only a living entity, but about to reproduce—as many individuals—and, indeed, many cellular groups arranged into individuals—have done "before."[4]

However, at the Cathedral of St. John the Divine in New York City in 1987, the thoughtful plant geneticist Wes Jackson protested the idea of Gaia on the basis of Gaia's "infertility." Jackson claimed there is no way the Earth could be an organism, since all known organisms, from microscopic amoebae to whales, reproduce. Since the Earth has no "kids," it cannot be a real organism. It is only a metaphor, he said—and it may even be a bad one. According to Jackson, we do not even know what the Earth is. ("What is God?" he asked provocatively, suggesting the questions were similar.) In a way I do agree with Jackson. The Earth seems indefatigable in its capacity to make us wonder about its true nature. Yet I had become convinced that the Earth is, in a sense, reproducing before ever hearing Jackson raise this counter-Gaian argument. The reason for my conviction that the biosphere is on the verge of reproduction has to do with two things: (1) The growing number of scientists and engineers involved in designing, for a variety of reasons, closed or self-sufficient ecosystems in which people or aggregates of life can live; and (2) My assumption that humanity is not special but part of nature. For, if we are part of the Earth, so is our technology, and it is through technology that controlled environments bearing plants, human beings, animals, and microbes will soon be built in preparation for space travel and colonization. In space these dwellings will have to be sealed in glass and metal or other materials so that life will be protected inside them. Such material isolation gives the recycling systems discrete physical boundaries—one of the best indications of true biological "individuality." Thus, the bordered living assemblages necessary for long-term space travel and planetary settlement by their very nature bear a resemblance to biological individuals at a new, higher scale of analy-

sis. They look startlingly like tiny immature "earths"—the biospheric offspring Jackson claims must exist for the Earth to be a true
organism.

We can trace a progression in size in these human-made containers
of recycling life. Claire Folsome of the University of Hawaii has kept
communities of bacteria enclosed in glass and they have remained
healthy and productive since 1967. There is no reason to think they
may not be immortal despite being materially isolated from the
global ecosystem. Similarly, Joseph Hansen of NASA has developed a
series of experimental desktop biospheres consisting of several
shrimp, algae, and other organisms in sealed orbs half filled with
marine water. These last for years, and in some crystal balls the hardy
animals have even reproduced. On a still larger scale, private and
governmental space administrations in the Soviet Union, the United
States, Japan, and other countries are developing the art of creating
materially closed perpetually recycling ecosystems. Crucial not only
to space travel and colonization, these miniaturized ecosystems could
also protect endangered species, maintaining air, water, and food
supplies, and allow, in the long term, the possibility of social,
cultural, and biological quasi independence on the ever more crowded
and homogenized Earth. If successful, controlled ecosystems will
carry a powerful educational message about the need for cooperation of
people with one another as well as with the other species that support
the global habitat. And, if perpetually recycling ecosystems can be
erected and maintained, a whole new scientific discipline may arise
from the possibility, for the first time ever, of comparing "parent" and
"offspring" biospheres. Former astronaut and physicist Joseph Allen
points out that the quantum mechanical revolution that so marks
modern physics derives from the comparison by Niels Bohr of helium
and hydrogen nuclei: Having more than a single biosphere to observe
may likewise revolutionize biology. Communication established between two semiautonomous biospheres may resemble in emotional
impact the relationship of a mother or father to a daughter or son. Yet
the "children" will teach: The safe modeling of potential ecological
disasters within a new biosphere may provide dramatic warnings and
even perhaps usable information on how to ward off the environmental
catastrophes—from acid rain to pesticide contamination of foods—
that potentially await us. New biospheres thus may serve as living

whole-Earth laboratories or "control worlds," inaugurating differential reproduction on the largest scale yet.

The importance of the development within the biosphere of such enclosed ecosystems cannot be overestimated. Whether or not individual, national, or private venture capital models succeed or fail is irrelevant. What we see, rather, is the *tendency* of the Earth (or Gaia, or the biosphere) to re-create itself in miniature. Since we, from an evolutionary perspective, are natural and not supernatural creatures, the Earth is, through the high-tech expedient of modern world civilization, re-creating versions of the global ecosystem on a smaller scale. To some the view of an Earth biospherically splintered into semiautonomous ecosystems would be a technocratic blunder equivalent to the formation of a planetary Disneyland. But even if the Earth is saved as a single biosphere, such materially closed ecosystem technology will be necessary for extended human voyages into space or the settlement of off-world sites for emigration or long-term exploration. Thus, we do seem to be caught in precisely that historical moment when the Earth is begetting its first, tentative batch of offspring. That humankind is currently the only tenable midwife for Gaian reproductive expansion is a gauge of our possible evolutionary longevity and importance—provided that the violently phallic technology that promises to carry life starward does not destroy its makers first.

The "Gaia hypothesis" is at once revolutionary science and an ancient worldview, with the power to spur not only scientific research but religious debate. If we take it to its logical extremes, it says not only that the Earth is alive but that it is on the verge of producing offspring. From a strict neo-Darwinian perspective this may be a mystery, for how can a giant organism suddenly appear *ex nihilo* and then just start reproducing? Yet, from a broader philosophical perspective, the reproduction of the biosphere makes perfect sense. We are animals whose reproduction is an elaboration of the reproductive efforts of cells: The organismic and reproductive antics of the Earth *have not* appeared in an evolutionary vacuum. Gaia's weak, immature attempts at "seed" formation and reproduction result from the sheer numbers of organisms reproducing at the Earth's surface. What before occurred in the living microcosm of cells is now transpiring in the larger world of animal communities. The Malthusian tendency to increase exponentially in a limited space beyond the resource base apparently may account for more than just the evolution of new species: It leads also to the appearance of individuality at ever greater levels and scales of analysis.

━━━

This essay broaches what might be termed a "Nietzschean ecology." That is, it attempts to hint at an art of biology whose unveiling may be as important as biology itself, at least as regards biological understanding as it applies to the "individual" in his, her, or its restless search for meaning. (Academicians, guard your territory!) The appearance of closed "offspring" biospheres from the original open biosphere repeats or continues the process by which "individual" plants, fungi, and animals appeared from communities of microbes. As the folk saying goes, *Plus ça change, plus c'est la même chose:* The more things change, the more they stay the same. As Nietzsche scrawled in one of his notebooks: "Everything becomes and recurs—forever!"

As we have seen, even a false idea may color our views of the world, and where there is a chance of changing the world, there is the chance of bettering it. Gaia is such an idea, yet one with the added punch that it may be proved true. (Oscar Wilde observed that "Even true things may be proved.") It was interesting to watch the debate develop in March 1988 as the Geophysical Union met in San Diego to "test" for the first time among polite scientific society the general validity of Lovelock's hypothesis. In fact, as everyone saw in the epistemology session (and *any* sort of philosophical discussions is rare at scientific meetings these days), it was fairly easy to show that Gaia is not, strictly speaking, testable. Whether one took him to be a very naïve epistemologist or an extremely sophisticated sophist, James W. Kirchner was correct when he compared the postulate that the Earth is alive to Hamlet's theory that "all the world is a stage." There is no way of proving or disproving such general notions. Kirchner pointed out that Gaia is not a valid hypothesis because it does not say something we can verify or falsify, something such as (Kirchner's example), "There are footlights at the edge of the world." In fact, Gaia is not a hypothesis. It is, like evolution, a metaphysical research program. The idea that the Earth is alive is extremely fruitful, able to suggest many scientific models and lines of inquiry. Yet ultimately it is unprovable, a matter, at bottom, of faith. It is, after all, a world-view. What positivists miss in their attack on Gaia is that they are also up to their necks in metaphor and metaphysics. There is no avoiding metaphor and metaphysics. When worldviews collide, weak ones are obliterated in the encounter. In my view, what happened at this conference was an encounter of worldviews. But it was no head-on collision. Rather, the old panbiotic or animistic worldview (at the center of the "Gaia hypothesis") sneaked its way into mainstream discussion. In a direct confrontation, the Gaian worldview would have been eaten alive by the prevailing worldview (atomistic science and its Platonic "laws" as absolute reality). But by disguising itself as a testable *hypothesis*, Gaia was smuggled into a prestigious scientific discussion. We would never expect the discussants at a serious scien-tific conference to bring up as the main question their own view of reality. But this is, in effect, what happened. Like the Trojan horse, the Gaian *worldview* sneaked past the well-armed guards of meta-physical realism ("science") by disguising itself as a *hypothesis*. And now the worldview Gaia, having lodged itself inside the worldview metaphysical realism, is impossible to extract without damage to both. Our entire conception of life and its environment is being called into question. What is life? Technology? The environment?

Perhaps another Greek myth, because it has not strayed onto the dangerous battlefield of truth, better sums up the present philosophi-cal situation: *Once Narcissus stood and eyed the still waves that reflected his own image. He had never seen himself before. He became infatuated. And now we gaze in the looking glass of satellite imaging technology. Again we see the water. Again . . . but what is "ourselves"? And who—or what—is this body?*

NOTES

[1] The quotation is from *We Are Three, New Rumi Translations*, by Coleman Barks. (Athens, Georgia: Maypop Books, 1987). Jalal ad-Din ar-Rumi

Rumi (1207–1273) was a Sufi love mystic who wildly spun around as he delivered his musical verses, which were transcribed by assistants. He was the first "Whirling Dervish," and it is claimed that his poetry read aloud in the Persian original is so musical it sends listeners into a trance by its aural quality alone.

2 The technique of leading people in certain directions and then "pulling the rug out from under them" resembles the method of the sleight-of-hand artist. Both the deconstructionist and the magician present signs that are typically organized or mentally ordered into a narrative of events. A difference is that, whereas the exponent of legerdemain presents approximately the minimal number of sensory stimuli to arrive prematurely and mistakenly at a certain impression of reality, and this impression is then revealed to be "wrong" (that is, clearly only an image), after the performance of the "trick," the deconstructionist uses language as the medium for the presentation of mirages that are more or less continuous; the deconstructionist does not entertain like the magician with a series of discrete and contained surprises, but reveals rather that the attribution of "finished" images and mirages from unfinished signs and stimuli proceeds unceasingly. The difficulty with deconstruction is that it shows offstage, whereas traditional magic shows onstage. But this difficulty has to do with the "broadening" of the stage, the spilling over of theater into the realms of everyday life: It cannot be gotten rid of by dismissing as unreadable all deconstructive prose. Clearly the conclusions arrived at through the use of language, and especially of "language with ordinary words," may be as bogus as the conclusions arrived at through the motions of a sleight-of-hand artist—and especially one manipulating not apparatus onstage (where the theatrical element is expected), but small ordinary objects such as cards and coins in the home space so normally above suspicion.

3 We say all this keeping in mind that our language—and our science—bears within it its own deeply embedded and usually unexamined set of metaphysical assumptions. Derrida has unequivocally shown this. Just as Nietzsche did not need thermodynamics to be affected by the idea of eternal recurrence, one need not justify the culturally marginal notion of a living Earth by reference to or with the sanction of a cultural mainstream, a tradition of knowledge not at home with such ideas. Nonetheless, the possibility of scientific sanction indicates the reality of the approach of this notion into the mainstream.

4 Part of the problem with the whole concept of evolution—and all narrative "explanations"—may be the unexamined reliance upon the unprovable

assumption of linear time, a logocentric assumption. The verb tenses of languages perpetuate the assumption of temporality. The relation of language to the bias of linear time is here dubbed "chronic." In fact, the relationship of life forms may be better seen as four- or multidimensional, in which case the evolutionary unfolding in linear time is better seen as only a "slice" through true spacetime.

Contributors

Morris Berman is an author, lecturer, and social critic. His published works include *Social Change and Scientific Organization* (Cornell University Press), and *The Reenchantment of the World* (Bantam). His essay in this issue is adapted from *Coming to Our Senses* (Simon & Schuster).

William H. Calvin, neurophysiologist at the University of Washington in Seattle is the author of *The Throwing Madonna: Essays on the Brain*, and *The River That Flows Uphill: A Journey from the Big Bang to the Big Brain*. His two essays in this volume are adapted from *Cerebral Symphony: Seashore Speculations on the Structure of Consciousness* (Bantam).

Wim Coleman, playwright and poet, is coeditor of *The jamais vu papers*. He is the coauthor of *PragMagic* (with Marilyn Ferguson and Pat Perrin; forthcoming, Pocket Books). His essay in this volume is excerpted from his forthcoming book *The jamais vu papers* (with Pat Perrin, Crown).

Mihaly Csikszentmihalyi, a research psychologist who studies "flow states," is Chairman, Department of Behavioral Sciences, University of Chicago, and author of *Flow: The Psychology of Optimal Experience* (Harper & Row).

Daniel C. Dennett, philosopher, is Distinguished Arts & Sciences Professor at Tufts University and Director, Center for Cognitive Studies. He is the author of *Brainstorms: Philosophical Essays on Mind and Psychology*, and coeditor of *The Mind's I: Fantasies and Reflections on Self and Soul* (with Douglas Hofstader).

Nicholas K. Humphrey, a theoretical psychologist from Cambridge, is the author of *Consciousness Regained*, *The Inner Eye*, and editor (with Robert Jay Lifton) of *In a Dark Time*.

Julius Korein, M.D., is a neurobiologist who studies brain states of death, vegetation, and life. He is professor of Neurology, New York University Medical Center.

Robert Langs, M.D., is a clinically trained psychoanalyst and author of twenty books on psychotherapeutic interaction, including *A Primer of Psychotherapy* (Gardner Press), and *Decoding Your Dreams* (Henry Holt).

Lynn Margulis is a biologist, Distinguished Professor, Department of Botany, University of Massachusetts at Amherst, and author of *Symbiosis in Cell Evolution* (W. H. Freeman), *Origins of Sex* (with Dorion Sagan; Yale), and *Microcosmos* (with Dorion Sagan; Summit).

Dan Ogilvie is a psychologist and researcher on aspects of life satisfaction over the life span. He is a member of the Department of Psychology at Rutgers University.

Pat Perrin, artist, is coeditor of *The jamais vu papers*. She is coauthor of *PragMagic* (with Marilyn Ferguson and Wim Coleman; forthcoming, Pocket Books). Her essay in this volume is excerpted from her forthcoming book *The jamais vu papers* (with Wim Coleman, Crown).

Dorion Sagan is a writer, author of *Origins of Sex* (with Lynn Margulis; Yale), *Microcosmos* (with Lynn Margulis; Summit), and *Biospheres* (McGraw-Hill).

Robert Sternberg is IBM Professor of Psychology and Education, Yale University, and author of *The Triarchic Mind: A New Theory of Human Intelligence* (Viking) and *The Triangle of Love* (Basic).

About the Editor

JOHN BROCKMAN, founder of The Reality Club and editor of *Speculations*, is a writer and literary agent. He is the author of *By the Late John Brockman* (Macmillan, 1969), *37* (Holt, Rinehart and Winston, 1970), *Afterwords* (Anchor Press, 1973), and editor of *About Bateson* (E. P. Dutton, 1977).